AFFIRMATIVE ACTION and PREFERENTIAL ADMISSIONS in HIGHER EDUCATION

An Annotated Bibliography

by KATHRYN SWANSON

THE SCARECROW PRESS, INC.
Metuchen, N.J., & London
1981

Library of Congress Cataloging in Publication Data

Swanson, Kathryn, 1938-
   Affirmative action and preferential admissions
in higher education.

   1. Universities and colleges--United States--
Admission--Bibliography.   2. Affirmative actions
programs--United States--Bibliography.   3. Discrimination in education--United States--Bibliog-
raphy.   I. Title.   II. Title: Preferential
admissions in higher education.
Z5814.U7S93 [LC212.2]   016.378'1056'0973   81-45
ISBN 0-8108-1411-0

TABLE OF CONTENTS

INTRODUCTION

The purpose of this bibliography is to familiarize readers with the literature relating to affirmative action and preferential admissions in higher education. Perhaps no other issue in recent times has created such widespread controversy as whether to grant preferential treatment to minorities and women as a means of overcoming generations of discrimination and opening up opportunities in education and employment previously denied to them.

Contributing to this controversy are the various federal laws and regulations issued over the last ten years or so consisting of formalized policies and procedures designed to improve the economic and educational conditions of the formerly "disadvantaged," including women.

But before discussing these various federal laws and regulations as they relate to higher education, the definitions of "affirmative action" and "preferential admissions" are necessary.

The federal government first used the term "affirmative action" in the issuance of Executive Order 11375 on October 13, 1967. In calling for equal employment opportunity in Government employment, and by Government contractors and subcontractors, the Presidential Order required that "the contractor will take affirmative action to ensure that applicants are employed, and that employees are treated during employment, without regard to their race, color, religion, sex, or national origin."[1]

As applied to higher education, the term "affirmative action" was first used in <u>Higher Education Guidelines, Executive Order 11246</u>, issued by the Office for Civil Rights, Department of Health, Education and Welfare, in October, 1972.[2] The premise behind affirmative action, the Office for Civil Rights wrote, was to take "positive action" to "overcome the effects of systematic institutional forms of exclusion and discrimination." In employment practices, the <u>Guidelines</u> continued, a "benign neutrality ... will tend to perpetuate the <u>status quo ante</u> indefinitely."[3]

The Guidelines required the employer "to make additional efforts to recruit, employ and promote qualified members of groups formerly excluded, even if that exclusion cannot be traced to particular discriminatory actions on the part of the employer."[4]

Thus, the affirmative action concept means that employers must take active steps to seek out qualified women and minorities for employment and promotion.

It could be said that the term "preferential admissions" is a form of affirmative action in that qualified women and minorities are sought out for admissions to higher education. As used in the literature, "preferential admissions" means the granting of priority or advantage on the basis of a person's race, sex, or both. The controversy arises over the importance given to race and sex in the admissions criteria in higher education. Preference may range from race and sex classification as the determining criteria if all other factors are equal among all the candidates. At the other extreme are special admissions programs designed to admit a fixed quota of minorities and women.

Much of the furor over preferential admissions centers on the issue of quotas, with critics charging that minorities and women are being admitted to higher education, including professional schools, even when they are not as qualified as white or male applicants. In the celebrated Bakke case, decided by the U. S. Supreme Court in June, 1978, one of the central issues is the constitutionality of the special admissions program at the University of California at Davis Medical School. [5] That school reserved 16 out of the 100 places in the entering class for disadvantaged students, although only minorities were admitted under the program. Applications under this special program were evaluated by a separate committee. This separate procedure allowed the admission of some minority students whose combined numerical ratings were lower than those of some rejected white applicants, including Allan Bakke. Twice Bakke had been denied admission to medical school, and subsequently sued for declaratory and injunctive relief to compel the university to admit him, alleging that the primary reason for his rejection was his race. [6]

The disposition of the Bakke case in the California courts and the issues before the U. S. Supreme Court will be discussed in greater detail in the introduction to Part One of this bibliography on the law and the courts.

The constitutionality of preferential admissions and affirmative action programs in education and employment is only one of several important issues in America today. At the heart of the controversy over these programs lies fundamentally opposing viewpoints over such terms as equality of opportunity and how best to bring about justice and racial harmony in America.

Whether affirmative action and preferential admissions provide the best means to achieve these long-held values of equality, justice, and harmony has produced sharp debate, which is particularly evident in the deep division between civil rights advocates who once stood firmly together during the turbulent racial strife of the 1960's.

On the one hand, it is argued that given the enduring and pervasive racist heritage in America, blacks and other minorities have never had the opportunity to compete fairly in the distribution of benefits and opportunities. Hence, to compensate for past injustices and to assist minorities so that they can compete fairly, race must be taken into account. Special opportunities, the argument goes, should be provided for minorities in education and employment so that they can achieve parity with the white majority. Racially neutral or color-blind laws and institutions can only perpetrate the severe handicaps and deep-seated discrimination under which minorities have historically found themselves.

Yet it is precisely this color-blind society which opponents of affirmative action and preferential admissions espouse as the only standard for a democratic society. Special treatment based upon race (or sex) destroys the ideal of being judged on the basis of individual merit and violates the constitutional guarantee of equal protection under the laws. The substitution of group rights over individual rights, the argument goes, contributes to racial polarization and stigmatizes those given preferential treatment. "Making it" thus becomes the result of membership in a group rather than because of individual merit.

It is within this broad philosophical framework that friends and foes of affirmative action and preferential admissions tend to operate. Such emotion-laden terms as "reverse discrimination" and "institutional racism" mask the very agonizing moral dilemma about how best to achieve justice and equality in America.

As explained earlier, this bibliography is limited to affirmative action and preferential admissions in higher education, the latter defined as four-year colleges and professional schools. I have concentrated upon the literature of these topics from 1970 to the present not only because of the vast literature involved, but primarily because it was not until the early 1970's that the application of federal affirmative action guidelines and regulations became more stringent, resulting in more opposition to them within the academic community.

This bibliography is divided into three parts:

1) The Law and the Courts;
2) The Academic Community Response;
3) The Philosophical Debate.

Included in the bibliography are government publications, books, periodical articles, newspaper articles, and selected chapters within collected works relating to affirmative action and preferential admissions in higher education.

Attached to the sections on the law and the courts and the academic community response is material selected from Resources in Education, a monthly abstract journal comprising recent report literature, both published and unpublished, relating to the field of education. Its sponsors are Educational Resources Information Center (ERIC); National Institute of Education (NIE); and the U. S. Department of Health, Education, and Welfare. ERIC is a nationwide information network for acquiring, selecting, abstracting, indexing, storing, retrieving, and disseminating significant and timely education-related reports.

Resources in Education consists of resumes and indexes, with the former providing descriptions of each document and abstracts of their content. Resumes are numbered sequentially by an accession number beginning with the prefix ED (ERIC Document). Documents are retrieved through this accession number and are available from the ERIC Document Reproduction Service (EDRS) in microfiche (MF) copy.

Although every effort has been made to annotate material throughout this bibliography, I was unable to obtain some sources, for various reasons. Nevertheless, several unannotated sources are included because of their promising titles or because they appeared several times as citations in the literature, quoted by other authors.

I wish to thank Robert B. Harmon, Reference and Special Collections Librarian at San Jose State University, for his encouragement and helpful suggestions in the compilation of this bibliography. I would also like to thank the Documents staff at San Jose State University Library, particularly Christine Simpson. Finally, this bibliography could not have been completed without the excellent and prompt service provided by King Wah Moberg and her Interlibrary Loan staff and also the able assistance offered by Helen Lee at San Jose State University Library.

References

1. "Executive Order 11246, as amended by Executive Order 11375." Federal Register. 32 (October 13, 1967) 14303.
2. U. S. Department of Health, Education and Welfare. Office of the Secretary. Office for Civil Rights. Higher Education Guidelines Executive Order 11246. October 1, 1972.
3. Ibid. , p. 3.
4. Ibid.
5. Bakke v. Regents of the University of California, 18 Cal. 3d 34, 553 p. 2d 1152, 132 Cal. Rptr. 680 (1976), cert. granted, 45 U. S. L. W. 3555 (U. S. February 22, 1977) (No. 76-811), 51 L Ed 2d 535.
6. Ibid. at 43-44, 553 P. 2d at 1158-59, 132 Cal. Rptr. at 686-687.

PART ONE:

THE LAW AND THE COURTS

An Analysis of the Law and the Courts in Affirmative

Action and Preferential Admissions in Higher Education

This section on affirmative action and preferential admissions in higher education pertains to federal laws, regulations, Executive Orders, legislative hearings, court cases, and interpretations of these laws and cases by legal scholars and laymen.

Although several court cases concern claims of race and sex discrimination in higher education, there have been only two cases which have reached the U. S. Supreme Court relating to the constitutionality of special admissions for minorities in higher education. In both cases, a white male contended that he was denied admission solely because of his race and that he was better qualified than minority group applicants who were successfully admitted to professional schools. One of these cases has already been mentioned: Bakke v. The Regents of the University of California. [1] In filing a complaint with the California courts, Bakke alleged that he was qualified for admission and that he had been the victim of invidious discrimination because of his race, in violation of the equal protection clause of the Fourteenth Amendment. [2] Bakke also alleged that all students admitted under the special admission program at the University of California at Davis Medical School were members of racial minorities, that the program applied separate, i. e. , preferential standards of admissions as to them, and that the use of separate standards resulted in the acceptance of minority applicants who were less qualified for the study of medicine than Bakke and other nonminority applicants not selected. [3]

The University, in seeking court validation for its special admissions program, filed a cross-complaint. The complaint averred that the University used the minority status of an applicant as only one factor in selecting students for admission, and that the purposes of the special program were to promote diversity in the student body and the medical profession, and to expand medical education opportunities to persons from economically or educationally disadvantaged backgrounds. [4]

On September 16, 1976, the California State Supreme Court issued its landmark decision on the Bakke case. By a vote of 6 to 1, the court held preferential treatment of racial minorities in admission to state professional schools unconstitutional under the equal protection clause of the United States Constitution. The court found that the separate admissions program for disadvantaged minority applicants adopted by the University resulted in the exclusion of white applicants who, using the University's own criteria, were more qualified than some minority applicants admitted under the program. The University, moreover, failed to demonstrate that basic goals could not be substantially achieved by less detrimental means. [5]

The Regents of the University of California subsequently appealed the case to the U. S. Supreme Court, where the case was decided on June 28, 1978. The high court affirmed the California Supreme Court's judgment that the medical school's special admissions program was unlawful and that Bakke must be admitted. At the same time, the Court agreed that the California Supreme Court's judgment must be reversed insofar as it prohibited the University of California from giving any consideration to race in its future admissions process. [6]

But before discussing the U. S. Supreme Court's decision in the Bakke case, let us turn to an earlier case relating to the constitutionality of special admissions for minorities, Marco DeFunis v. Charles Odegaard. [7] The case was argued before the U. S. Supreme Court on February 25, 1972, and decided on April 23 of that same year. The facts of the case are these: In 1972, Marco DeFunis had been denied admission to the University of Washington Law School. When seeking a mandatory injunction to compel his admission, DeFunis contended that the school's policy invidiously discriminated against him on account of his race in violation of the equal protection clause of the Fourteenth Amendment. That policy was the special admissions program whereby preferential treatment was extended to applicants from certain minority racial groups, even though such applicants did not rate as highly as other, nonminority applicants under the school's evaluation procedure based on testing results and undergraduate grades. The trial court granted DeFunis requested relief, whereupon the Supreme Court of Washington reversed the trial court's judgment, upholding the constitutionality of the school's admission policy. The case was appealed to the U. S. Supreme Court. The high court, by a 5-4 decision, declared the case moot because DeFunis had been admitted to the law school and was about to graduate. [8]

In studying the literature on affirmative action and preferential admissions in higher education, the basic constitutional questions raised in the court cases and by legal scholars are as follows:

1) Are racial classifications constitutionally permissible?
2) Can a distinction be made between "invidious" and "benign" racial classifications?
3) What is to be the standard of judicial review in questions relating to racial classifications under the Equal Protection Clause?
4) What is the relationship between racial classification, governmental purpose, and past record of discrimination?

1. Are racial classifications constitutionally permissible?

The more precise question posed in the legal literature is: for what purposes are racial classifications used? Legal scholars have long debated the distinctions between "invidious" and "benign" racial classifications. The former is generally defined as stigmatizing a racial group with a stamp of inferiority; the latter generally means discriminating in favor of minorities in order to achieve some institutional or societal goal, such as achieving a more representative student body or increasing the percentage of minority doctors or lawyers. [9]

The arguments made on behalf of affirmative action programs and preferential admissions in higher education focus on this distinction between "invidious" and "benign" racial classification. Such programs, the argument goes, are constitutional because the government's purpose was not to racially discriminate against all members of a certain racial group by denying them the benefits of higher education. Rather, the state's purpose in affirmative action programs, including preferential admissions, is to integrate the races and provide the benefits of higher education to qualified members of all racial groups.

One of the most forceful arguments in favor of "benign" racial classification was by Justice Matthew O. Tobriner, the lone dissenting voice in the Bakke case before the California Supreme Court. Tobriner criticized the majority opinion for its "two fundamentally flawed premises:" one, for failing to distinguish between "invidious" racial classification and remedial or "benign" racial classification; and, second, for incorrectly asserting that the minority students accepted under the special admission program are "less qualified" than nonminority applicants rejected by the medical school. [10] Tobriner added that "numerous court decisions recognize that as a practical matter racial classifications frequently must be employed if the effects of past discrimination and exclusion are to be overcome" and if integration of institutions is to be achieved. Remedial racial classifications are not forbidden by the Constitution, he added. [11]

The majority of the California State Supreme Court, in turn, questioned "benign" racial classifications because while the special admission program was favorable to minorities, "it certainly cannot be said to favor the majority." The equal protection clause, the majority added, "by its literal terms applies to 'any person,' and its lofty purpose, to secure equality of treatment of all, is incompatible with the premise that some races may be afforded a higher degree of protection against unequal treatment than others." [12]

2. What should be the standard of judicial review to test whether racial classifications are in accordance with the Equal Protection Clause?

Legal scholars emphasize three standards of review: 1) "compelling interest" test; 2) "rational basis" test; and 3) "substantive interest" test.

(1) "Compelling interest" test

As the literature brings out, the courts have consistently recognized that race is a "suspect" classification, hence subject to a "strict scrutiny" test. Such a classification must have its purpose serve a "compelling state interest. " Any state action employing a racial classification is "constitutionally suspect ... subject to the most rigid scrutiny ... and in most circumstances irrelevant to any constitutionally acceptable legislative purpose. " It can be justified only by "some overriding statutory purpose. " Without this purpose the racial classification "is reduced to an invidious discrimination forbidden by the Equal Protection Clause. "[13]

In both cases involving preferential admissions in higher education, DeFunis v. Odegaard and Bakke v. Regents of the University of California, the "compelling interest" test became the standard of review. The Washington State Supreme Court, in DeFunis, held that "the burden is upon the Law School to show that its consideration of race in admitting students is necessary to the accomplishment of a compelling state interest. "[14] The California State Supreme Court, in the Bakke case, held that "it must be demonstrated by rigid scrutiny that there are no reasonable ways to achieve the state's goals by means which impose a lesser limitation on the right of the group disadvantaged by the classification. The burden in both respects is upon the Government. "[15]

Whereas the state supreme court of Washington accepted the university's contention that racially preferential admissions met the "compelling interest" test, and upheld the constitutionality of preferential admissions, the California State Supreme Court found that the University of California had not proven that there were no alternatives to a special admissions program for minorities.

In the DeFunis case, the court found compelling state interests in the elimination of "racial imbalance within public legal education, " the production of "a racially balanced student body at the law school, " and the alleviation of a nationwide "shortage of minority attorneys. "[16]

The California State Supreme Court in the Bakke case assumed arguendo that several objectives which the University sought to achieve by its special admissions program "met the exacting standards required to uphold the validity of a racial classification insofar as they establish a compelling governmental interest. "[17]

The University of California justified its program as meeting the compelling interest test on the grounds that minority admissions are necessary to integrate the medical school and the profession. To accomplish this, the "presence of a substantial number of minority students will ... provide diversity in the student body ... will influence the students and the remainder of the profession so that they will become aware of the medical needs of the minority community" and minority doctors will "provide role models for younger persons in the minority community. " Black doctors will have "a greater rapport with patients of their own race. "[18]

The majority of the court responded by holding that the University had not established that "a program which discriminates against white applicants because of their race" is necessary to achieve the goals of integrating the medical school and the profession. [19]

Both state supreme courts had considered, then rejected a second standard of judicial review, the "rational basis" test.

(2) "Rational basis" test

This level of review holds that a classification to be valid must bear a "rational relationship to some legitimate legislative objective. "[20] As applied to preferential admissions, such a test would have to prove that special admissions are a rational means to serve the legitimate purpose of compensating for injustices promoting diversity within law schools, and ameliorating racial stereotypes. [21]

In both the DeFunis and Bakke cases, the proponents of preferential admissions argued for the application of the "rational basis" test. In the DeFunis case, the Law School contended that the rational basis test should be applied, and not the most stringent "compelling interest" test because the minority admissions program was not constitutionally suspect in that it was not "invidious" or "stigmatizing" toward racial minorities. [22]

In the Bakke case, the University argued that it was only sufficient to prove that the special admissions program "has a rational relationship to the University's goals, " and that "white applicants denied admission are not stigmatized in the sense of having cast about them an aura of inferiority. " "Invidious" discrimination, the University contended, "occurs only if the classification excludes, disadvantages, isolates, or stigmatizes a minority or is designed to segregate the races. "[23]

The majority of the court rejected the implication that "invidious" discrimination can only be directed against a minority. It was "abundantly clear, " the court maintained, that "whites suffer a grievous disadvantage by reason of their exclusion from the University on racial grounds. " Race as a suspect classification applies equally to the majority if the consequences of the classification are detrimental, the court suggested. [24]

(3) "Substantial interest" test

The California State Supreme Court had briefly considered, then dismissed, a third standard of review, the "substantial interest" test. In the Bakke case, the University had used a New York case, Alevy v. Downstate Medical Center (1976), in an effort to persuade the court that the "compelling interest" test need not apply, and that a "substantial interest" test was sufficient. That case involved a white medical student who alleged that he had been discriminated against in admission to a public medical school because of preferences accorded to black and Puerto Rican applicants in the admission program. [25] The New York appellate court, in discussing the permissibility of preferential minority admissions, contended that the question to be considered was whether the state had a substantial interest in special admissions programs and if such an interest be found, the gain on balance outweighs its possible detrimental effects. [26]

The California State Supreme Court concluded that the language of the New York court in the <u>Alevy</u> case and their decision was "more apparent than real. "[27]

3. What is the relationship between racial classification, governmental purpose, and past record of discrimination?

Closely related to the question of "invidious" vs. "benign" discrimination, as the literature shows, is the issue of intention or purpose behind such discrimination and whether there exists a record of past discrimination. At least one legal scholar has suggested that the constitutionality of affirmative action programs, like those found in the <u>DeFunis</u> and <u>Bakke</u> cases, will turn on the Supreme Court's clarification of "racially discriminatory intention or purpose. "[28]

In the <u>Bakke</u> case before the California State Supreme Court, the University of California cited various U. S. Supreme Court decisions which had, according to the University, upheld the validity of a preference to minorities on the basis of race even if the classification resulted in detriment to the majority. [29]

The majority of the California court responded to the University's claims by pointing out that in all the cases cited by the University, "the defendant had practiced discrimination in the past and that the preferential treatment of minorities was necessary to grant them the opportunity for equality which would have been theirs but for the past discriminatory conduct. [30]

The majority of the court reemphasized that federal court decisions had upheld the validity of preferential treatment of minorities if it had been proven that the employer was guilty of prior discrimination. [31]

This issue of what constitutes "prior discrimination, " was a focal point not only in the California courts but also in the arguments before the U. S. Supreme Court, as we shall see.

The California State Supreme Court addressed the question of whether the University of California had discriminated against minority applicants in the past. The test for such prior discrimination had been raised in a brief on behalf of the University. That

brief claimed that the University's reliance on grade point averages
and the Medical College Admission Test in evaluating applicants
amounted to discrimination against minorities.   The application of
these tests, the brief asserted, "resulted in the exclusion of a disproportionate number of minority applicants. "   The test scores,
moreover, "were not significantly related to a student's performance
in medical school or in the profession, and that the test is culturally biased. "[32]

As the literature shows, these same arguments against standardized tests continue to be raised in defense of minority admissions to higher education.

The California State Supreme Court, however, responded to
these charges by citing cases in which the U. S. Supreme Court had
decided that "absent a racially discriminatory purpose, a test is
not invalid solely because it may have a racially disproportionate
impact. "   Underrepresentation of minorities at the University, the
Court continued, was not sufficient to prove that the University was
guilty of past racial discrimination. [33]   In addition, there was no
evidence in the record to indicate that the University had engaged
in racial discrimination in the past. [34]

Whether a record of past racial discrimination justifies preferential treatment of minorities was also an issue before the U. S.
Supreme Court in the oral arguments on the Bakke case (October
12, 1977).   Archibald Cox, representing the University of California,
talked of the need for increasing representation of qualified minority
group members in professional schools so as to train them for the
professions "from which minorities are long excluded because of
generations of pervasive racial discrimination. "   Cox continued that
"there is no racially blind method of selection, which will enroll
today more than a trickle of minority students in the nation's colleges and professions. "[35]

I have gone into some detail on the issues raised in the
DeFunis and Bakke cases relating to the constitutionality of preferential admissions in higher education because these are the same
issues raised by legal scholars and laymen in discussing affirmative
action programs.

An additional issue raised in court cases is whether such
programs, including preferential admissions, are "stigmatizing" to
those participating in them.   Justice William Douglas raised this
point in his dissent in the DeFunis case:

> A segregated admission process creates suggestions of
> stigma and caste no less than a segregated classroom,
> and in the end it may produce that result despite its con-
> trary intentions. . . .   [T]hat Blacks or Browns cannot make
> it on their individual merit . . . is a stamp of inferiority
> that a state is not permitted to place on any lawyer. [36]

Others have argued, however, that not to have special admissions programs for minorities in higher education contributes to the perpetuation of a permanent racial underclass in America and a continuing stigma attached to being a minority. [37] As the Solicitor General of the United States, Wade McCree, Jr., argued before the U.S. Supreme Court in the Bakke case, "It is not enough ... to look at the visible wound imposed by unconstitutional discrimination based upon race or ethnic status, because the very identification of race or ethnic status in America today is, itself, a handicap."[38] Affirmative action programs, such as preferential admissions, which take race into consideration, McCree argued, only means to eliminate pervasive discrimination. Such programs, moreover, are consistent with the intent and purpose of the Fourteenth Amendment. [39]

That the Fourteenth Amendment sanctioned affirmative action programs was also a theme running through the arguments of Archibald Cox, representing the University before the U.S. Supreme Court during the Bakke case.

The Fourteenth Amendment, Cox told the Supreme Court Justices, "does not outlaw race-conscious programs where there is no invidious purpose or intent, or where they are aimed at offsetting the consequences of our long tragic history of discrimination and achieving greater racial equity."[40]

To achieve greater racial equity, is it necessary to grant preferential treatment to blacks over apparently more qualified whites?

The U.S. Supreme Court addressed this question in its long-awaited decision on June 28, 1978, Regents of the University of California v. Bakke. [41] The sharply divided Court issued six separate decisions, with Justice Lewis Powell casting the deciding vote on the two major holdings. He joined with Justices Brennan, White, Marshall, and Blackmun in upholding the constitutionality of race-conscious admissions programs whose aim is to increase minority student enrollment in higher education. The U.S. Supreme Court thus reversed the California Supreme Court's ruling which prohibited any consideration of race in its admissions process. [42] Powell then joined with Justices Stevens, Chief Justice Burger, Stewart, and Rehnquist in affirming the California Supreme Court's holding that the special admissions program at Davis was unlawful and that Bakke should be admitted. [43]

But unlike Powell, the Stevens group, as it came to be called, did not address the constitutional issues of whether Davis' special admissions program violated the equal protection principles or whether race could ever be considered in an admissions program. The only issue before the Court, the Stevens group held, was the validity of the admissions program as applied to deny Bakke entry to medical school. Thus confining their judgment to the statutory question of whether Title VI of the Civil Rights Act of 1964 allowed the special admissions program at Davis, the Stevens group ruled

that the program clearly violated Title VI by excluding Bakke because of his race. Title VI had clearly prohibited such exclusion,
on the basis of race, of "any" individual from a federally funded
program, regardless of whether or not such exclusion carried with
it a racial stigma or resulted from an "affirmative action" program. 44

The question of whether Title VI was distinct from the Fourteenth Amendment equal protection clause was answered by Justices
Powell, Brennan, White, Marshall, and Blackmun in their holding
that the prohibition of discrimination in Title VI was coextensive
with the Fourteenth Amendment and that Congress intended that Title VI's standard was that of the Constitution. The Brennan group
held that Title VI does not bar preferential treatment of racial
minorities as a means of remedying past societal discrimination to
the extent that such action is consistent with the Fourteenth Amendment. 45

The five justices who addressed the constitutional issues in
the Bakke case were essentially asking the question: under what
circumstances are racial classifications permissible under the equal
protection clause? Justices Powell and the Brennan group (Brennan, White, Marshall, and Blackmun) arrived at different conclusions, based upon their different standards of review.

Justice Powell invoked the traditional "strict scrutiny" test
for racial classifications by which under the equal protection clause,
racial distinctions "of any sort were inherently suspect and thus
call for the most exacting judicial examination. "46

Under the strict scrutiny test, racial classifications could be
justified if such classifications were "precisely tailored to serve a
compelling governmental interest. "47 The Davis special admissions
program, Powell held, did not meet a compelling governmental interest or purpose and was therefore invalid under the equal protection clause. 48   Powell specifically cited the following purposes of
the special admissions program at Davis and explained why all but
one did not meet a compelling governmental interest:

1) Assuring a specified percentage of a particular racial
group within the student body, since such racial preferences were facially invalid as discrimination for its own
sake. 49
2) Countering the effects of past societal discrimination,
while legitimate and substantial, the University, nevertheless, cannot institute racial classifications, at least in
the absence of judicial, legislative, or administrative
findings of constitutional or statutory violations. 50
3) Increasing the number of doctors in communities currently underserved, but the record gave virtually no evidence
that the special admissions program was needed or geared
to promote this goal. 51
4) Obtaining the educational benefits that derive from an eth-

nically diverse student body is a constitutionally permissible goal in view of the First Amendment's special concern for academic freedom, particularly which includes
the freedom of a university to make its own judgments
as to the selection of its student body.   But the University of California at Davis had not met its burden in
proving that the program's reserving a fixed number of
seats in each class solely on the basis of race was necessary to achieve diversity. [52]

Powell indicated that a more flexible admissions program
would be constitutional if it took race into account without reserving
a fixed number of seats for minorities.   The key difference between
the admissions program at Davis and the admissions program at
Harvard, which Powell singled out as a model, was that the latter
"treats each applicant as an individual. "[53]

In summary, a majority of the Supreme Court had upheld as
lawful under Title VI of the Civil Rights Act of 1964 and the Fourteenth Amendment an admissions program which considers race and
even a numerical balance of the class; but such a program could
not assign a fixed number of seats for minorities, as the Davis
program had done.

While the Brennan group (Justices Brennan, White, Marshall,
and Blackmun) had also approved the Harvard admissions program
they had gone much farther in upholding the constitutionality of race-
conscious admissions programs than had Powell, and in so doing
had used a different standard of review than Powell's utilization of
the "strict scrutiny" test. [54]

Justices Brennan, White, Marshall, and Blackmun ruled that
"racial classifications designed to further remedial purposes 'must
serve important governmental objectives and must be substantially
related to achievement of these objectives. '"[55]

This "substantial interest" test is an intermediate standard
of review because racial classifications must serve "important"
rather than "compelling" governmental interests or purposes.   Racial classifications under this test, moreover, are not required to
be "necessary" to achieve these interests.   Justice Powell ruled
that the goal of achieving a diverse student body, while sufficiently
compelling to justify consideration of race under some circumstances, nevertheless, the assignment of a fixed number of places
to a minority group is not a necessary means toward achieving educational diversity. [56]   The California Supreme Court had previously
ruled that even if the special admissions program served a compelling interest, alternate means were available to accomplish that
interest.

Under the "substantial interest" test, the Brennan group emphasized that a racial classification would be declared invalid if it
"stigmatizes any group or ... singles out those least well repre-

sented in the political process to bear the brunt of a benign program" or it were not justified by "an important and articulated purpose. "[57]

The Brennan group thereupon concluded that the Davis "articulated purpose of remedying the effects of past societal discrimination is ... sufficiently important to justify the use of race-conscious
admissions programs when the school had a sound basis for concluding that minority underrepresentation is substantial and chronic, "
and that the handicap of past discrimination is impeding minority
access to the medical school. The Davis program met these two
tests in addition to the test that it did not stigmatize any discrete
group or individual. [58]

Justices Marshall and Blackmun, in separate opinions, reaf-
firmed the constitutionality of race-conscious admissions programs
to overcome past societal discrimination. In summarizing the
"sorry history of discrimination and its devastating impact on the
lives of Negroes, " Marshall wrote,

> bringing the Negro into the mainstream of American life
> should be a state interest of the highest order. To fail
> to do so is to insure that America will forever remain a
> divided society. [59]

The Negro experience in America, Marshall continued, makes
it difficult for him "to accept that Negroes cannot be afforded greater protection under the Fourteenth Amendment where it is necessary
to remedy the effects of past discrimination. " It is because of this
legacy of unequal treatment, Marshall insisted, that "we must now
permit the institutions of this society to give consideration to race
in making decisions about who will hold positions of influence, affluence and prestige in America. "[60]

Justice Blackmun also wrote of the original purpose of the
Fourteenth Amendment, and found it ironic that only preferential
admissions for minority groups have raised so much concern, given
other governmental preferences such as to veterans, Indians, the
handicapped, and the progressive income tax. It would be impos-
sible, Blackmun, suspects, "to arrange an affirmative action program in a racially neutral way and have it successful. "

> In order to get beyond racism, we must first take account
> of race. There is no other way. And in order to treat
> some persons equally, we must treat them differently.
> We cannot--we dare not--let the Equal Protection Clause
> perpetrate racial supremacy. [61]

The Brennan group disagreed not only with the proper standard of review to employ in ruling upon the constitutionality of affirmative action plans, but also whether such plans can be justified
without specific findings of past discrimination. As previously explained, Powell ruled that the Court had "never approved a classifi-

cation that aids persons perceived as members of relatively victimized groups at the expense of other innocent individuals in the absence of judicial, legislative, or administrative findings of constitutional or statutory violations. "[62] The Brennan group, on the other hand, wrote that "the presence or absence of past discrimination
by universities or employers is largely irrelevant to resolving
[Bakke's] constitutional claims. "[63] "The requirement of a judicial
interpretation of a constitutional or statutory violation as a predicate
for race-conscious remedial actions would be self-defeating. " Such
a requirement, the Brennan group emphasized, would severely undermine voluntary efforts to comply with the law, adding that the
value of voluntary efforts to further the objectives of the law have
always been stressed by our society and jurisprudence. [64]

In explaining why findings of past discrimination are largely
irrelevant, the Brennan group explained that prior cases

> ... unequivocally show that a state government may adopt
> race-conscious programs if the purpose ... is to remove
> the disparate racial impact its actions might otherwise
> have and if there is reason to believe that the disparate
> impact is itself the product of past discrimination, whether
> or not that of society at large. [65]

To the Brennan group, therefore, preferential treatment for
those likely disadvantaged by societal discrimination was authorized
by Title VI of the Civil Rights Act of 1964 and permitted under the
equal protection clause of the Fourteenth Amendment.   Under such
an interpretation the quota system was permissible as used in the
special admissions program at Davis.

But the majority of the Supreme Court, as explained earlier,
held that the special admissions program was unlawful and that
Bakke should be admitted.

A comparable "Bakke" case in employment and a similar issue of the permissible use of racial quotas was taken up by the
U. S. Supreme Court in the Weber case, decided June 27, 1979. [66]
But unlike the Bakke decision, the Supreme Court in the Weber
case confined itself solely to the statutory question of whether Title
VII of the Civil Rights Act of 1964 left employers and unions in the
private sector free to take such race-conscious steps to eliminate
manifest racial imbalances in traditionally segregated job categories.

The background for the case is as follows: In 1974, the
United Steelworkers of America and Kaiser Aluminum & Chemical
Corporation (Kaiser) entered into a collective-bargaining agreement
covering terms and conditions of employment at 15 Kaiser plants.
One provision of the agreement called for an affirmative action plan
designed to eliminate conspicious racial imbalances in Kaiser's then
almost exclusively white craft workers by reserving for black employees 50 per cent of the openings in in-plant craft-training programs until the percentage of black craft workers in a plant is

commensurate with the percentage of blacks in the local labor force.
Brian Weber, a white production worker at a Kaiser plant in Louis-
iana, brought a class action suit in the Federal District Court, alleging that because the affirmative action plan resulted in black employees of less seniority than white workers receiving preferential
training, white workers had been discriminated against in violation
of Title VII of the Civil Rights Act of 1964.   Title VII had made it
unlawful to "discriminate ... because of ... race" in hiring and in
the selection of apprentices for training programs.   The District
Court held that the affirmative plan of Kaiser violated Title VII and
entered judgment in favor of Brian Weber.   Upon appeal, the U. S.
Court of Appeals affirmed, holding that all employment preferences
based upon race, including those preferences incidental to bona fide
affirmative action plans, violated Title VII's prohibition against racial discrimination. [67]

Upon appeal to the U. S. Supreme Court, in a 5-2 vote, the
Court held that Title VII does not condemn all private, affirmative
action plans, since any contrary interpretation would bring about an
end completely at variance with the purpose of the statute, the in-
ference that Congress did not wish to ban all voluntary, race-conscious affirmative action. [68]   Both the language and legislative history of Title VII supports this conclusion, according to the majority
decision, particularly section 703(j) of Title VII which provides that
nothing contained in Title VII "shall be interpreted to require any
employer ... to grant preferential treatment ... to any group because of the race ... of such ... group on account of" a de facto
racial imbalance in the employer's work force.

Kaiser's affirmative action plan, designed to break down
traditional patterns of conspicuous racial segregation and hierarchy
and structured to open up employment opportunities for Blacks in
occupations which have been traditionally closed to them, was permissible under Title VII.   The Plan, moreover, did not unneces-
sarily trammel upon the interests of white employees: it did not
require the discharge of white employees and their replacement by
black hirees; it did not create an absolute bar to the advancement
of white employees since half of those trained in the program would
be white, and the plan was only temporary, intended to eliminate a
manifest racial imbalance rather than attempting to maintain a previously achieved racial balance. [69]

In their sharply dissenting opinions, Chief Justice Burger and
Justice Rehnquist pointed out how the clear and explicit language of
Title VII prohibited discrimination based upon race; hence the quota
used in the collective-bargaining agreement was an "unlawful employment practice. "   As Chief Justice Burger explained, the majority opinion "under the guise of statutory 'construction' ... effectively rewrites Title VII to achieve what it regards as a desirable result and 'amends' the statute to do previously what its sponsors and
its opponents agreed the statute was not intended to do. "[70]   The
plain language of Title VII, Rehnquist echoed, "flatly prohibits"
Kaiser's racially discriminatory admissions quota. [71]   Justice Rehnquist acerbicly wrote:

> Thus, by a tour de force, reminiscent not of jurists such
> as Hale, Holmes, and Hughes, but of escape artists such
> as Houdini, the Court eludes clear statutory language,
> 'uncontradicted' legislative history, and uniform precedent
> in concluding that employers, are, after all, permitted to
> consider race in making employment decisions. [72]

In both the Weber and the Bakke cases, a majority of the
U. S. Supreme Court declined to settle the question of what kinds of
affirmative action programs would be constitutionally permissible.
The Court's failure to rule upon acceptable racially preferential
programs in education and employment perhaps reflects upon the
larger societal dilemma in how best to eliminate racial injustice in
America. On the one hand, it is argued that constitutional principles and the democratic concept revolve around individual, not
group rights, and that justice requires the elimination of artificial
barriers (e. g. , discrimination based upon race or sex) in order to
achieve a true equality of opportunity whereby individuals are free
to compete equally for society's benefits and rewards. Thus, racially preferential programs are as violative of individual rights as
are racially discriminatory programs because both violate the right
of individuals to be judged according to their abilities rather than
by such genetically determined characteristics as race, ethnicity,
and sex.

On the other hand, proponents of preferential treatment for
women and minorities argue that discrimination aimed not at individuals but at an entire race or sex and which acts to deny these
groups an equal opportunity to compete for society's benefits and
rewards makes imperative affirmative action programs to remedy
the "disparate racial [and sexual] impact" produced by societal discrimination. Justice thus requires that society at large compensate
or make amends to those against whom it has discriminated. [73]

The vast literature on affirmative action and preferential admissions in higher education reflects these conflicting viewpoints and
the complex legal and philosophical questions raised by preferential
admissions measure the travail in how best to bring about racial and
sexual justice in America.

References

1. Bakke v. Regents of the University of California, 18 Cal. 3d
        34, 553 P. 2d 1152, 132 Cal. Rptr. 680 (1976). The Cali-
        fornia Reporter citation will hereafter be used.
2. 132 Cal. Rptr. at 683.
3. Ibid.
4. Ibid.
5. Ibid. at 680. Background of the trial court record is ibid. ,
        at 683-684.
6. Regents of the University of California v. Bakke, 51 L Ed 2d
        535, 57 L Ed 2d 750, 98 S. Ct. 2733 (1978).

7.   82 Wash. 2d 11; 507 P. 2d 1169 (1973).
8.   DeFunis v. Odegaard, vacated and remanded per curiam as
     moot, 416 U. S. 312, 40 L Ed 2d 1964, 94 S Ct. 1704
     (1974).
9.   For representative articles discussing "benign" and "invidious"
     racial classifications, see the bibliographic citations under
     Ely, "The Constitutionality of Reverse Racial Discrimina-
     tion"; Greenawalt, "Judicial Scrutiny of 'Benign' Racial
     Preference in Law School Admissions"; and Morris, "Con-
     stitutional Alternatives to Racial Preferences in Higher Edu-
     cation Admissions. "
10. Bakke v. Regents of the University of California, 132 Cal.
     Rptr. at 701.
11. Ibid.
12. Ibid. , at 690n and 691.
13. McLaughlin v. Florida, 379 U. S. 184, 191-193 (1964); Loving
     v. Virginia, 388 U. S. 1, 11 (1967), quoted in Larry M.
     Lavinsky, "DeFunis v. Odegaard: The 'Non-Decision' with
     a Message, " Columbia Law Review, 75 (April, 1975), 525.
     The last time the U. S. Supreme Court sustained a racial
     classification was the wartime cases of Korematsu v.
     United States, 323 U. S. 214 (1944) and Hirabayashi v.
     United States, 320 U. S. 81 (1943) which involved the relo-
     cation of Japanese-Americans.
14. 82 Wash. 2d at 32, 507 P. 2d at 1182.
15. Bakke v. Regents of the University of California 132 Cal.
     Rptr. at 690.
16. 82 Wash. 2d at 507, 507 P. 2d at 1182, 1184.
17. Bakke v. Regents of the University of California, 132 Cal.
     Rptr. at 693.
18. Ibid. , at 692-693.
19. Ibid. , at 693.
20. Greenawalt, "Judicial Scrutiny of 'Benign' Racial Preference
     in Law School Admissions, " Columbia Law Review, 75
     (April, 1975), 561.
21. Ibid. , 562.
22. Quoted in Lavinsky, p. 526.
23. 132 Cal. Rptr. at 691.
24. Ibid.
25. 384 N. Y. S. 2d 82, 348 N. E. 2d 537, quoted in ibid. , 697.
26. Ibid. , at 698n. A leading exponent of applying the "substantial
     interest" test to preferential admissions is Kent Greenawalt.
     See "Judicial Scrutiny of 'Benign' Racial Preference in Law
     School Admissions. "
27. 132 Cal. Rptr. at 698n. The New York court had not decided
     whether the minority preference was constitutional. It held
     that the petitioner had not demonstrated his right to relief
     because he had failed to show that he would have been ad-
     mitted if no preference had been extended to minorities.
     Ibid.
28. Morris, "Constitutional Alternatives to Racial Preference in
     Higher Education. " p. 302n.
29. 132 Cal. Rptr. at 696.

30. Ibid.
31. Ibid., at 696, 697.
32. Ibid., at 697.
33. Ibid.
34. Ibid.
35. Regents of the University of California v. Bakke, 46 U.S.L.W.
    3249, 3250.
36. DeFunis v. Odegaard. (J. Douglas, dissent), 40 L Ed 2d 184.
37. The idea of a permanent racial underclass is a theme in John
    Kaplan, "Equal Justice in an Unequal World: Equality for
    the Negro--the Problem of Special Treatment," Northwest-
    ern University Law Review, 61 (July-August, 1966), 363,
    374.   See also Morris, "Constitutional Alternatives to Ra-
    cial Preferences in Higher Education Admissions."
38. Regents of the University of California v. Bakke 46 U.S.L.W.
    3253.
39. Ibid.
40. Ibid., 3252.
41. 98 S. Ct. 2733 (1978).
42. Ibid. at 2764, 2767 (opinion of Powell, J.); ibid. at 2766
    (opinion of Brennan, White, Marshall, and Blackmun, JJ.).
43. Ibid. at 2764 (opinion of Powell, J.); ibid. at 2815 (opinion of
    Stevens, J.).
44. Ibid. at 2811-2815 (opinion of Stevens, J.).   For the text of
    Title VI of the Civil Rights Act of 1964, see p. 25.
45. Ibid. at 2745-47 (opinion of Powell, J.); ibid. at 2768-2774
    (opinion of Brennan, White, Marshall, and Blackmun, JJ.).
46. Ibid. at 2749 (opinion of Powell, J.).
47. Ibid. at 2753 (opinion of Powell, J.).
48. Ibid. at 2764 (opinion of Powell, J.).
49. Ibid. at 2757 (opinion of Powell, J.).
50. Ibid. at 2757-2759 (opinion of Powell, J.).
51. Ibid. at 2759-2760 (opinion of Powell, J.).
52. Ibid. at 2760-2764 (opinion of Powell, J.).
53. Ibid. at 2762-2763 (opinion of Powell, J.).
54. The Brennan group, however, found no constitutional distinction
    between the Harvard and Davis plans and suggested that the
    Harvard program is more acceptable to the public than is
    the Davis "quota." (Ibid. at 2793-2794.).
55. Ibid. at 2784 (quoting Califano v. Webster, 430 U.S. 313, 316
    (1977) (quoting Craig v. Boren, 429 U.S. 190, 197 (1976)
    (opinion of Brennan, White, Marshall, and Blackmun, J.).
56. Ibid. at 2761-2762 (opinion of Powell, J.).   The Brennan group
    declined to use the compelling interest test because no
    fundamental rights were at stake and because whites as a
    class lack the traditional idicia of suspectness: they have
    not been historically subjected to unfair treatment or ren-
    dered politically powerless which required special protec-
    tion from the ordinary political process.   The preference
    involved in the Bakke case, moreover, does not presume
    the inferiority of one race or place the government in sup-
    port of racial hatred and separatism, an event in which
    such classification would be "invalid without more." (Ibid.

at 2782-2783 (opinion of Brennan, White, Marshall, and
Blackmun, JJ.)).

57.   Ibid. at 2785 (opinion of Brennan, White, Marshall, and Blackmun, JJ.).   The Brennan group rejected the "rational basis" test for racial classification, a standard of review
whereby a classification to be valid must bear a rational
relationship to some legitimate legislative objective.   An
intermediate test was needed because state programs osten-
sibly designed to ameliorate the effects of past racial discrimination "obviously create ... a hazard of stigma, since
they may promote racial separation and reinforce the views
of those who believe that members of racial minorities are
inherently incapable of succeeding on their own. " (Ibid. at
2783-2784.)

58.   Ibid. at 2785, 2789-2793 (opinion of Brennan, White, Marshall,
and Blackmun, JJ.).

59.   Ibid. at 2803 (opinion of Marshall, J.).

60.   Ibid. at 2805 (opinion of Marshall, J.).

61.   Ibid. at 2808 (opinion of Blackmun, J.).

62.   Ibid. at 2757-2758 (opinion of Powell, J.).

63.   Ibid. at 2787 (opinion of Brennan, White, Marshall, and Blackmun, JJ.).

64.   Ibid. at 2786.

65.   Ibid. at 2789 (opinion of Brennan, White, Marshall, and Blackmun, JJ.).

66.   United Steelworkers of America, AFL-CIO-CLC v. Brian F.
Weber et al. No. 78-432. Argued March 28, 1979. De-
cided June 27, 1979. Together with No. 78-435, Kaiser
Aluminum & Chemical Corporation v. Weber et al, and
No. 78, 436, United States et al v. Weber et al. 99 S. Ct.
2721 (1979).

67.   For the text of Title VII of the Civil Rights Act of 1964, see
p. 25.

68.   Ibid. at 2722, 2727. Justice Brennan wrote the majority opinion. Justices Stewart, White, Marshall, and Blackmun
joined Justice Brennan in the majority opinion. Brennan
filed a concurring opinion. Chief Justice Burger dissented.
Justice Rehnquist filed a dissenting opinion in which Chief
Justice Burger concurred. Justices Powell and Stevens
took no part in the consideration or decision of the case.

69.   Ibid. at 2722, 2729 (opinion of Brennan, Stewart, White, Marshall, and Blackmun, JJ.).

70.   Ibid. at 2734 (opinion of Burger, J.).

71.   Ibid. at 2740 (opinion of Rehnquist, J.).

72.   Ibid. at 2737 (opinion of Rehnquist, J.).

73.   The foregoing section focused on the constitutional issues
raised in the Bakke case; for the philosophical issues of
preferential treatment pertaining to justice and equality,
see pp. 260-263.

Notes on the Sources

GOVERNMENT PUBLICATIONS

Monthly Catalog of U. S. Government Publications.   Jan. 1895-
Washington, Superintendent of Documents, U. S. Govt. Print. Off.
       This is the most important source to gain access to govern-
ment publications of the United States.   It is arranged by agency,
with monthly, semi-annual, and annual indexes arranged by title,
subject, and Series/Report.

Public Affairs Information Service.   Bulletin.   1915- New York.
       Source contains books, pamphlets, periodical articles, and
government documents relating to current public affairs such as
laws, legislation, and political and economic issues of the day.   It
is issued weekly, with quarterly and annual cumulations.   The Bulletin is arranged by subject.

LEGAL SOURCES

Court Cases--United States

United States.   Supreme Court.   United States Reports; cases ad-
    justed in the Supreme Court.   v. 1-   1754-   Washington [etc.]
    U. S. Govt. Print. Off.
       Contains the official reports of the U. S. Supreme Court.
The bound volumes are up-dated by pamphlets.

U. S. Supreme Court.   United States Supreme Court Reports.   Law-
    yer's Edition.   Book 1-100, 1790-1955; 2d ser. v. 1-   1956-
       Contains the full reports of each case argued in the U. S.
Supreme Court, as well as annotations, table of reported cases,
subject index, and a table of federal laws and regulations cited.

Preview of United States Supreme Court Cases.   Philadelphia: As-
    sociation of American Law Schools.   1976-
       Contains memoranda by law school professors, describing the
background, significance, and the issues pending before the U. S.
Supreme Court.   Published weekly, September through April.

United States Law Week.   Washington, D. C. :   Bureau of National
    Affairs.   1933-
       Weekly.   Contains sections on General Laws and the U. S.
Supreme Court.   General Laws section contains statutes, summary

and analysis, and federal agency rulings and new court decisions.
Supreme Court section is divided into Supreme Court Proceedings
and Supreme Court Opinions.   Oral arguments before the Court also included, although not verbatim.

Court Cases--California

Wests' California Reporter.   Cases argued and determined in the
  Supreme Court, District Courts of Appeal, Appellate Department
  Superior Court.   St. Paul: West Pub. Co., 1960-
        Each volume has a cross reference table among different re-
porting systems, list of judges, table of cases reported, table of
statutes cited, table of words and phrases defined, and an alphabetical digest of each law topic discussed in the volume.

Periodical Indexes to Legal Articles

Index to Legal Periodicals.

  New York: Wilson.   1908-
        Issued monthly, and arranged by subject and author in one
alphabetical arrangement.   Each issue contains a separate section
on "Table of Cases" which cites articles dealing with specific cases.
There is also a sub-heading "cases" under the subject.

Index to Periodical Articles Related to the Law.

  Dobbs Ferry, New York: Glanville Pub. 1958-
        Quarterly, and includes only the substantial and relevant
articles in English that are not cited in the Index to Legal Periodicals.   Arrangement is by subject.   A separate author index refers
to page numbers within the subject index.

Statutory Law

U.S. Laws, statutes, etc.   United States Statutes at Large, Containing the Laws and Concurrent Resolutions....   Washington,
  D.C.:   U.S. Govt. Printing Office.   v. 1-   1789-
        Contains all the laws enacted by the U.S. Congress in chrono-
logical order.   Each volume has a subject index and a table of laws
affected (amendments or repeals of prior statutes).

U.S. Laws, statutes, etc.   United States Code, Containing the General and Permanent Laws of the United States.   Washington,
  D.C.:   U.S. Govt. Printing Office, 1925-
        Permanent public laws enacted by Congress are arranged by
subject in 50 titles.   Volumes 12-15 contain a popular name index
and a general index.   Vol. 11 provides cross reference tables from
the U.S. Statutes to respective sections of the Code.   Kept up to
date by revisions and supplemental volumes.

U. S. Laws, statutes, etc. United States Code Annotated. St. Paul:
    West Publishing Co., 1927-   . 45 vols.
    Contains the annotated version of the U. S. Code, under the
same classification, including the digests of court decisions and administrative rulings which interpreted the various sections of the
code. Includes State and Federal court interpretations. Kept up
to date by revisions and cumulative annual pocket supplements.
    Of particular importance to the issues of affirmative action
programs in education and industry is Title 42, The Public Health
and Welfare Code. Section 2000d includes the provisions and interpretations of the Civil Rights Act of 1964; section 2000e on Equal
Employment Opportunities includes Executive Order 11246, as
amended.

Highlights of Major Legislation, Executive Orders, and Federal Regulations Pertaining to Affirmative Action, Race and Sex Discrimination in Institutions of Higher Education

Civil Rights Act of 1964   Public Law 88-352   78 Stats. 241

Title VI

Prohibits discrimination against any person on the grounds of race, color, or national origin in programs receiving Federal funds. Title VI and related case law prohibit discrimination on the basis of race in student admissions, access to courses and programs, and student policies and their applications. Any institution or agency receiving Federal funds is covered by Title VI.

Title VII of the Civil Rights Act of 1964 as amended by the Equal Employment Opportunity Act of 1972

Public Law 92-261   86 Stats. 103

Prohibits discrimination on the basis of race, color, religion, sex, or national origin by all private employers of 15 or more persons, all public and private educational employment agencies, labor unions with 15 or more members, and labor-management apprenticeship programs. Religious institutions or associations are exempt with respect to the employment of individuals of a particular religion in work connected with carrying on their activities.

Title VII prohibits discriminatory practices in all terms and conditions of employment including recruitment, selection, assignment, transfer, layoff, opportunities for promotion, wages and salaries, sick leave, vacation time and pay, medical insurance, retirement plans and benefits.

Affirmative action is not required unless charges have been filed, in which case it may be included in conciliation agreement or be ordered by the court.

Executive Order 11246, as amended by Executive Order 11375 (effective October 14, 1968)

Executive Order 11246 of September 24, 1965 (30 Federal Register

12319) provided a program of equal employment opportunity in Government employment, employment by Federal contractors and subcontractors and employment under Federally assisted construction contracts regardless of race, creed, color, or national origin.

Executive Order 11375 (32 Federal Register 14303), issued October 13, 1967, added the classification of sex to the above categories; contractors were prohibited from discriminating against any employee or applicant for employment in these categories, and for the first time, the term "affirmative action" was used, although not defined. As stated, "The contractor will take affirmative action to ensure that applicants are employed, and that employees are treated during employment, without regard to their race, color, religion, sex or national origin." Such action included, but was not limited to, employment, upgrading, demotion, or transfer; recruitment or recruitment advertising, layoff or termination; rates of pay or other forms of compensation, and selection for training, including apprenticeship.

Enforcement of the Executive Order and related policy guidelines are the responsibility of the Office of Federal Contract Compliance Programs (OFCCP) of the U.S. Department of Labor. The OFCCP is responsible for ensuring compliance by government contractors with the equal employment opportunities established by Executive Order 11246 and its amendments. During the height of the furor over affirmative action guidelines as applied to institutions of higher education, the OFCCP designated the Department of Health, Education, and Welfare as the agency responsible for enforcement of the order as it affected educational institutions and agencies. HEW, in turn, designated its agency, the Office for Civil Rights (OCR) as responsible for enforcement of Executive Order 11246, as amended. Effective as of October 8, 1978, any functions concerned with responsibility for enforcement of the equal employment provisions under Executive Order 11246, as amended, were transferred or reassigned to the Secretary of Labor. He, in turn, delegated most enforcement duties to the OFCCP. (Executive Order 12086, "The Consolidation of Contract Compliance Functions for Equal Employment Opportunity." Federal Register, October 5, 1978, 46501-46504.)

Both the Office of Federal Contract Compliance Programs and the Office for Civil Rights have regularly issued guidelines and detailed regulations implementing Executive Order 11246. The regulations which have caused the greatest furor among employers and educators in higher education are the following:

Revised Order No. 4, issued on December 4, 1971, by the Office of Federal Contract Compliance, Department of Labor. (36 Federal Register 23152)

Higher Education Guidelines, Executive Order 11246, issued October 1, 1972 by the Office for Civil Rights, Department of Health, Education, and Welfare.

Revised Order No. 4.

Requires each contractor or subcontractor with 50 or more employees and a contract in excess of $50,000 to develop and main-
tain a written affirmative action program within 120 days of receipt
of such a contract.   Contractors are further required to determine
whether women and minorities are "underutilized" in its employee
work force, and if that is the case, to develop specific goals and
timetables designed to overcome that underutilization.   Underutilization is defined as "having fewer women or minorities in a particular
job than would reasonably be expected by their availability. "

    In addition to providing detailed regulations concerning the
contents of affirmative action programs, the program itself is defined as "a set of specific and result-oriented procedures to which
a contractor commits himself to apply every good faith effort. "
The objective of the procedures and efforts is "equal employment
opportunity. "

Higher Education Guidelines, Executive Order 11246. 1

The Office for Civil Rights, under the leadership of J. Stanley Pottinger, issued the Guidelines in October, 1972.   A distinction was
made between nondiscrimination and affirmative action.

    Nondiscrimination requires the "elimination of all existing
    discriminatory conditions, whether purposeful or inadvertent. "

    Affirmative action "requires the employer to make additional
    efforts to recruit, employ and promote qualified members of
    groups formerly excluded, even if that exclusion cannot be
    traced to particular discriminatory actions on the part of the
    employer.   The premise of the affirmative action concept of
    the Executive Order is that unless positive action is under-
    taken to overcome the effects of systematic institutional
    forms of exclusion and discrimination, a benign neutrality in
    employment practices will tend to perpetuate the status quo
    ante indefinitely. "2

    In applying Revised Order No. 4 to institutions of higher edu-
cation, the Office for Civil Rights required the same affirmative
action program of determining underutilization and setting goals and
timetables, with the purpose of furthering employment opportunities
for women and minorities, the latter defined by the Department of
Labor as "Negroes, Spanish-surnamed, American Indians, and Ori-
entals. "   Goals were defined as "projected levels of achievement
resulting from an analysis by the contractor of its deficiencies, and
of what it can reasonably do to remedy them, given the availability
of qualified minorities and women.... "3

    The Guidelines then went on to explain:

nothing in the Executive Order requires that a university
contractor eliminate or dilute standards which are necessary to the successful performance of the institution's
educational and research functions.   The affirmative action concept does not require that a university employ or
promote any persons who are unqualified.   The concept
does require, however, that any standards or criteria
which have had the effect of excluding women and minorities be eliminated, unless the contractor can demonstrate
that such criteria are conditions of successful performance
in the particular position involved. 4

As we shall see in the second part of this bibliography on
responses to affirmative action programs in higher education, critics severely denounced these guidelines and charged that they sub-
stituted quotas for goals, forced universities to hire unqualified
women and minorities into professional positions, and imposed ar-
bitrary and unrealistic requirements upon universities, thus violat-
ing the integrity and independence of these institutions.

Additional federal regulations and legislation relating to affirmative action programs and anti-discrimination on college campuses are the amendments to the Public Health Service Act, the
Education Amendments of 1972, and the Rehabilitation Act of 1973.

Title VII (Section 799A) and Title VIII (Section 845) of the Public
Health Service Act as amended by the Comprehensive Health Man-
power Training Act and the Nurse Training Amendments Act of 1971
(Citations for the 1971 laws: Public Law 92-157, 85 Stats. 431;
Public Law 92-157, 85 Stats. 465.)

Titles VII and VIII of the Public Health Service Act state that funds
for their health personnel training programs may not discriminate
on the basis of sex in admissions or in employment practices relating to employees working directly with applicants or students.
Every institution receiving or benefiting from a grant, loan guarantee, or interest subsidy to its health personnel training programs
or receiving a contract under Titles VII or VIII is covered.

Election Amendments of 1972   Public Law 92-318, 86 Stats. 235

Title IX

Prohibits discrimination on the basis of sex in educational funds or
activities which receive Federal funds.   This prohibition covers educational programs, employment, health benefits, housing, athletics,
admissions, and financial aid, and all other programs and services
of the institution.

The Office for Civil Rights in the Department of Health, Education and Welfare is charged with enforcement of Title IX.   On

June 4, 1975, that office issued effectuating regulations for Title IX, to go into effect on July 21, 1975. These regulations are entitled

Final Title IX Regulation Implementing Education Amendments of 1972: Prohibiting Sex Discrimination in Education (40 Federal Register 21428)

The affirmative action regulations called for the following:

> In the absence of a finding of discrimination on the basis of sex in an education program or activity, a recipient may take affirmative action to overcome the effects of conditions which resulted in limited participation therein by persons of a particular sex. Nothing herein shall be interpreted to alter any affirmative action obligations which a recipient may have under Executive Order 11246.

Equal Pay Act of 1963 as amended by the Education Amendments of 1972

The Equal Pay Act prohibits sex discrimination in salaries and most fringe benefits. The above Amendments extended coverage to all employees of educational institutions and agencies, including those in professional, executive and administrative positions.

Rehabilitation Act of 1973   Public Law 93-112, 87 Stats. 355

Section 504 provided that no otherwise handicapped individual "shall, solely by reason of his handicap, be excluded from the participation in, be denied the benefits of, or be subject to discrimination under any program or activity receiving Federal financial assistance."

Affirmative Action for the Handicapped

On April 9, 1976, the U.S. Department of Labor issued the final affirmative action regulations relating to Section 503 of the 1973 Rehabilitation Act. The regulations were codified in the Code of Federal Regulations, Title 41 section 60-741. (See below for explanation of this source.) These regulations require all contractors with a Federal government contract or subcontract in excess of $2,500 to take affirmative action to hire qualified handicapped individuals, and to treat those individuals without discrimination based upon their physical or mental handicap in all employment practices.

Additional regulations aiding the handicapped were issued January 13, 1978 entitled "Implementation of Executive Order 11914, nondiscrimination on the basis of handicap in Federally assisted programs." (43 Federal Register 2132.)

Vietnam Era Veterans' Readjustment Assistance Act of 1974
                                     Public Law 93-508, 88 Stats. 1578

Increases vocational rehabilitation subsistence allowances, educational and training assistance allowances, and special allowances for Vietnam era veterans. Section 402 provides for affirmative action programs to employ and advance in employment veterans of the Vietnam era for contractors of a Federal government contract in the amount of $10,000 or more.

Federal Affirmative Action Regulations to Desegregate the Systems of Public Higher Education in Six Southern States

The most massive effort by the Department of Health, Education, and Welfare to apply affirmative action regulations to institutions of higher education grew out of the litigation of Kenneth Adams, et al v. Joseph A. Califano, Jr. [5] On April 1, 1977, Judge John Pratt in the U.S. District Court for the District of Columbia issued a Second Supplemental Order directing the Department of Health, Education, and Welfare to transmit to the six Southern states of Arkansas, Florida, Georgia, North Carolina, Oklahoma, and Virginia "specifying the ingredients of acceptable desegregation plans for their institutions of higher education. " The Court further directed that HEW require each state to submit, within 60 days of receipt of the criteria, a revised desegregation plan and to accept or reject such plan within 20 days thereafter. [6]

The Court's order arose out of a lawsuit filed in 1970 to require HEW to take action to enforce the Title VI provisions of the Civil Rights Act of 1964. [7]

The Department of Health, Education, and Welfare, in citing its criteria for acceptable desegregation plans, asserted that the Fourteenth Amendment "calls for more than mere abandonment of discrimination through the states adoption of passive or neutral policies. "[8] In its imposition of desegregation criteria upon the six Southern states, HEW used as its authority the court cases requiring public school officials to eliminate racial discrimination, including higher education systems, and HEW's regulations implementing Title VI of the Civil Rights Act of 1964. According to departmental regulations, if the recipient of federal funds has previously discriminated against persons on the ground of race, "the recipient must take affirmative action to overcome the effects of prior discrimination. "[9]

As with previous HEW affirmative action regulations, the six Southern states were required to submit to HEW numerical goals and timetables with the former "established as indices by which to measure progress toward the objective of eliminating ... racial segregation and of providing equal educational opportunity for all the citizens of these states. " HEW emphasized that these goals were not quotas and that "failure to achieve a goal is not sufficient evidence, standing alone, to establish a violation of Title VI. " The States' efforts, moreover, to meet the criteria "need not and should not lead to lowering academic standards, " the criteria were intended to allow all student applicants to compete successfully. 10

In HEW's detailed criteria for desegregating the South's higher education system, we can see the deep involvement of the federal government in attempting to bring about equal educational opportunity through the use of affirmative action regulations. This involvement is particularly evident in HEW's numerical goals in desegregating students and faculty, as seen by the following requirements:

> Adopt the goal that for two year and four year undergraduate public higher education institutions in the state system, taken as a whole, the proportion of black high school graduates throughout the State who enter such institutions shall be at least equal to the proportion of white high school graduates throughout the State who enter such institutions.

> Adopt the goal that the proportion of black state residents who graduate from undergraduate institutions in the state system and enter graduate study or professional schools in the state system shall be at least equal to the proportion of white state residents who graduate from undergraduate institutions in the state system and enter such schools.

> Assure hereafter and until the foregoing goals are met that for the traditionally white institutions as a whole, the proportion of blacks hired to fill faculty and administrative vacancies shall not be less than the proportion of black individuals with the credentials required for such positions in the relevant labor market area. 11

As evidence that the six Southern states were accomplishing these criteria, they were required to submit annually to the Office for Civil Rights (HEW) "comprehensive narrative assessment of its desegregation efforts. "

The same District Court Judge John Pratt who ordered HEW to submit criteria for desegregation plans also ordered the six Southern states to submit acceptable desegregation plans to HEW by February 3, 1978; those plans called for increased black enrollment at predominantly white institutions and a strengthening of black colleges. By May, 1979 all of the six Southern states had submitted acceptable plans to HEW, thus averting millions of dollars worth of Federal aid which they would possibly have lost without acceptable plans. 12

In summarizing the history of affirmative action legislation and regulations in higher education, it can readily be seen how powerful federal agencies have become in implementing (some critics would argue creating) Congressional legislation and Presidential Executive Orders. Whether one views these regulations as justifiable implementation of Congressional and Presidential mandates, or unwarranted intrusion by unrepresentative and unelected federal bureaucrats, depends to a large extent on how one views affirmative action regulations. Whether these regulations are favored or opposed, they are closely watched as they appear in the Federal Register and the Code of Federal Regulations.

Federal Register

Contains all Executive Orders, proclamations, and other edicts of the President, as well as the rules and regulations of executive departments and agencies and the independent agencies. Published daily Monday through Friday, with a separate monthly, quarterly, and annual index. Entries are by agencies and broad subject references.

Code of Federal Regulations

Codification of the general and permanent rules in the Federal Register by the Executive departments and agencies of the Federal government. The Code is divided into 50 titles which represent broad subject areas to Federal regulations. Each title is divided into chapters which usually bear the name of the issuing agency. Each chapter is further subdivided into parts covering specific regulatory areas. The Code is prima facie evidence of the text of the original documents. It is kept up to date by the individual issues of the Federal Register. Relevant portions dealing with affirmative action and sex and race discrimination are

> Title 29 Labor
> Part 1604   Equal Employment Opportunity Commission. Guidelines on discrimination because of sex.
>
> Title 41 Public Contracts and Property Management
> Part 60   Office of Federal Compliance Programs, Equal Employment Opportunity, Department of Labor.   (60-2, Affirmative Action Programs)
>
> Title 45 Public Welfare
> Part 80   Nondiscrimination under programs receiving Federal assistance through the Department of HEW effectuation of Title VI of the Civil Rights Act of 1964.
>
> Part 86   Department of HEW.   Nondiscrimination on the basis of sex in education programs and activities receiving or benefiting from Federal financial assistance.

References

1. U. S. Department of Health, Education, and Welfare. Office
    of the Secretary. Office for Civil Rights. Higher Educa-
    tion Guidelines Executive Order 11246. October 1, 1972.
2. Ibid., p. 3.
3. Ibid.
4. Ibid., p. 4.
5. U. S. District Court for the District of Columbia, Civil Action
    No. 3095-70, cited in Kenneth Adams, et al v. Joseph A.
    Califano, Jr., Amended Criteria Specifying Ingredients of
    Acceptable Plans to Desegregate State Systems of Public
    Higher Education, Federal Register, 42, August 11, 1977,
    40780.
6. Ibid.
7. Ibid.
8. Ibid.
9. 45 Code of Federal Regulations 80. 3(b) (6) (1), in ibid.
10. Ibid., 40781.
11. Ibid., 40783, 40784.
12. The Chronicle of Higher Education, 17 (February 20, 1979), 13;
    The New York Times, May 13, 1979, p. 21.

U. S. Government Publications

These federal government publications pertain to affirmative action, equal opportunity, and discrimination in higher education. Classification numbers are provided for easy access to the documents. Several documents are also available on microfiche from Educational Resources Information Center (ERIC), Resources in Education. Access to these microfiche copies is through ERIC's accession numbers (e. g., ED 144 518). ERIC documents are included, whenever possible.

1. U. S. Civil Service Commission. Bureau of Intergovernmental Personnel Programs. Goals and Timetables for Effective Affirmative Action: A Guide for State and Local Government. Washington, D. C., 1976. 12 p.
   CS 1. 7/4: G 53

   The purpose of the pamphlet is to assist in the development of employment goals and timetables to achieve equal opportunity. Sections are divided into U. S. government policy on employment goals; work force analyses; setting your employment goals and timetables; charting your progress, and evaluation.

2. _____. Guidelines for the Development of an Affirmative Action Plan. Washington, D. C., 1975. 78 p.
   CS 1. 7/4: Ac 8/3/975-2

   Includes guidelines to aid in the development of affirmative action plans for public employers. Sections include: evaluation of current EEO program to identify areas in need of updating, amending or improving; basics of developing a written plan, including its administration; outline of personnel management principles and practices to aid in the analysis of employer's personnel practices; methods for internal evaluation of the operation of the EEO program as compared to the objectives and actions contained in the written plan; and supplementary and supportive record keeping and reports.

3. _____. Library. Equal Opportunity in Employment. Washington, D. C., 1978. 52 p. (Personnel Bibliography Series No. 95)
   CS 1. 61. 3: 95

Chapters in this bibliographical series include employment of
minority groups, employment of specific minority groups, employment of women; and a section on affirmative action.

4. U. S. Commission on Civil Rights. Affirmative Action in Em-
    ployment in Higher Education; a consultation sponsored by the
    U. S. Commission on Civil Rights. Washington, D. C. , Sept.
    9-10, 1975. Prepared by Frederick B. Routh and Everett A.
    Waldo. Washington, D. C. , 1977. 239 p.
    (ERIC ED 144 518)   CR 1. 2: Em 7/9 item 288-A

Includes four separate sessions, with different speakers in
each session. Topics: Historical background; federal regulations and case law; HEW guidelines and actions; reactions of
colleges and universities; arguments for and against affirmative action in higher education. Focuses upon faculty recruitment, promotion, and tenure policy and practice in higher
education.

5. _____ . The Federal Civil Rights Enforcement Effort--1974.
    Volume 3: To Ensure Equal Educational Opportunity. Wash-
    ington, D. C. , 1975. 1115 p.
    (ERIC ED 102 071)   CR 1. 2: En 2/2/974/v. 3

Report evaluates efforts to ensure equal educational opportunity by three federal agencies, including the Department of
Health, Education, and Welfare. Chapter 3 deals with HEW's
responsibility for equal opportunity.

6. _____ . The Federal Civil Rights Enforcement Effort--1974.
    Volume 5: To Eliminate Employment Discrimination. Wash-
    ington, D. C. , 1975. 709 p.
    (ERIC ED 109 291)   CR 1. 2 En 2/2/974/v. 5

Includes sections on the role of colleges and universities in
eliminating employment discrimination and how affirmative action laws and regulations affect institutions of higher education. Contains major weaknesses in the federal government's
efforts to eliminate discrimination, including the problem of
diffusion of authority for the enforcement of equal employment
mandates.

7. _____ . A Guide to Federal Laws and Regulations Prohibit-
    ing Sex Discrimination. Rev. ed. Washington, D. C. , July,
    1976. 189 p.
    (ERIC ED 145 329)   CR 1. 10: 46/2

Sections divided into employment discrimination (laws, Executive Orders), federal programs (including section on higher
education), federal regulatory system, advisory and informa-
tional programs, and sex discrimination guidelines. Describes
the major provisions of each law and regulation and the complaint procedures established under each.

8. _____ . HEW and Title VI: A Report on the Development of the Organization, Policies, and Compliance Procedures of the Department of Health, Education, and Welfare Under Title VI of the Civil Rights Act of 1964. Washington, D. C., 1970. 80 p.
5 (ERIC ED 067 441)   CR 1.10: 22

Discusses the changes during the last five years of Title VI program at HEW and how they affected the compliance program of the federal government.

9. _____ . Statement on Affirmative Action for Equal Employment Opportunities. Washington, D. C., 1973.   26 p.
(ERIC ED 090 338)

Position paper on Title VII of the Civil Rights Act of 1964 and the basis for affirmative action, including responses to the debate on possible reverse discrimination and the quota system.

10. _____ . To Eliminate Employment Discrimination: A Sequel: The Federal Civil Rights Enforcement Effort--1977: A Report. Washington, D. C., Dec. 1977.   335 p.
(ERIC ED 150 224)   CR 1.2 En 2.2/977

Reviews the Federal effort by several government agencies, including HEW, to end discrimination in employment.   Sequel to The Federal Civil Rights Enforcement Effort--1974.   Latest report covers the period from July, 1975 to August, 1977.

11. _____ . Toward Equal Educational Opportunities: Affirmative Admissions Programs at Law and Medical Schools. Edited by Larry Riedman. Washington, D. C., June, 1978.   55 p.
(ERIC ED 159 980)   CR 1. 10: 55

Examines affirmative action admissions programs at law and medical schools, traces the history of past discrimination in education, describes some of its continuing effects, including underrepresentation of minorities in the legal-medical professions.   Examines traditional admissions processes at law and medical schools, describes affirmative action admissions programs currently in operation.

12. U. S. Congress.   House.   Committee on Education and Labor. Ad Hoc Subcommittee on Discrimination Against Women. Oversight Hearings on Discrimination against Women: hearings, on April 26-May 10, 1972, on investigation of discrimination on the basis of sex in the Office of Education and Office of Education grant and contract procedures.   92d Cong., 2d sess., 1973.   409 p.
                              Y 4. Ed 8/1: W84/4

Statements presented by government officials, group representatives, and individuals; articles on the subject of discrimination against women, particularly in institutions of higher education.

13. _____ . Committee on Education and Labor. Hearings on
Title IX Regulations, hearings before Subcommittee on Equal
Opportunities on House Concurrent Res. 330, 94th Cong., 1st
sess., July 14, 1975. 71 p.
                            Y 4. Ed 8/1: R 31

Includes prepared statements for and against Title IX guidelines applied to higher education, including statements relating
to intercollegiate athletics.

14. _____ . Committee on Education and Labor. Higher Education Amendments of 1971, hearings on H.R. 32. H.R.
5191-93, 92nd Cong., 1st sess., 1971.
                            Y 4. Ed 8/1: Ed 8/26/971/pt. 2

Contains bills to extend and amend the Higher Education Act
of 1965 and other acts dealing with higher education, statements relating to amendment included.

15. _____ . Committee on Education and Labor. Special Subcommittee on Education. Discrimination Against Women;
hearings on Section 805 of H.R. 16098, to prohibit discrimination against women in federally assisted programs and in
employment in education.... 91st Cong., 2d sess., 1970.
2 parts (1261 p.)
                            Y 4. Ed 8/1: W84/3, pts. 1-3

Includes statements of individuals, groups, articles, statistics,
citing extent of sex discrimination in higher education and employment, including medical schools. Source popularly called
the "Green hearings" for the subcommittee chairwoman, Edith
Green.

16. _____ . Committee on Education and Labor. Special Subcommittee on Education. Federal Higher Education Programs
Institutional Eligibility: hearings on August 8-September 25,
1974. 93rd Cong., 2d sess., 1975. Parts 2A and 2B, Civil
Rights Obligations, 1975.
                            Y 4. Ed 8/1: Ed 8/49/pt. 2AB

Contains statements, letters, reports, articles by individuals,
group representatives, and government officials on recruitment
of minorities and women in higher education and opinions both
attacking and defending affirmative action guidelines of the
federal government.

17. _____ . Committee on Education and Labor. Subcommittee
on Equal Opportunities. Oversight Hearings on Federal Enforcement of Equal Employment Laws. Hearing, 94th Cong.,
2d sess., 1976. 356 p.
                            Y 4. Ed. 8/1: Em 7/18/pt. 3

Contains statements by individuals, group representatives on
how well various agencies of the Federal government are en-

forcing equal opportunity laws, which includes those for higher education. Articles, letters, reports also included.

18. _____. Committee on Education and Labor. Subcommittee
on Equal Opportunities. The Women's Educational Equity Act:
hearings on H. R. 208, a bill to authorize the Secretary of
Health, Education, and Welfare to make grants to conduct special educational programs and activities designed to achieve
educational equity for all students, men and women, and for
other related educational purposes. 93rd Cong., 1st sess.,
1973. 629 p.
                          Y 4. Ed 8/1: W84/5/pt. 1

Includes prepared statements of individuals, group representatives, reports, letters, newspaper articles, and government
reports citing sex discrimination in higher education with the
purpose of passing legislation providing for educational equity
for women.

19. _____. Committee on Education and Labor. Subcommittee
on Postsecondary Education. Sex Discrimination Regulations:
hearings, review of regulations to implement Title IX of Public Law 92-318. 94th Cong., 1st sess., 1975. 664 p.
                          Y 4. Ed 8/1: Se 9/2

Concerns legislation banning sex discrimination in any educational program or activity assisted by the Federal government;
emphasis on college athletics.

20. U. S. Congress. Senate. Labor and Public Welfare Committee. Legislative History of the Equal Employment Opportunity
Act of 1972 (H. R. 1746, P. L. 92-261). 1976? 2067 p.
                          Y 4. L 11/2: Em 7/21

Includes the history and legislative background of the Equal
Employment Opportunity Act of 1972, text of Congressional
reports, and Congressional debates.

21. _____. Committee on Labor and Public Welfare. Subcommittee on Education. Prohibition of Sex Discrimination, 1975:
hearings on S. 2106, to amend Title IX of the Education
amendments of 1972. 94th Cong., 1st sess., 1976. 441 p.
                          Y 4. L 11/2: Se 9/975

Concerns primarily athletic programs in colleges, and whether
sex discrimination exists in such programs.

22. _____. Committee on Labor and Public Welfare. Subcommittee on Education. Women's Educational Equity Act of
1973; hearings on S. 2518. 93rd Cong., 1st sess., 1973.
426 p.
                          Y 4. L 11/2: W84

Includes prepared statements of individuals, group representatives, reports, letters, newspaper and periodical articles on sex discrimination in higher education.

23.   U. S. Department of Health, Education, and Welfare.   Education Division.   National Center for Educational Statistics.
       Barriers to Women's Participation in Post-Secondary Education: A Review of Research and Commentary as of 1973-74.
       Prepared by Esther Manning Westervelt.   Washington, D. C.,
       1975.   74 p.
       (ERIC ED 111 256)   HE 19. 311: W84

Discusses extent and magnitude of institutional barriers, social constraints, and psychological factors in women's participation in higher education.   Excellent bibliography included.

24.   _____ .   Office for Civil Rights.   Final Title IX Regulation
       Implementing Education Amendments of 1972:   prohibiting sex
       discrimination in education, effective date: July 21, 1975.
       Washington, D. C., 1975.   44 p.
                                     HE 1. 6:   Ed 8

Final regulations barred discrimination in varied ways--from admissions policies in undergraduate and graduate schools, housing, classes, and employment.   Each institution is required to evaluate its policies within one year, and to take remedial action to eliminate the effects of any past discrimination.

25.   _____ .   Office for Civil Rights.   Higher Education Guidelines Executive Order 11246.   October 1, 1972.   Washington,
       D. C., 1973.   116 p.
       (ERIC ED 074 893)   HE 1. 6 /3: G1

Concerns the legal provisions of the Executive Order, personnel policies and practices, development of affirmative action programs (including the setting of goals and timetables), and steps to overcome the "underutilization" of women and minorities.

26.   _____ .   Office for Civil Rights.   "Nondiscrimination in
       Federal Assisted Programs; Title VI of the Civil Rights Act
       of 1964; Policy Interpretation. "   Federal Register.   44 (October 10, 1979), 58509-58511.

Includes a policy interpretation by HEW of regulations under Title VI of the Civil Rights Act of 1964 concerning nondiscrimination in federally assisted programs.   The policy statement was also prompted by the U. S. Supreme Court decision in Bakke.   Encourages institutions of higher education to continue to expand voluntary affirmative action programs to increase their enrollment of minority students and to attain a diverse student body.   Identifies permissible techniques to achieve these objectives consistent with Title VI and the Supreme Court decision in Bakke.

27. _____. Office for Civil Rights. Racial, Ethnic, and Sex Enrollment Data From Institutions of Higher Education, Fall, 1976. 2 vols. Washington, D. C., 1979.
                                        HE 1. 2: R 11/2/976/v. 1-2

Includes data from institutions of higher education receiving federal financial assistance. Based upon degrees conferred by race, ethnicity, and sex, during the academic year, 1975-76.

28. _____. Statement on Guidelines for Application of Executive Order 11246 to Higher Education Institutions Receiving Federal Funds. Washington, D. C., Oct. 1972. 4 p. (ERIC ED 069 225)   HE 1. 6/3: G1

Introductory remarks by J. Stanley Pottinger, Director of the Office for Civil Rights, Department of Health, Education, and Welfare in the document, Higher Education Guidelines Executive Order 11246 (October 1, 1972). Includes the legal requirements to develop affirmative action programs by institutions of higher education to attract more women and minority applicants for employment considerations. Distinguishes between goals and quotas (the latter not required nor permitted), denies that affirmative action requires the hiring of unqualified persons, but that affirmative action does require the elimination of any standards or criteria that has the effect of excluding women and minorities unless such criteria are conditions of successful performance in the particular position involved.

29. _____. Office of Education. A Look at Women in Education: Issues and Answers for HEW. Report of the Commissioner's Task Force on the Impact of Office of Education Programs on Women. Washington, D. C., 1972. 148 p. (ERIC ED 091 957)

Examines sex discrimination in institutions of higher education and the implications for all Office of Education programs.

30. _____. Office of Education. Programs for Educational Equity: Schools and Affirmative Action, by Shirley McCune and Martha Matthews. Washington, D. C., 1975. 56 p. (ERIC ED 123 701)   HE 5. 2: P94/9

Contents: Origin and foundation of affirmative action in employment, why needed in educational employment, elements of an affirmative action program in education, and related topics.

31. _____. Office of Education. Research Reports on Affirmative Action Programs in Colleges and Universities: An Annotated Bibliography, by S. Macpherson Pemberton. Washington,

D. C., 1977.   16 p.
(ERIC ED 147 247)

Provides narrative summaries of 31 articles and books dealing
with affirmative action in higher education that appeared between 1972 and 1977.

32.　　　　　　. Office of Education.   Resources in Women's Educational Equity.   Washington, D. C., Dec. 1977- Vol. 1-
　　　　　　　　　　　　　　　　HE 19. 128: W84/2/v. 1-

Semi-annual publications funded by Federal programs established to promote educational equity for women and authorized
by the Women's Educational Equity Act of 1974 (Public Law
93-380) and the Education Amendments of 1978 (Public Law
95-561).   Special issues are also published (two by March,
1980).   Volumes include material pertaining to women's educational equity drawn from 13 or more computerized data
bases from 1970 to the present (e. g., ERIC, MEDLARS,
ABI/INFORM, Psychological Abstracts, Sociological Abstracts,
Public Affairs Information Service (PAIS).   Materials are annotated, if the data base provided such annotations.

33.　　　　　　. Office of Education.   Title IX Grievance Proce-
dures: An Introductory Manual, by Martha Matthews and
Shirley McCune.   Washington, D. C., 1977.   102 p.
(ERIC ED 135 296)　　　　　HE 19. 108: T53

Detailed step-by-step study of identifying grievance standards
for grievance procedures, and administering grievances.

34.　　　　　　. Office of Education.   Federal Interagency Commit-
tee on Education.   Keeping Your School or College Catalog in
Compliance with Federal Laws and Regulations.   Washington,
D. C. June, 1978.   17 p.
　　　　　　　　　　　HE 19. 108: C28

Provides information to assist institutions in bringing their
publications into Federal compliance.   Summarizes applicable
laws and regulations but does not attempt to interpret them.
Includes names and mailing addresses of those agencies responsible for administering these laws, regulations, and Executive Orders.   Includes information on nondiscrimination on
the basis of sex or handicap.

35.　　　　　　. Office of Education.   Resource Center on Sex
Roles in Education.   National Foundation for the Improvement
of Education.   Complying with Title IX: Implementing Insti-
tutional Self-Evaluation, by Martha Matthews and Shirley Mc-
Cune.   Washington, D. C., 1976.   141 p.
　　　　　　　　　　　HE 19. 102: T53/4

Chapters include access to courses, counseling, treatment of
students, athletics, financial assistance, employment, and
conducting an institutional self-evaluation.

36.   .   Office of Education.   Resource Center on Sex
Roles in Education.   National Foundation for the Improvement
of Education.   Identifying Discrimination: A Review of Federal Antidiscrimination Laws and Selected Case Examples, by
Shirley McCune and Martha Matthews.   Washington, D. C. ,
1976.   14 p.
                              HE 19. 102: D63

Includes a summary of federal laws and regulations prohibiting
discrimination in education; lists governmental agencies with
which to file charges of possible discrimination; gives case
examples of discrimination policies and practices.

37.   .   Office of Education.   Resource Center on Sex
Roles in Education.   National Foundation for the Improvement
of Education.   Selecting Professionals in Higher Education:
A Title IX Perspective, by Emily Taylor and Donna Shavlik.
Washington, D. C. , 1977.   25 p.
(ERIC ED 136 699)   HE 19. 102: P94 /3

Purposes of booklet are to review briefly data and legislation
relating to issues of equal employment opportunity in postsecondary educational institutions and to provide some specific
suggestions for personnel involved in the selection of professional employees in these institutions regarding strategies for
ensuring greater equity in the selection process and compliance with Title IX.

38.   .   Office of Education.   Resource Center on Sex
Roles in Education.   National Foundation for the Improvement
of Education.   A Student Guide to Title IX, by Myra Sadker.
Washington, D. C. , 1976.   45 p.
                              HE 19. 108: St9 /2

Topics include physical education courses, counseling, mar-
ried and pregnant students, student financial treatment of students, vocational education, working, and admissions policies.

39.   .   Office of Education.   Resource Center on Sex
Roles in Education.   National Foundation for the Improvement
of Education.   Title IX and Physical Education: A Compliance
Overview.   Washington, D. C. , 1977.
(ERIC ED 135 790)   HE 19. 102: T53 /7

Reviews Title IX requirements and how to insure compliance;
includes checklist for evaluating Title IX compliance programs.

40.   .   Office of Education.   Title IX of the Education
Amendments of 1972--A Summary of the Implementing Regula-

tions. Washington, D. C. , 1976. 21 p.
                              HE 19. 102: T53 /3

Presents a summary of the regulations grouped into five major sections, including those on admissions, employment, programs, and activities.

41.   . Title IX: Selected Resources. Washington, D. C. ,
    1976. 14 p.
    (ERIC ED 125 465)   HE 19. 102: T53

Annotated list of 57 resources on Title IX; includes Office for
Civil Rights documents, guidelines, policy statements, and di-
rectives developed by various state departments and general
assistance centers.

42.   . Public Health Service, Health Resources Adminis-
    tration, Bureau of Health Manpower. Minorities & Women in
    the Health Fields: Applicants, Students, and Workers, pre-
    pared by Marion Altenderfer. Washington, D. C. , 1976. 101 p.
                              HE 20. 6602: M66

Includes statistics on all disciplines of medicine, data on sex,
racial, and ethnic members for the years 1970-1975.

43.   . Women's Action Program. Exploratory Study of
    Women in the Health Professions Schools, prepared by Urban
    and Rural Systems Associates, San Francisco, 1976. 11 v.
                              HE 1. 2: W84 /3 /v. 1-11

Deals with eight health professions. Purpose of study is to
identify and explore barriers to success women face as school
applicants and students and to describe the discrimination
process which limit women's entry into medicine. Volume 10
is an annotated bibliography.

44. U. S. Department of Labor. Employment Standards Adminis-
    tration. OFCCP: Making EEO and Affirmative Action Work.
    Washington, D. C. , June, 1979. 16 p.
                              L 36. 2: C 76. 2

Describes the function of the Office of Federal Contract Compliance Programs which, as of October 1, 1978, has all enforcement as well as administrative and policy making authority for the entire contract compliance program and authority
to enforce equal job opportunity and affirmative action on government contract work, including institutions of higher education.

45.   . Employment Standards Administration. Survey of
    Executive Order 11246, As Amended, Nondiscrimination under
    Federal Contracts. Washington, D. C. , 1975. 6 p.
                              L 36. 2: Ex3

Describes the functions, enforcement techniques, and complaint procedures of the Office of Federal Contract Compliance.

46.   _____. Employment Standards Administration.   Office of Federal Contract Compliance Programs Task Force.   Preliminary Report on the Revitalization of the Federal Contract Compliance Program.   Washington, D. C. , Sept. 1977.   301 p.
L 36. 2: C76 /prelim.

Purpose of the Task Force is to assess and evaluate the entire operation of the Office of Contract Compliance Program and develop recommendations for change.   Parts are divided into overview of the OCCP, administration of the federal contract compliance program in the federal system and within the Department of Labor, regulatory standards, application of enforcement systems, interagency and public relationships, and appendix.   Contains a 22-page summary of findings and recommendations to improve the organizational structure and procedures to ensure equal job opportunity for minorities, women, veterans, and the handicapped.

47.   _____. Women's Bureau.   Brief Highlights of Major Federal Laws and Orders on Sex Discrimination in Employment. Rev. ed.   Washington, D. C. ,   Feb. 1977.   6 p.
L 36. 102: Se9 /977

Discusses the law, regulations, and enforcement procedures of major laws as the Equal Pay Act of 1963, Title VII as amended by the Equal Employment Opportunity Act of 1972, Executive Order 11246, and Title IX of the Education Amendments of 1972.

48.   _____. Women's Bureau.   Laws on Sex Discrimination In Employment,   Federal Civil Rights Act,   Title VII,   State Fair Employment Practices Laws,   Executive Orders.   Washington, D. C. ,   rev. May, 1973.   39 p.
L 36. 102: Em7

Describes the coverage and exemptions, unlawful employment practices, excerpts from the Code of Federal Regulations on laws relating to sex discrimination.

49.   _____. Women's Bureau.   References and Data Sources for Implementing an Affirmative Action Program.   Washington, D. C. ,   Aug. 1978.   5 p.
L 36. 102: R25

Presents a list of sources to aid in formulating and implementing programs of equal employment opportunity and affirmative action.   Contains sources of information on legislation, educational attainment, labor force analysis, and individuals who may qualify as prospective applicants.

50.   U. S. Equal Employment Opportunity Commission.   Affirmative
       Action and Equal Employment: A Guidebook for Employers.
       Washington, D. C. , Jan. 1974.   2 vols.
                                      Y3. Eq2. 8 Em 7/3/v. 1, 2

       Describes affirmative action programs, legal basis for affirm-
       ative action and basic steps to develop effective programs.
       The second volume includes sample reporting forms, data and
       recruitment sources, and guidelines and regulations.

51.   _____ . Directory of Resources for Affirmative Recruit-
       ment.   Washington, D. C. , Mar. 1975.   97 p.
       (ERIC ED 127 723)   Y3. Eq2. 2 R24

       Sections divided into Directories and Professional Rosters; Or-
       ganizational Referral Sources (which is divided into national,
       regional, and local referral sources).   Source is a supplement
       to the document named above.

52.   _____ . Guide to Resources for Equal Employment Oppor-
       tunity and Affirmative Action.   Washington, D. C. , Mar. 1976.
       61 p.
       (ERIC ED 127 722)

       Lists more than 200 publications and other resource material
       helpful to develop equal employment and affirmative action pro-
       grams.   Majority of publications published by various state
       and federal agencies.

53.   _____ . Legislative History of Title VII and XI of the Civil
       Rights Act of 1964.   Washington, D. C. , 1968.   3487 p.
                                      Y3. Eq2: 2C49 /2

       Includes the history and legislative background of Titles VII
       and XI annotated, text of Congressional Reports, Congressional
       debates, and tabulation of amendments adopted and rejected.

54.   U. S. General Accounting Office.   A Compilation of Federal
       Laws and Executive Orders for Nondiscrimination and Equal
       Opportunity Programs: Study. Washington, D. C. , Aug 1978. 72 p.
                            GA 1. 13: HRD-78-138

       Describes the provisions of the major laws and Executive Or-
       ders such as 11246 on affirmative action and equal opportunity
       in employment and education.

55.   _____ . The Equal Employment Opportunity Program for
       Federal Nonconstruction Contractors Can Be Improved.   Wash-
       ington, D. C. , May, 1975.   89 p.
                            GA 1. 13: MWD-75-63

       Contents include improvements needed in administration of the
       program; program implementation by compliance agencies;

problems in coordination between EEOC and the Department of
Labor; agency comments and unresolved issues.

56. _____. More Assurances Needed that Colleges and Univer-
sities with Government Contracts Provide Equal Employment
Opportunities. Washington, D. C., Aug. 1975. 39 p.
(ERIC ED 112 805)   GA 1.13: MWD-75-72

Includes series of critical comments that the Department of
Health, Education, and Welfare has made minimal progress in
certifying that colleges and universities have acceptable affirmative action programs and are in compliance with Executive
Orders establishing such programs. Criticisms focus on inconsistent "show-cause" notices to universities held in noncompliance with affirmative action regulations; absence of preaward reviews of institutions; noncompliance of universities
with Department of Labor's timetables for acceptable affirmative action programs; absence of definitive program guidance
to HEW's field officers; absence of a uniform nationwide training program for its compliance officers; needed clarification
of the Department of Labor's affirmative action guidelines.
Includes a series of recommendations to correct above weaknesses.

57. U. S. President's Committee on Employment of the Handicapped.
Affirmative Action for Disabled People: A Pocket Guide on
Sections 503 and 504 of the Rehabilitation Act of 1973 and the
Vietnam Era Readjustment Assistance Act of 1974. Washing-
ton, D. C., [1978?] 12 p.
                         PrEx 1.10/8: D 63

Cites the law and regulations governing affirmative action for
the handicapped and Vietnam War veterans.

58. _____. Affirmative Action to Employ Disabled Veterans
and Veterans of the Vietnam Era. A Pocket Guide to the
Regulations of the Affirmative Requirements of Section 402 of
the Vietnam Era Veterans' Readjustment Assistance Act of
1974. (P. L. 93-508). Washington, D. C., 1977. 18 p.
                         PrEx 1.10/8: V64

Describes the laws and regulations related to affirmative action as applied to veterans.

59. _____. Affirmative Action to Employ Handicapped People.
How the New Law on Federal Contracts Affects the Employer,
Protects the Jobseeker & Employee. Washington, D. C., 1974.
7 p.
                         PrEx 1.10: Af2

Describes the laws and regulations for federal contractors related to the hiring of handicapped persons.

60. U.S. Superintendent of Documents. <u>Civil Rights and Equal Opportunity</u>. Washington, D.C., Feb. 1979. 21 p.
GP 3.22/2: 207/3

One of a series of subject bibliographies issued by the Superintendent of Documents. List of sources, including a section on equal educational opportunity.

Court Cases

Regents of the University of California v. Allan Bakke (1978)

Marco De Funis v. Charles Odegaard (1974)

BIBLIOGRAPHY

Bakke v. Regents of the University of California
    18 Cal. 3d 34
    553 P. 2d 1152
    132 Cal. Rptr. 680 (1976)

Regents of the University of California, Petitioner v. Allan Bakke
    45 U. S. Law Week 3555 (U. S. Feb. 22, 1977) (No. 76-811)
    51 L Ed 2d 535
    57 L Ed 2d 750
    98 S Ct 2733
    Argued October 12, 1977. Decided June 28, 1978

BOOKS, PERIODICALS, AND NEWSPAPER ARTICLES

61.   Abernathy, Charles F. "Affirmative Action and the Rule of Bakke. " American Bar Association Journal. 64 (August, 1978), 1233-1237.

    Analyzes how the U. S. Supreme Court justices voted on the Bakke case, discusses the blocs on the high court, the breakdown of the liberal-conservative dichotomy, and court politics. Concludes that the only lasting legacy of the Bakke case may be evisceration of Title VI.

62.   Adelson, Joseph. "Living with Quotas. " Commentary. 65 (May, 1978), 23-29.

    Discusses the basic assumption of the quota system and the Bakke case: whether quotas are successful (e. g. , do they help the disadvantaged, are minority students qualified under the quota system).

63.   "Admitting and Assisting Students After Bakke: Symposium. " Edited by Alexander W. Astin and others. New Directions for Higher Education. No. 23, 1978. 110 p.

Discussions include such topics as increasing minority access to higher education in light of the Supreme Court Bakke ruling. Authors include Alexander Astin, Patrick Callan, Richard Donovan, Bruce Fuller, Patricia McNamara, and Robert O'Neil.

64. "Aftermath of Bakke Decision." USA Today. 107 (February, 1979), 6-7.

Discusses the analysis of the Bakke decision made by a joint committee of the American Council on Education and the Association of American Law Schools and the committee's recommendations on affirmative action programs in higher education after Bakke.

65. Allen, Bernadene V. "Bakke vs. Minority Students: Did the Success of Minority Recruitment Programs Create the Bakke Case?" San Jose Studies. 4 (November, 1978), 97-107.

Examines the compelling need for affirmative action programs in education and employment; affirmative action represented as the first conscious effort made by Americans since Reconstruction both to acknowledge educational and economic inequalities of racial and ethnic citizens to work vigorously toward correcting these inequalities.

66. Allen, Robert L. "Bakke Case and Affirmative Action." Black Scholar. 9 (September, 1977), 9-16.

Brief review of the Bakke case, institutional racism, effectiveness of affirmative action, and the necessity to rebuild the mass movement against racism.

67. American Council on Education. The Bakke Decision: Implications for Higher Education Admissions. A Report of the ACE-AALS Committee on Bakke. Edited by Wayne McCormack. Washington, D. C.: American Council on Education, 1978. 69 p.

Analyzes the principal opinion of the Supreme Court justices in the Bakke case, both at the state and federal levels. Discusses implications of the decision of the U. S. court concerning Title VI coverage and discretion in constructing admission plans. Report concludes that the U. S. Supreme Court recognizes the authority of higher educational institutions to continue under certain circumstances their affirmative action programs.

68. "Amici Curiae Brief: Anti-Bakke." Cross Reference: A Journal of Public Policy and Multicultural Education. 1 (March-April, 1978), 124-141.

Presents argument on behalf of preferential admissions: race must be specifically considered in choosing a student body in order to achieve the racial and ethnic diversity important to educational institutions.

69.   "Amici Curiae Brief: Pro-Bakke. " Cross Reference: A
      Journal of Public Policy and Multicultural Education.   1
      (March-April, 1978), 142-155.

      Presents argument against preferential admissions: there will
      be an impetus to develop admissions procedures that are both
      nondiscriminatory and humanitarian only after the Supreme
      Court has made clear that experimentation with racially dis-
      criminatory programs is not permissible.

70.   Arkes, Hadley.   "Bakke, the Legal Profession in Crisis. "
      American Spectator.   11 (February, 1978), 5-8.

      Explains how affirmative action strikes at the very principles
      that underlie our laws on civil rights, but our most respected
      jurists are unable to clarify questions of principle, and in that
      sense Bakke marks a serious crisis for the legal profession
      itself.

71.   Aspen Institute for Humanistic Studies, Palo Alto, California.
      Bakke and Beyond.   Invitational Regional Seminar.   Collected
      Papers.   Palo Alto: Aspen Institute for Humanistic Studies,
      1978.   173 p.

      Includes a collection of papers and programs from a series of
      regional seminars conducted in 1978 and entitled "Bakke and
      Beyond. "   Programs focus on various impacts of the Bakke de-
      cision, including the educational impact of affirmative action
      in higher education, the historical background of the Bakke
      case, the validity of test scores as a measure of merit, equity
      issues in admissions, the constitutionality of special admis-
      sions programs, and policies and programs in the admission
      and retention of minority students.

72.   Bakaly, Charles G. and Krischer, Gordon E.   "'Bakke': Its
      Impact on Public Employment Discrimination. " Employee Re-
      lations Law Journal.   4 (Spring, 1979), 471-484.

      Explains how the Bakke case decision may be expected to di-
      minish the use of inflexible goals and quotas based on racial
      preference, at least in those cases in which there has been no
      official finding of past discrimination.

73.   Bakke, Allan Paul, petitioner.   Allan Bakke versus Regents
      of the University of California, edited by Alfred A. Slocum
      for the Council on Legal Education Opportunity (CLEO).
      Dobbs Ferry, N.Y.:   Oceana Publications, 1978- .   6 vols.

      Multi-volume set of the entire judicial record of the litigation
      of the Bakke case from the trial court to the U.S. Supreme
      Court.

74.   "Bakke v. The Regents of the University of California. " California Law Review. 65 (March, 1977), 506-509.

Summary of the case before the California State Supreme Court, in which by a 6-1 vote, the Court held that a racially conditioned admissions procedure used by the University of California at Davis Medical School violated the equal protection clause of the Fourteenth Amendment.

75.   "Bakke v. Board of Regents: Symposium. " Santa Clara Law Review. 17 (Spring, 1977), 271-404.   Contents:

76.   Galloway, Russell W. and Hewitt, Henry.   "Bakke Below: A Constitutional Fallacy. " Pp. 385-404.

Traces development of strict scrutiny test as applied to discrete and insular minorities.   Concludes strict scrutiny test is inappropriate for reviewing classifications that treat minorities preferentially.

77.   Morris, Arval A.   "Constitutional Alternatives to Racial Preferences in Higher Education Admissions. " Pp. 279-328.

Criticizes California Supreme Court decision, argues court's use of equal protection clause is inconsistent with dominant purpose of Fourteenth Amendment.   Strict scrutiny test should not have been applied and court misapplied reasonable alternative test.   Points out practical difficulty of administering alternative admissions procedures.

78.   Sedler, Robert Allen.   "Racial Preference, Reality and the Constitution: Bakke v. Regents of the University of California. " Pp. 329-384.

Argues that reality of black underrepresentation in medical profession because of economic and educational conditions created need for racially preferential admissions program to alleviate effect of these conditions.

79.   "Bakke v. The University of California: Symposium. " Change. 9 (October, 1977), 18-25+

Viewpoints presented by Lee Daniels and Francesta E. Farmer who support preferential admissions; Malcolm J. Sherman opposes preferences.

80.   "Bakke v. The Board of Regents of the University of California.   Arguments Before the U. S. Supreme Court (October 12, 1977), Editorial Summary. " United States Law Week. 46 (October 18, 1977), 3249-3256.

Excellent summary of the oral arguments of both sides of the controversy.

81. "Bakke Battle. " Newsweek.   90 (October 24, 1977), 45-47.

Oral arguments before the U. S. Supreme Court described.

82. "Bakke Case: An Exchange of Letters. " The New York Review of Books. 24 (January 26, 1978), 42-45.

Six writers respond to Ronald Dworkin's article in the same source (November 10, 1977), "Why Bakke Has No Case. "

83. "Bakke Case Analysis. " The New York Times.   November 1, 1977, p. 42.

Describes the background and basic issues of the case.

84. [Bakke Case Symposium.] Freedomways. 18 (1978), 4-27.

Four writers discuss the Bakke case.

85. "Bakke: Pro and Con. " Phi Delta Kappan. 59 (March, 1978), 447-455.

Excerpts of the amicus curiae briefs submitted by the National Education Association and the American Federation of Teachers before the U. S. Supreme Court.

86. The Bakke Symposium. Edited by Mary Ten Thor, and others. Sacramento: Uncommon Lawyers Workshop, 1977. 282 p.

Results of a symposium held May 20-22, 1977 in Chicago by the Uncommon Lawyers Workshop.

87. "Bakke Symposium: Civil Rights Perspectives. " Harvard Civil Rights-Civil Liberties Law Review. 14 (Spring, 1979), 1-327.

88.   Bell, Derrick A., Jr. "Introduction: Awakening Bakke. " Pp. 1-6.

Explains how the post-Bakke minorities must rely on the interest of schools to admit a small number of minority students, based upon the school's interest in diversity, rather than on either the magnitude of past racial wrongs or on the minority students' potential for future achievement.

89.   Gertner, Nancy. "Bakke on Affirmative Action for Women: Pedestal or Cage?" Pp. 173-214.

Identifies and analyzes the conceptual flaws in Justice Powell's treatment of sex discrimination; considers the implications of his analysis for affirmative action for women and rejects the application of the Court's approach to affirmative action for blacks to affirmative action for women; outlines an alternative framework for reviewing gender-based affirmative action classifications under the fourteenth amendment.

90.   Ginger, Ann Fagan.   "Who Needs Affirmative Action?" Pp. 265-313.

Discusses the issues in the Bakke case, facts that did and did not get into the record, how the law in Bakke differs from that in Brown, what the Supreme Court decision leaves unsettled, and the future course of action by lawyers in education and employment cases.

91.   Jones, Emma Coleman.   "Intervention to Affirm Affirmative Action."   Pp. 31-87.

Criticizes the absence of minority participation in the Bakke case in the state and federal courts.   Such absence imperiled significant minority interests.   Describes several existing but largely overlooked procedural devices to correct the absence of minority representation, particularly the intervention principle.

92.   Karst, Kenneth L. and Horowitz, Harold W.   "The Bakke Opinions and Equal Protection Doctrine."   Pp. 7-29.

Concludes that the Bakke decision lacks a coherent doctrinal underpinning, but provides a how-to-do-it handbook for the admission of minority applicants to professional schools. Explains the remarkable degree of doctrinal convergence between Justice Powell and the Brennan group.   In relating equal protection theory to the Bakke decision, authors conclude that Justice Powell's opinion may be the culmination of a generation of equal protection decisions in which substantive doctrinal development has been sacrificed to other concerns; the Brennan group's opinion may be the beginning of a long overdue effort to reconstruct equal protection doctrine on a substantive foundation.

93.   Larson, E. Richard.   "Race Consciousness in Employment after Bakke."   Pp. 215-263.

Considers race-conscious employment programs in two contexts: governmental measures designed to remedy governmentally identified past discrimination or underrepresentation of minority employees and voluntary implementation of remedial, race-conscious measures by private employers. In both areas, author views Justice Powell's opinion as allowing race-conscious employment programs in a broad range of cases.

94.   Motley, Constance Baker.   "From Brown to Bakke: The Long Road to Equality."   Pp. 315-327.

Analyzes the Bakke decision, views it as a small step for-
ward in that it established that race is a factor which may
constitutionally be considered in university admissions.

95.   Sedler, Robert A.   "Beyond Bakke: The Constitution and
        Redressing the Social History of Racism. "   Pp. 133-
        171.

        Explains why the Constitution permits, and in some cir-
        cumstances requires, governmental entities to take action
        in overcoming the present consequences of past discrimina-
        tion.   Emphasizes the link between the past history of ra-
        cism and its present efforts, and on the constitutional
        significance of that link.

96.   White, David M.   "Culturally Biased Testing and Predictive
        Invalidity: Putting Them on the Record. "   Pp. 89-132.

        Explores predictive validity in admissions criteria and the
        problem of cultural bias in standardized tests.   Explains
        the Bakke court's treatment of the theory of cultural biased
        test scores, and describes the theory's broader societal
        implications.

97.   "Bakke Wins, Quotas Lose. "   Time.   112 (July 10, 1978), 8-
        16.

        Describes the Supreme Court ruling as giving something to
        everybody, outlawing strict racial quotas but permitting race
        to be considered in college admissions policies.

98.   Baldwin, Fletcher N. Jr., and Nagan, Winston P.   "Board of
        Regents v. Bakke: The All-American Dilemma Revisited. "
        University of Florida Law Review.   30 (1978), 843-866.

        Authors focus upon Justice Powell's opinion in the Bakke case.
        Case analyzed within the larger context of reconciling social
        justice (affirmative action programs having as their purpose
        to bring this about) with principles of individual justice.

99.   Barry, Stan.   "A Post Bakke Assessment. "   College and Uni-
        versity.   54 (Winter, 1979), 85-88.

        Suggests that the Court is most concerned about the formaliza-
        tion of rules and regulations which affect different classes and
        groups of people in different ways and cautions universities
        from relying too heavily upon academic performance or test
        scores alone to determine who is to be admitted to college.
        Concludes that since all admissions requirements are discrim-
        inatory, admissions offices must be certain that discrimination
        is not based on prejudgment of groups or types of people but
        rather on logical and fair attempts to provide society with a
        product most beneficial to that society.

100. Bennett, William J. and Eastland, Terry. "Why Bakke
      Won't End Reverse Discrimination. " Commentary. 66
      (September, 1978), 29-35.

      Examines the Supreme Court's ruling on Bakke, concludes
      that the decision undermines the principles of equal protec-
      tion of the laws and that all men are created equal.

101. Blank, Melody B. "One Small Step for Man, One Missed
      Step for Mankind: Regents of the University of California
      v. Bakke. " Southwestern University Law Review. 10 (1978),
      617-649.

      Comment focuses upon the notion of equal protection as an
      individual right and that the Supreme Court in its Bakke
      ruling had the opportunity, but failed to take it, to create
      a landmark decision by striking race as a relevant consid-
      eration with respect to the distribution of benefits and bur-
      dens by the state.

102. Block, Gertrude. "The Semantics of the Bakke Decision. "
      ETC.: A Review of General Semantics. 35 (Winter, 1978),
      348-353.

      Analyzes the way the Supreme Court in its Bakke decision
      dealt with the meanings of key words: "quotas, " "stigma, "
      "equality, " "discrimination, " and others.

103. Bowden, Henry L. "A Lawyer's Advice to a College about
      Bakke: Adopt a Program and Live Up to It. " Vital Speeches
      of the Day. 44 (September 1, 1978), 687-690.

      Legal counsel to Emory University analyzes the decision and
      advises universities to reexamine admissions programs to
      make them conform to the Supreme Court decision.

104. Braveman, Marilyn. Beyond Bakke: Our Stake in the Urban
      Condition. Pertinent Papers No. 2. New York: American
      Jewish Committee, 1978. 10 p.

      Bakke case explained as well as a description of traditional
      admissions procedures and current trends and admissions
      criteria of six selective current programs.

105. Bundy, McGeorge. "Beyond Bakke: What Future for Af-
      firmative Action?" Atlantic Monthly. 242 (November, 1978),
      69-73.

      Describes the Supreme Court judgment in the Bakke case as
      helpful but incomplete and that the opinions of the justices
      form a reasonably clear and hopeful guide to action for those
      who believe in increasing the number of racial minorities in
      the professions.

106.   _____. "The Issue Before the Court: Who Gets Ahead
in America?" Atlantic Monthly. 240 (November, 1977),
41-54.

Reviews the issues, distinguishes between goals and quotas,
argues that there is no racially neutral process of choice
that will produce more than a handful of minority students
in college and professional schools.   Concludes that it would
be cruel irony for Supreme Court to interpret equal protection clause as to cripple efforts of higher education to eradi-
cate racism.

107.   Bunzel, John H. "Bakke vs. University of California. "
Commentary. 63 (March, 1977), 59-64.

Discusses the three possible choices open to the Supreme
Court; believes that the fundamental conflict concerns whether
preferential treatment serves a compelling state interest.
Discusses the broader philosophical questions of individual
vs. group rights, and the appropriate application of academic
standards.   Concludes that Americans will reject the granting
of special privileges to some groups at the expense of others
but will assist all the disadvantaged.

108.   Calabresi, Guido. "Bakke as Pseudo-Tragedy. " Catholic
University Law Review. 28 (Spring, 1979), 427-444.

Discusses the Supreme Court Bakke ruling within the context
of conflicting conceptions of egalitarianism: the universalist,
meritocratic notion of equality of opportunity versus reparations to disadvantaged groups.

109.   California. Legislature. Assembly. Permanent Subcom-
mittee on Postsecondary Education. The Bakke Decision:
Disadvantaged Graduate Students, Transcript and Statements.
Sacramento, March 2, 1977. 111 p.

Testimony taken on the issues of the Bakke case from people
representing students, health services education, legal services, particularly at the University of California, and from
the University of California president's office.   Questions
focused on minority representation in graduate schools, why
special admissions programs were started, alternatives to
such programs, and how the Legislature might help in better
serving graduate students of different cultures.

110.   California. University. Berkeley. School of Law (Boalt
Hall). Report on Special Admissions at Boalt Hall. After
Bakke. October 5, 1976. Journal of Legal Education. 28
(1977), 363-402.

Report presents history of the development of the Special Admissions program at Boalt Hall, describes the prevailing

criteria and procedures for both general and special admissions, analyzes the Bakke decision of the California Supreme Court in terms of its implication for admissions at Boalt and possible alternative admissions programs which would be constitutionally permissible.

111.   California. University. Los Angeles. Chicano Studies Center. The Bakke Decision: The Question of Chicano Access to Higher Education. Document No. 4 for the MALDEF-Higher Education Task Force. Carlos Manuel Haro, editor. Los Angeles: University of California at Los Angeles, 1977. 189 p.

Discusses the California Supreme Court decision and the impact of the case on the Chicano community. Includes statements of the Mexican American Legal Defense and Education Fund and the National La Raza Lawyers' Association.

112.   Callan, Patrick M. "The State Role after Bakke: Toward Collaborative Action." New Directions for Higher Education. 6 (1978), 53-60.

Posits that the state concern in professional and graduate admissions encompasses the distribution of human services (such as medical care and legal representation) as well as enhancement of educational opportunities.

113.   Carnegie Council on Policy Studies in Higher Education. The Relevance of Race in Admissions: A Summary of the Position of the Carnegie Council on Policy Studies in Higher Education as Reported in "Selective Admissions in Higher Education: Public Policy and Academic Policy." Berkeley: Carnegie Council on Policy Studies in Higher Education, 1977. 9 p.
(ERIC ED 151 465)

The Carnegie Council's position on public and academic policy issues involved in the Bakke case is summarized in this publication. The racial experience of an academically qualified student is among the criteria relevant to admissions decisions.

114.   Carty-Bennia, Denise. "Bakke: Some Views, Extraordinary Split." Civil Rights Digest. 10 (Summer, 1978), 10-11.

Describes the differences among the justices in their perceptions, reasoning, and conclusions about the issues raised.

115.   Clark, Ramsey. "The Bakke Decision." Nation. 227 (July 8, 1978), 37-39.

Former Attorney General of the United States criticizes the justices who would not or could not address the obvious and

pervasive presence of inequality in America, caused by racial prejudice and enforced by law and government.

116.   Cohen, Carl.   "Who Are Equals?" National Forum.   58
        (Winter, 1978), 10-14.

        Explains that the issue in the Bakke case is not "affirmative
        action" but preference by race.   Two arguments in favor of
        preferential treatment, the argument for compensation and
        the argument from integration, fail utterly.   Racial prefer-
        ence is to be condemned as both unjust and unwise.

117.   Current, Gloster B.   "The 69th--The Post-Bakke Conven-
        tion. " Crisis.   85 (October, 1978), 259-276.

        Annual convention of the National Association for the Ad-
        vancement of Colored People (NAACP) discusses the effect
        of the Bakke decision on future college admission and af-
        firmative action programs.

118.   Daniels, Lee and Farmer, Francesta E.   "Bakke: The
        Case for Preference. " Change.   9 (October, 1977), 19, 58.

        Claims that a pro-Bakke decision would devastate blacks'
        efforts to gain equality of opportunity.   Discusses inept
        defense by the University of California in the state court;
        Bakke's questionable right to sue; weaknesses of standardized
        tests; and judicial interpretation of the Fourteenth Amend-
        ment which permits affirmative use of racial classifications
        to eliminate discrimination.

119.   Denenberg, R. V.   "Uncertain Trumpet--the Bakke Deci-
        sion. " International and Comparative Law Quarterly.   28
        (April, 1979), 280-288.

        Reviews the U. S. Supreme Court ruling in Bakke, focusing
        upon Justice Powell's opinion.   Points out that the main
        justification for racial preference is expediency but such
        preference is socially divisive and difficult to administer.
        Concludes that the Court's ability to gain broad acceptance
        for the principle of racial preference is probably limited.

120.   Dershowitz, Alan.   "Powell's Beau Ideal (Harvard's admis-
        sions program vs. Bakke case). " New Republic.   179
        (July 22, 1978), 14-18.

        Harvard law professor describes the Supreme Court decision
        as a triumph of ambiguity and discretion over clarity and
        candor.   Deems unfortunate that Harvard was chosen as
        model for affirmative action programs because the program
        differs from reality in its emphasis upon race as a prime
        criteria for admissions.

121. Donovan, Richard A.   "Bakke and 'Qualified' Undergradu-
      ates."   New Directions for Higher Education.   6 (1978), 85-
      94.

      Suggests that colleges will have to discover or design addi-
      tional, racially neutral ways to measure a student's aptitude,
      if only to prepare themselves for possible court challenges.

122. Dreyfuss, Joel, and Lawrence, Charles III.   The Bakke
      Case: The Politics of Inequality.   New York: Harcourt
      Brace Jovanovich, 1979.   278 p.

      Analyzes the Bakke case within the broader social framework
      of economic inequality and racial injustice in America.

123. Dworkin, Ronald.   "The Bakke Decision: Did It Decide Any-
      thing?"   The New York Review of Books.   25 (August 17,
      1978), 20-26.

      Emphasizes Justice Powell's arguments; his compromise,
      while popular, may lack strength in principle to furnish the
      basis for a coherent and lasting constitutional law of affirma-
      tive action.   Concludes that later cases will have to address
      general principles and detailed applications of the issues in-
      volved.

124. _____.   "Why Bakke Has No Case."   The New York Re-
      view of Books.   24 (November 10, 1977), 11-15.

      Argues that the long-term goal of affirmative action programs
      is to reduce the degree to which America is a racially con-
      scious society.   Bakke was excluded because of a "rational
      calculation about the socially most beneficial use of limited
      resources for medical education."   Denies that affirmative
      action will produce racial and ethnic subnations or that it
      is a denial of the merit principle.

125. Eastland, Terry and Bennett, William J.   Counting By Race:
      Equality from the Founding Fathers to Bakke.   New York:
      Basic Books, 1979.   243 p.

      Authors' purpose is to inquire into the history of the idea of
      equality in America and to present an argument on a ques-
      tion of public policy, specifically on the issue of equality
      present in the Bakke case.   Two ideas of equality are em-
      phasized: "moral equality" and "numerical equality," and
      how these ideas are relevant to the Bakke case.

126. "Editorial: NAACP Statement on Implications of the Bakke
      Decision."   Crisis.   86 (February, 1979), 41-43.

      Concludes that the Supreme Court has upheld the use of race
      as an important factor to be considered in school admission
      and admission to the professions.

127.   [Editors of the New Republic] "The Court's Affirmative Action. " New Republic. 179 (July 8, 1978), 5-8.

Analyzes the Supreme Court decision and suggests that the crucial moral issue in the debate over affirmative action is protection of the individual. Quota systems substitute simplistic group identification for evaluations of individual worth.

128.   "Education and Minorities: After Bakke. " The New York Times, July 6, 1978, p. 18.

Letters to the editor responding to the Supreme Court decision include Alan H. Goldman, Ira Glickstein, and David I. Evans, the latter being the admissions officer for Harvard-Radcliffe.

129.   "Educators Welcome Bakke Ruling as Signal to Retain Current Policy. " The New York Times, June 29, 1978, p. 23.

Most U.S. educators see the Bakke decision as no threat to their admissions policies, except that some programs will need to be reexamined for evidence of unconstitutional quotas.

130.   Etzioni, Amitai. "Making Up for Past Injustices: How Bakke Could Backfire. " Psychology Today. 11 (August, 1977), 18.

Views the dangers of reverse discrimination: legitimizing discrimination based upon ascribed status will open the door to all kinds of discrimination and could lead toward quota systems. Considers strategy for correcting past injustice that is compatible with democratic societies.

131.   Fagan, Marilyn. "Preferential Admissions and the Constitutional Course of Bakke. " Ohio North Law Review. 5 (April, 1978), 444-478.

Examines some of the social and legal problems concerning the use of preferential admissions in higher education and the constitutional propriety of such admissions. Includes a proposition that a new equal protection standard of review should be articulated and applied to preferential admissions programs.

132.   Fields, Cheryl. "Conflicting Reactions to the Bakke Decision. " The Chronicle of Higher Education. 16 (July 3, 1978), 12.

Various civil rights leaders and government officials give opposing viewpoints on the impact of the Bakke decision.

133.   _____. "In Bakke's Victory, No Death Knell for Affirmative Action. " The Chronicle of Higher Education. 16 (July 3, 1978), 1, 12.

Describes the Supreme Court decision and the reactions to it by educators, civil rights leaders, and government officials.

134.   . "In the Wake of Bakke." The Chronicle of Higher Education. 16 (July 10, 1978), 1.

Article cites opinions of lawyers and university officials on the impact of the Bakke decision; includes the planned conferences discussing the decision.

135.   Finkin, Matthew W.   "Some Thoughts on the Powell Opinion in Bakke." Academe: Bulletin of the AAUP.   65 (April, 1979), 192-196.

Analyzes Justice Powell's reasoning in the Bakke case, with its disturbing misidentification of the autonomy of the institution per se with academic freedom.   By obliterating the distinction between the two, Powell would give educational institutions virtual autonomy from judicial scrutiny, which professors might well consider detrimental.

136.   Fisher, B. Jeanne.   "The Bakke Case: Part I--The Issues." Journal of College Student Personnel.   19 (May, 1978), 174-179.

Discusses the facts and issues of the case before the U.S. Supreme Court.

137.   . "The Bakke Case: Part II--An Analysis and Implications."   Journal of College Student Personnel.   20 (May, 1979), 264-271.

Analyzes the six different opinions of the Supreme Court justices and suggests that the absence of a majority opinion might later produce a different case with a different decision.   Discusses the implications for admissions, financial aid, and affirmative action programs.

138.   Flygare, Thomas J.   "Bakke: Implications for Federal Affirmative Action." Phi Delta Kappan.   59 (February, 1978), 418-419.

Concludes that the special admissions program at the University of California at Davis goes so far beyond federal affirmative action requirements that a decision for Bakke would not affect current federal programs.

139.   Foner, Eric.   "Bakke Reconstructed." The Chronicle of Higher Education.   16 (March 13, 1978), 48.

Explains the remarkable analogy which exists between the issues raised by the Bakke case and debates over a century ago between the abolitionists and the beginning labor move-

ment in the Civil War era. The major difference between
the First and Second Reconstruction was the rise of the black
middle class in the latter period. The heart of the Bakke
controversy is whether the contemporary condition of blacks
is unique or an extreme example of the deep and pervasive
injustices that cut across racial lines. The Bakke case
presents the challenge of addressing the interrelated questions of race and class in America.

140.   Fort, Edward. "Around the Bend from Bakkeism. " Journal
        of Negro Education. 47 (Fall, 1978), 317-322.

        Describes the Bakke decision as legitimizing the use of race
        as one of a number of criteria in admissions criteria.

141.   Fromm, David H.   "Bakke v. Regents of the University of
        California: the Ghost of DeFunis Arises. " California West-
        ern Law Review. 13 (1977), 588-619.

        Examines the California Supreme Court decision in Bakke
        and prior decisions which appear to sanction preferential
        treatment for minority groups. Demonstrates that when a
        racial classification totally deprives an individual of a bene-
        fit that he might otherwise have received, the strict scrutiny
        test is the only standard of review that can guarantee equal
        protection.

142.   Fromm, Paul. "Bakke: The Choices that Remain. " The
        New York Times, July 9, 1978, IV, p. 17.

        Explains the Bakke decision as giving little definitive guid-
        ance in the field of racial preference; outer contours of the
        problem can be drawn by judges, but its resolution lies
        within spectrum of moral and practical choices to be made
        by all Americans.

143.   Fuller, Bruce, and others. "Alternative Admissions Proce-
        dures. " New Directions for Higher Education. 6 (1978),
        1-27.

        Explains the Supreme Court Bakke decision as setting limits
        to what institutions could not do regarding the use of race
        and ethnicity in admissions. Describes alternative proce-
        dures developed by Michigan State University, the Medical
        College of Ohio, Temple University, McMaster University,
        and Florida State University which focus on assessing indi-
        vidual applicant disadvantagement rather than ethnic or racial
        group membership.

144.   _____, and McNamara, Patricia P. "Defining and As-
        sessing Disadvantagement. " New Directions for Higher Edu-
        cation. 6 (1978), 61-73.

Outlines the parameters of the Supreme Court decision in Bakke in permissible admissions procedures and explains how institutions must now attempt to balance conventional admissions criteria with a careful assessment of disadvantagement among both minority and majority applicants.

145.   Furniss, W. Todd.   "Professional Education After Bakke."
       Educational Record.   60 (Spring, 1979), 137-145.

Suggests that in response to the Bakke decision, efforts must be made to enlarge and improve the pool of qualified minority applicants to colleges and professional schools.   The problem could be alleviated with certain improvements in elementary and secondary schools and increased community efforts.

146.   "The Furor Over 'Reverse Discrimination.'"   Newsweek.   90
       (September 26, 1977), 53-58.

Describes the pending Bakke case before the U.S. Supreme Court and the debate over preferential hiring of blacks.

147.   Ginsburg, Ruth Bader.   "Women, Equality, and the Bakke
       Case."   Civil Liberties Review.   4 (November-December,
       1977), 8-16.

Explains how doctrine, programs, and remedies which are directed toward racial discrimination are not necessarily applicable or transferable to gender discrimination.   Special minority admissions are conceived as transitional in order to allow socially and economically disabled groups to catch up.

148.   Glazer, Nathan.   "Why Bakke Won't End Reverse Discrimination."   Commentary.   66 (September, 1978), 36-42.

Reviews the Bakke decision and approves the idea that Congress makes a clear statement that no American can be discriminated against on the grounds of race or ethnicity.

149.   Gold, Bertram.   "Bakke: Some Views.   Both Sides Won."
       Civil Rights Digest.   10 (Summer, 1978), 12-13.

Claims that both sides of the Bakke issue have escalated rhetoric and predictions of doom if the Supreme Court failed to support their particular view.   Court decision upholds the tradition of the American promise and both sides must come together to make that promise a reality.

150.   Goode, Victor M.   "The Bakke Decision: The Failure of
       Policy and the Limitations of the Law."   Cross Reference:
       A Journal of Public Policy and Multicultural Education.   1
       (March-April, 1978), 115-123.

Explains how the Bakke case, with its political and legal
controversy, indicates the rise and fall of affirmative action
as law and policy, all within the span of the last 15 years.

151.   Greenberg, Jack. "The Meaning of Bakke's 'Window.'"
         Nation. 227 (July 22, 1978), 72-74.

         Describes the Bakke case as involving basic philosophical
         differences over how to distribute power, prestige, and
         wealth. Because of the divided Court, the struggle to bring
         racial minorities into the mainstream of American life will
         continue.

152.   "The Harvard Admissions Plan: Acceptable Affirmative Ac-
         tion, In Justice Powell's View." The Chronicle of Higher
         Education. 16 (July 10, 1978), 9.

         Text of the description of the University's admissions pro-
         gram as it appeared in a friend-of-the-court brief before the
         U. S. Supreme Court, and cited by Justice Lewis F. Powell,
         Jr.

153.   "Harvard Admissions Plan Held a Model of Flexibility."
         The New York Times, June 29, 1978, p. 23.

         Explains the Harvard plan for entering students as only part-
         ly filled on the basis of academic merit; the rest are ad-
         mitted as qualified students who can bring diversity to the
         student body, such diversity seen as adding to the learning
         process.

154.   Hazard, William R. "The Bakke Decision: Mixed Signals
         from the Court." Phi Delta Kappan. 60 (September, 1978),
         16-19.

         Concludes that race can probably be considered in admissions
         decisions but not in disregard of constitutionally protected
         rights and that further Supreme Court decisions are needed
         to know what it means for affirmative action programs.

155.   "High Court Backs Some Affirmative Action by Colleges, But
         Orders Bakke Admitted." The New York Times, June 29,
         1978, p. 1.

         Describes the 5-4 decision by the U. S. Supreme Court on the
         Bakke case.

156.   Holloway, Charles M. The Bakke Decision: Retrospect and
         Prospect. Summary Report on Six Seminars Held by the
         College Board in July-August, 1978. New York: College
         Entrance Examination Board, 1978. 87 p.

         The six seminars provided a forum for discussion of the
         Supreme Court's decision on the Bakke case. Appended are

three background papers: "Legal Implications for the College Admissions Process," by Alfred B. Fitt; "Some Educational and Social Implications of University of California v. Bakke," by Warren W. Willingham; and "Implications of the Bakke Decision for Undergraduate Admissions Policies and Practices," by a team of practicing admissions officers.

157.   Hook, Sidney.   "Bakke, Equal Opportunity, Affirmative Action, Quotas."   The Chronicle of Higher Education.   16 (March 13, 1978), 18.

Hook, Chairman of the Committee on Academic Nondiscrimination and Integrity, along with 124 college and university professors, signed this letter reaffirming their hope that the Supreme Court will leave unweakened the basic constitutional right to equal opportunity and nondiscriminatory treatment. Affirmative action not only violates equal opportunity, in principle and in effect, but also is unreasonable, patronizing, and in some cases, tinged with racist pre-judgment of the capacity of minorities to make it on their own.

158.   "How Justices Explain Their Bakke Ruling."   U.S. News & World Report.   85 (July 10, 1978), 18.

Excerpts from Justice Powell, Stevens, Brennan, and Marshall.

159.   Howe, Harold, II.   "The Effects of Bakke on Selective Admissions."   Change.   10 (September, 1978), 13, 61.

Notes that the Supreme Court merely allows affirmative action, not requires it.   The Court's support for the use of race as a permissible criterion in university admissions is no guarantee that minority persons will receive special consideration in competition with whites.   Future legal challenges by minorities will raise new definitions of discrimination in higher education.

160.   "The Impact [of the Bakke Supreme Court decision] Is Discussed on U. of California Campus."   The New York Times, June 30, 1978, p. 10.

University of California administrators, faculty members, and attorneys discuss the impact of the Bakke ruling on admissions programs.

161.   "Impact of Bakke Decision."   U.S. News & World Report. 85 (July 10, 1978), 14-17.

Describes the Supreme Court decision, public reaction, and its effect upon education and industry.

162.   Jordan, Vernon E.   "How Far We Still Must Go."   AGB Reports.   21 (July-August, 1979), 10-14.

Contends that higher education's commitment to equal educational opportunity has eroded in the past decade in that blacks are still underrepresented in faculty posts, in administration, and on governing boards. Black colleges, the credibility crisis, and overcoming past discrimination are discussed.

163.   Kahng, Anthony I. "The Bakke Decision: University of California v. Bakke ... Who Won?" Bridge, An Asian American Perspective. 6 (Fall, 1978), 4-14.

Presents overview of the Bakke decision and the effects the decision will have on the future of affirmative action and on the potential civil rights achievements of minority groups, particularly Asian Americans.

164.   Katz, Alan M. "Benign Preferences: An Indian Decision and the Bakke Case." American Journal of Comparative Law. 25 (Fall, 1977), 611-640.

Compares a Supreme Court case in India (State of Kerala v. Thomas, 1975) with the Bakke case. Indian case provides an opportunity to see how another government and its courts deal with state preference as a tool for the betterment of backward groups, in the author's opinion. The Indian Supreme Court ruled that a state employment preference has a reasonable basis only if the beneficiary class is severely backward, underrepresented, and will receive no more than adequate representation, and the preference will not prevent the maintenance of administrative efficiency.

165.   Knowlton, Robert E. "Regents of the University of California v. Bakke." Arkansas Law Review. 32 (Fall, 1978), 499-504.

Analyzes the opinions rendered in the Bakke case and concludes that the final resolution of the issue remains the prerogative of Congress and the Executive department. Educational administrators who use race as an admissions factor will have their actions cloaked with the presumption of legality that will discourage spurious suits every time race is considered.

166.   Kohn, Janet. "Bakke: Some Views. Two Rulings." Civil Rights Digest. 10 (Summer, 1978), 14.

The Bakke decision demonstrates that, like the society around it, the Court is deeply split on the issues presented and unable to formulate a clear approach to the affirmative redress of racial discrimination.

167.   Kurland, Philip B. "Bakke's Wake." Chicago Board Record. 60 (September-October, 1978), 66-83.

Describes the major points of the amicus curiae brief the author filed on behalf of the Anti-Defamation League in the Bakke case before the U.S. Supreme Court.   Analyzes the Bakke ruling and concludes that the case will have no broad consequences because it did not set any precedents.

168.   "The Landmark Bakke Ruling." Newsweek.   92 (July 10, 1978),   19-29.

Describes the Bakke decision of the Supreme Court, questions yet to be settled, key opinions, and the next major steps to come in business and employment.

169.   Landmark Briefs and Arguments of the Supreme Court of the United States: Constitutional Law.   1977 Term Supplement, Vol. 99-100.   (Regents of the University of California v. Bakke).   Edited by Philip B. Kurland and Gerhard Casper. 2 vols.   Washington, D.C.:   University Publications of America, Inc., 1977.

Includes the more than 60 briefs filed in the Bakke case before the U.S. Supreme Court.   Invaluable source presenting the complex issues of the case.

170.   Lavinsky, Larry M.   "A Moment of Truth on Racially Based Admissions." Hastings Constitutional Law Quarterly.   3 (Fall, 1976), 879-890.

Compares the Bakke and DeFunis cases, with a brief analysis of other court cases dealing with racially preferential programs in higher education and employment.   Concludes that the Bakke case is potentially destructive in that special admissions programs utilize racial quotas and preference, the traditional engines of discrimination, as vehicles for social progress, accompanied by a very high social cost to blacks and whites in the form of stigmatization and victimization of persons because of their race.

171.   Lawrence, Charles L. 3rd.   "Bakke Case: Are Racial Quotas Defensible?" Saturday Review.   5 (October, 1977), 10-16.

Criticizes the University's mishandling of the case, the California Supreme Court's refusal to hear all the evidence, the assumption by opponents and supporters that white applicants are automatically "better qualified" and that minorities must therefore be arbitrarily "preferred."   True equality depends upon how much privilege white Americans are willing to relinquish in exchange for racial parity.

172.   Lawrence, Charles.   "When the Defendants Are Foxes Too: The Need for Intervention by Minorities in 'Reverse Discrimination' Suits Like Bakke." Guild Practitioner.   34 (Winter, 1976), 1-20.

Examines the California Supreme Court's decision in view of the need for intervention by the real parties in interest in suits that challenge affirmative action programs. Author sets forth several essential arguments that were not made by defendants in the Bakke case and indicates the kind of evidence that might have been presented to support them.

173. Leventhal, Harold. "ACES Back to Bakke. " American Bar Association Journal. 65 (February, 1979), 214-217.

Comments on American Conservative Enterprise Society's raising of the issue of the applicability of the Bakke decision to hiring practices; based on address.

174. Lewis, Anthony. "Bakke May Change a Lot While Changing No Law. " The New York Times, July 2, 1978, IV, 1.

Comments on the Bakke decision in that it may lead to great social changes, but should allow most existing policy in the field to continue.

175. Lipset, Seymour Martin and Schneider, William. "The Bakke Case: How Would It Be Decided at the Bar of Public Opinion?" Public Opinion. 1 (March/April, 1978), 38-44.

Survey of American attitudes toward racial equality reveals that most Americans favor equal rights and equal opportunity but they overwhelmingly reject the use of conventional affirmative action and preferential treatment to achieve them.

176. _____. "Disadvantaged Groups, Individual Rights. " New Republic. 177 (October 15, 1977), 5-9.

Analyzes the arguments for quotas, including the concept of proportionality. Framework includes such questions as what groups should be helped, how shall group membership be defined and enforced, and how much help is called for, and at whose expense is help to be given? Defines the purpose of affirmative action: to break down patterns of prejudice and discrimination and to make sure that talented individuals have a chance to shine.

177. McAlmon, George A. "A Critical Look at Affirmative Action. " Center Magazine. 11 (March/April, 1978), 43-55.

Discusses the Bakke case and affirmative action. Author is Director of the Fund for the Republic. Viewpoints are also presented by Harold Fleming, President of the Potomac Institution and Director of the Fund for the Republic; Maxwell Greenberg, Chairman of the National Executive Committee of the Anti-Defamation League; and Maurine Rothschild, Director of the Fund for the Republic.

178.   McHugh, Michael J.   "Constitutional Law--Equal Protection--
       Effect of Minority Preference in Graduate School Admissions
       Upon Equal Protection Rights of Non-minority. " Suffolk Uni-
       versity Law Review.   11 (Spring, 1977), 1143-1158.

       Provides detailed analysis of the California Supreme Court
       decision in Bakke, with emphasis upon the application of the
       strict scrutiny test to affirmative action programs, the re-
       sult of which presents seemingly insurmountable burdens for
       advocates of such programs to overcome.

179.   McKay, Robert B.   "'Act in Good Faith. '"   AGB Reports.
       21 (March-April, 1979), 15-16.

       Argues that the Supreme Court in its Bakke decision gives
       wide latitude for devising programs that take race and ethnic
       background into account if colleges are acting in good faith.

180.   Maguire, Daniel C.   "The Triumph of Unequal Justice. "
       Christian Century.   95 (September 27, 1978), 882-886.

       Explains how the Bakke decision by the Supreme Court re-
       flects the conflict between the traditional ideology of indi-
       vidualism and equality and the pressing claims of social jus-
       tice for corrective inequality.   Defends affirmative action
       for blacks because they are the lower caste in America and
       meet the criteria for discerning groups in need of prefer-
       ential relief: bias against blacks is depersonalizing, in-
       grained and institutionalized, and facilitated by their visibil-
       ity.

181.   _____.   "Unequal But Fair. "   Commonweal.   104 (October
       14, 1977), 647-652.

       Explains how Bakke was treated unequally but not unjustly in
       being excluded from medical school and how blacks deserve
       preferential treatment based upon legal and distributive justice
       principles.

182.   Maltz, Earl M.   "Bakke Primer. "   Oklahoma Law Review.
       32 (Winter, 1979), 119-137.

       Comment examines the various opinions in the Bakke Supreme
       Court ruling with a view toward determining the current state
       of the law on the question of affirmative action and what is-
       sues remain to be resolved.   The opinions perhaps should be
       viewed as more favorable to the advocates of affirmative ac-
       tion programs, but the extent to which race may be used is
       still very unclear.

183.   Margolis, Emanuel.   "Aching Bakke: Is There a Cure?"
       Connecticut Bar Journal.   51 (December, 1977), 417-434.

Presents the issues of the Bakke case before the U.S. Supreme Court, cites previous court cases in which racial preferences were not per se unconstitutional, and suggests that the Bakke case calls for judicial restraint rather than judicial arrogation of educational expertise.

184.   Martin, Ben L. "The Parable of the Talents." Harper's Magazine. 256 (January, 1978), 21-24.

Discusses the Bakke case as a contemporary parable of liberal thought. Divides recent history of changing racial values in America into five states, ranging from color blindness in society and state action to implicit and explicit compulsory discrimination.

185.   Maynard, Robert C. "The Politics of Being Equal." Black Enterprise. 8 (September, 1977), 39-43.

Concerns the legality of a two-track admissions system in professional schools and cites the Bakke case.

186.   Middleton, Lorenzo. "Amid Debate Over Impact of Bakke, Colleges Rewrite Admission Policies." The Chronicle of Higher Education. 17 (October 16, 1978), 1, 18.

Describes how institutions of higher education are devising affirmative action programs and policies to protect themselves against reverse discrimination lawsuits.

187.   _____. "Bakke Ruling Seen Having Little Effect." The Chronicle of Higher Education. 18 (July 30, 1979), 1, 13.

Cites various opinions of educational and professional organizations that have been monitoring the reaction to the Bakke decision. Concludes that the ruling has virtually no effect on minority group enrollment at most colleges and universities.

188.   _____. "Those Vanishing Quotas." The Chronicle of Higher Education. 16 (July 10, 1978), 8.

Discusses how quotas have all but disappeared in America's colleges, including medical schools, and how the U.S. Supreme Court ruling in the Bakke case has forced colleges, particularly law and medical schools, to reexamine their minority admissions programs to see how far they can go in using race in admissions criteria.

189.   "Minority Leaders, After Review, Regard Bakke Ruling as Setback." The New York Times, July 9, 1978, p. 14.

NY Times survey finds minority leaders see Bakke ruling as setback for educational equity, while white leaders, including traditional liberals, approve decision that would permit affirmative action to continue while outlawing quota system.

190.   Morris, Arval A.   "Bakke Decision: One Holding or Two?"
        Oregon Law Review.   58 (1979), 311-335.

        Analyzes the U. S. Supreme Court's Bakke ruling and concludes that the six opinions gave something to everyone at the expense of decisiveness, clarity, and legal predictability. Gives examples of some kinds of affirmative action admissions programs that might be upheld in future Supreme Court opinions.

191.   Morse, Thomas R. and Rusciano, Anthony J.   "Bakke v. Regents of the University of California: Preferential Admissions, an Unconstitutional Approach Paved with Good Intentions?"   New England Law Review.   12 (Winter, 1977), 719-761.

        Purpose of comment is to demonstrate that the California Supreme Court need not have found the medical school's minority admissions policy unconstitutional, that the Equal Protection Clause is broad enough to encompass a preferential admissions program.

192.   Nathanson, Nathaniel and Bartnik, Casimir J.   "The Constitutionality of Preferential Treatment for Minority Applicants to Professional Schools."   Chicago Bar Record.   58 (May-June, 1977), 282-286.

        Presents the issues supporting and opposing preferential treatment for minority candidates to law schools.   Compares the Bakke case with the New York case, Alevy v. Downstate Medical Center of New York (1976) and the decisions rendered by the state and appellate courts in both cases.   Cites standard of review for reviewing "benign" racial classifications and why it would be unwise to abandon strict judicial scrutiny of racial classifications.

193.   Newton, Lisa H.   "Bakke and Davis: Justice, American Style."   Phi Kappa Phi Journal.   58 (Winter, 1978), 22-23.

        Attacks special minority quotas for medical school admissions because such quotas are unfair to all minority groups not selected for special treatment, reinforce the stereotype of inferior ability to preferred minorities, and adds vast weights of nonproductive bureaucracy to the economy.

194.   Nisbet, Lee.   "Reverse Racism: the Bakke Case."   Humanist.   38 (January-February, 1978), 60-61.

        Discusses the arguments by proponents of affirmative action, particularly their use of racial criteria in college admissions on the grounds that blacks are intellectually inferior to members of other racial or ethnic groups.

195. Norton, Eleanor Holmes. "Comment on the Bakke Decision. "
      Personnel Administrator. 23 (August, 1978), 26-28.

      Chairman of the U. S. Equal Employment Opportunity Commission discusses the Bakke decision.

196. O'Neil, Robert M. "What Bakke Leaves to the States: Preliminary Thoughts. " New Directions for Higher Education.
      6 (1978), 47-52.

      Suggests that Justice Powell's opinion in the Bakke case stressed educational diversity over state responsibility. Even where diversification fails as a goal, author believes that the desire to overcome the effects of past discrimination may still avail.

197. "125 Professors Oppose Support for Bakke View. " The New
      York Times, February 9, 1978, p. 16.

      Professors of the Committee on Academic Nondiscrimination and Integrity oppose a November, 1977 statement by 90 other university professors supporting special hiring and admissions programs for minorities; note implication of stand in Bakke case for other civil rights issues.

198. Payne, Charles. "The Bakke Case and Its Implications for
      Schools of Education. " Teacher Education. 14 (Spring,
      1979), 20-29.

      Author lists the implications of the Bakke ruling for the educational system and presents alternatives that include the development of an educational system beginning in kindergarten that prepares minority students for professional schools.

199. Picott, J. Rupert. "Beyond Bakke: Assessment and Future. "
      Negro History Bulletin. 41 (September-October, 1978), 875.

      Suggests that the Court's approval of the principle of affirmative action may prove to be the heart of the landmark compromise in Bakke, but that the U. S. must wait for supplemental decisions on the Bakke case which will provide needed clarification and historical perspective.

200. Pollak, Louis. "Race as a 'Permissible Touchstone. '"
      The Center Magazine. 11 (January/February, 1978), 14-16.

      Dean of the University of Pennsylvania Law School argues for a Supreme Court reversal of the California Supreme Court decision. Defends race as a permissible touchstone for remedial government action in a broad range of situations.

201.   Pottinger, Stan. "The Bakke Case: How to Argue about
         'Reverse Discrimination.'" Ms. Magazine. 6 (January,
         1978), 59-60.

         Former Director of the Office for Civil Rights (HEW) sug-
         gest various ways in which the U. S. Supreme Court could
         rule in the Bakke case, why race and sex are legitimate
         criteria for admission to professional schools, and why it is
         a myth that government, under its affirmative action laws,
         is forcing colleges and universities to admit unqualified stu-
         dents.

202.   Pulliam, Roger I. "Allan Bakke vs. Regents of the Univer-
         sity of California: Analysis and Implications." Western
         Journal of Black Studies. 2 (March, 1978), 18-23.

         Discusses the Bakke case in relation to the role of affirma-
         tive action programs, the problem of quotas, the relevance
         of admission criteria to minority group applicants, and public
         opinion concerning affirmative action.

203.   Rabinove, Samuel. Bakke's Implication. New York: Amer-
         ican Jewish Committee, 1978. 6 p.

         Analyzes the Supreme Court decision in the Bakke case, em-
         phasizing the uncertainties and ambiguities remaining in the
         wake of the Court's findings that racial and ethnic quotas are
         unacceptable, although race can be a valid factor in applying
         affirmative action remedies. Also discussed are cases pend-
         ing which challenge the validity of affirmative action pro-
         grams which discriminate against whites.

204.   Ravenell, Mildred W. "DeFunis and Bakke ... The Voice
         Not Heard. " Howard Law Journal. 21 (1978), 128-174.

         Analyzes the Bakke and DeFunis cases before the U. S. Su-
         preme Court in the context of the proper use of race in ad-
         missions criteria, particularly to achieve the compelling edu-
         cational goals of training competent lawyers and doctors from
         diverse backgrounds for all Americans. Consideration of
         race in admissions to professional schools is legally and
         educationally defensible, morally correct, and consistent with
         "racial neutrality" in contemporary reality.

205.   _____. "Issues in Admissions after Bakke. " Journal of
         the National Association of College Admissions Counselors.
         23 (December, 1978), 12-26.

         Author was a member of the joint committee on behalf of the
         American Council on Education and the Association of Amer-
         ican Law Schools, which prepared an interpretative working
         document on the Bakke ruling. Explains how, in the light of
         the Bakke decision, institutions of higher education can achieve
         diversity as the goal in admissions.

206.   _____. "Untangling the Bakke Decision. " AGB Reports.
          21 (March-April, 1979), 10-14.

          Examines the Bakke ruling, emphasizing Justice Powell's
          opinion.

207.   Regan, Richard J. "Reflections on Bakke and Beyond. "
          Thought. 54 (March, 1979), 58-66.

          Contends that the Bakke case raises fundamental questions
          about the vitality of the American social compact.   Bakke's
          supporters ignore the social goals of racial integration and
          broader distribution of resources and rewards.   Minority
          supporters fail to recognize sufficiently society's interest in
          the highest standards of excellence for doctors.   Both sides
          should recognize responsibilities to society.

208.   Regents of the University of California vs. Allan Bakke.   3
          vols.   (United States Supreme Court Records and Briefs
          Series).   Englewood, Colorado: Information Handling Serv-
          ices, 1978.

          Presents the trial and appellate records, along with the
          U. S. Supreme Court decision, briefs before the court.

209.   Roark, Anne C. "Post-Bakke Admission Plan Adopted at
          Davis. " The Chronicle of Higher Education. 17 (October
          30, 1978), 13.

          University of California at Davis medical school officials an-
          nounce the beginning of a complex new screening procedure
          for medical school applicants which consider the latter's race
          and "disadvantage" along with traditional academic qualifica-
          tions.   The new procedures do not use a quota system for
          minorities.

210.   Rogers, Rich, and Harper, Judy. "Why the Bakke Case
          Has the University Under Siege: Affirmative Action vs. Re-
          verse Discrimination. " California Journal. 8 (May, 1977),
          171-172.

          Discusses the two basic tests concerning any violation of the
          Fourteenth Amendment: the Bakke effect on higher educa-
          tion; and that the question before the Court is how to provide
          equal opportunity for minority groups without denying equal
          protection to individuals within the majority.

211.   Roos, Peter D. "Bakke: Some Views. Expansion or De-
          struction?" Civil Rights Digest. 10 (Summer, 1978), 17-19.

          Examines two questions regarding the Bakke decision: does
          the decision really say "yes" to race and "no" to quotas; and
          what criteria, in addition to race, may be used in an admis-

sions program to advance the cause of minority participation in higher education.

212.   Routh, Frederick B.   "Affirmative Action after Bakke. " Journal of Intergroup Relations.   7 (May, 1979), 31-35.

Analyzes the impact of the Bakke ruling on affirmative action programs in education and employment.

213.   Scherer, Douglas.   "Bakke Revisited. "   Human Rights.   7 (Summer, 1978), 22-29.

Author views the Bakke decision and its three predecessor cases during the 1976 and 1977 Supreme Court terms as confirming the fundamental purposes of the equal protection clause of removing badges and incidences of slavery and of permitting black Americans to obtain opportunities equal to those of white Americans.

214.   Schoch, Dorothy W.   "Fourteenth Amendment--Equal Protection: Preferential Admissions--Race as an Admissions Criterion. "   Case Western Reserve Law Review.   28 (Fall, 1977), 238-265.

The purpose of article is to state the legal issues the Supreme Court faces in its pending Bakke ruling, analyze the few lower court decisions which expressly dealt with preferential admissions programs, and suggest appropriate standard of review to determine the validity of racially preferential admissions programs.

215.   Sedlacek, William E.   "Bakke Decision: Should We Use Race in Admissions? "   Howard Law Journal.   22 (1979), 327-334.

Considers the various ways race can legitimately be used in admissions to higher education, in light of the Bakke Supreme Court ruling.

216.   Segal, Phyllis.   "Bakke: Some Views.   A Feminist Perspective. "   Civil Rights Digest.   10 (Summer, 1978), 15-16.

Author believes that while Bakke won his challenge, so did proponents of affirmative action.   The solid foundation for affirmative action laid in the Bakke case should apply to sex as well as to race discrimination, and to employment as well as to university admissions.

217.   Sexton, John.   "Minority-Admissions Programs after Bakke. " Harvard Educational Review.   49 (August, 1979), 313-339.

Describes the special admissions program challenged in the Bakke case and outlines the reaction to it by the Supreme

Court.   Argues that while Bakke is an instance of judicial
intrusion into educational policy, it is simultaneously an invitation to greater autonomy for educators.   Examines the
desirability of an affirmative action component in an en-
lightened admissions program, considers the appropriate role
of such objective indicators as standardized test scores and
college grades, and describes the factors that would affect
the legality of admissions programs.   Author offers two
models of special admissions programs that would meet the
requirements of the Bakke decision.

218.   Shapiro, Herbert.   "The Bakke Decision: Illusion and Real-
        ity in the Supreme Court. "   Crisis.   86 (February, 1979),
        62-66.

        Examines the opinions of the Justices in the Bakke case, and
        the issue of "reverse discrimination. "

219.   Sharrow, Conrad.   "Legal Technicalities and Interpretation
        of the Bakke Decision. "   Journal of the National Association
        of College Admissions Counselors.   23 (December, 1978),
        17-26.

        Paper clarifies several questions regarding the Bakke case
        decision.   Describes the case as a direct collision between
        affirmative action and equal protection.   Commends the Su-
        preme Court for recognizing the social service function of
        universities to integrate for a pluralistic society that seeks
        equality for all.

220.   Sherman, Malcolm.   "Bakke: The Case Against Prefer-
        ence. "   Change.   9 (October, 1977), 19, 60-61.

        Concludes that merit, not race, should be the criteria for
        university admissions.   Suggests that white applicants are
        required to have substantially higher grades and test scores
        than blacks for law school admissions.   Gives possible rea-
        sons for the Supreme Court to decide for or against Bakke.

221.   Simms-Brown, R. Jean.   "After Caution Comes Red: The
        Bakke Decision and Its Threat to Black Educational Institu-
        tions. "   Crisis.   86 (February, 1979), 67-69.

        Describes the reactions to the Bakke ruling and suggests that
        students become more self-reliant so that they will not need
        special programs in the future.

222.   Sindler, Allan P.   Bakke, DeFunis, and Minority Admis-
        sions: The Quest for Equal Opportunity.   New York: Long-
        man, 1978.   358 p.

        Analyzes the public policy and legal issues surrounding pref-
        erential admissions of minorities in higher education, specif-

ically the cases of Marco DeFunis and Allan Bakke.   Topics
considered are divergent notions of equal opportunity, increasing number of applicants and rising standards of admission, racial preference, special admissions of discretion-
ary selection, goals and quotas, legal strategies, comparative
academic qualifications, an increasing supply of qualified
minority applicants, equal protection of the laws and racial
classifications, and political implications.   A final chapter
focuses upon an analysis of the U.S. Supreme Court's ruling
in the Bakke case.

223.   Smith, Ralph R.   "Bakke's Case vs. the Case for Affirma-
       tive Action. " New York University Education Quarterly.   9
       (Winter, 1978), 2-8.

       Claims that the Bakke case is weak, that admissions are
       best left to university discretion, and that whatever the Court
       decides, the questions raised by Bakke will not be put to
       rest.

224.   _____.   "The Road Not Taken: More Reflections on the
       Bakke Case. " Southern University Law Review.   5 (Fall,
       1978), 23-60.

       Analyzes the U.S. Supreme Court decision in the Bakke case
       with the thesis that the Justices had the opportunity and
       principled bases for disposing of the litigation in a- manner
       which would have more readily accomodated the competing
       interests involved.

225.   Spitzer, Matthew L.   "Multicriteria Choice Processes: An
       Application of Public Choice Theory to Bakke, the FCC and
       the Courts. " Yale Law Journal.   88 (March, 1979), 717-
       779.

       Applies public choice analysis to the U.S. Supreme Court
       decision in the Bakke case, and demonstrates that Justice
       Powell's proposed admissions process violates at least one
       of a specified set of characterizations of that process, and
       that the most likely violation directly supports the critique
       in the Brennan opinion.

226.   Stevens, John M.   "The Good News of Bakke. " Phi Delta
       Kappan.   59 (September, 1977), 23-27.

       Discusses the Bakke case within the context of the necessity
       to expand the numbers of professionals, particularly in medi-
       cine, and to guarantee admissions to professional schools to
       all qualified applicants.

227.   Stone, Julius.   "Equal Protection in Special Admissions Pro-
       grams: Forward from Bakke. " Hastings Constitutional Law
       Quarterly.   6 (Spring, 1979), 719-750.

The author's purpose is to analyze Bakke's equal protection
holding and to offer an assessment of what the decision
means for academic special admissions programs.   Discussion focuses on how race may be used as a factor in admissions decisions consistently with the equal protection clause
of the Constitution.

228.   "The Supreme Court, 1977 Term: Equal Protection, Affirmative Action: Regents of the University of California v.
Bakke. "   Harvard Law Review.   92 (November, 1978), 131-
148.

Explains why the severely fragmented Court left many issues
unresolved, and the overall impact on equal protection doctrine remains to be seen.   The crucial question left unan-
swered by the case is what types of affirmative action programs would be approved by the Court in education and other
contexts.

229.   "Symposium: Regents of the University of California v.
Bakke. "   California Law Review.   67 (January, 1979), 1-229.

230.   Bell, Derrick A. Jr.   "Bakke, Minority Admissions, and
the Usual Price of Racial Remedies. "   Pp. 3-19.

Criticizes the exclusion of minorities from meaningful
participation in the Bakke litigation and from much of the
scholarly debate over the case.   Contends the real issue
would have been clarified by more attention to history and
less reliance on legal precedent or moral philosophy.
Compares the condition of slaves with that of blacks today, and concludes that in both eras blacks can progress
in society only when that progress is perceived by the
white majority as a clear benefit to whites, or at least
not a serious risk.   Also sketches the main problems
confronting proponents or minority admissions in the post-
Bakke era.

231.   Blasi, Vincent.   "Bakke as Precedent: Does Mr. Justice
Powell Have a Theory? "   Pp. 21-68.

Explores how the Supreme Court opinion in Bakke should
be interpreted by judges and administrators who are obligated to adhere to it as a precedent and what types of
race-conscious admissions programs should be upheld under this precedent.   Focuses upon the opinions of Justices
Powell and Stevens for precedents.

232.   Chen, Edward.   "The Case for Minority Participation in
Reverse Discrimination Litigation. "   Pp. 191-229.

Demonstrates the compelling political, jurisprudential, and
constitutional considerations that mandate the systematic

and full participation of minority beneficiaries in lawsuits
in which race-conscious affirmative action programs are
challenged.   The Federal Rules of Civil Procedure provide feasible means to facilitate such participation.

233.   Dixon, Robert G., Jr.   "Bakke: A Constitutional Analy-
            sis."   Pp. 69-86.

            Discusses the impact of Bakke on equal protection theory
            and on the statutory and executive order cases.   Suggests
            that all the opinions of the justices point up the need to
            clarify our thinking on the concept of discrimination itself
            and the emerging question of individual rights vs. groups
            rights in our constitutional order.   Author expresses deep
            reservations about a policy of ethnic proportionality be-
            cause it has no foundation in constitutional tradition of in-
            dividual rights, no foundation in the traditional western
            concept of equal citizenship, and no foundation in the cus-
            tomary imbalanced ethnic patterns in our country and
            among other nations.

234.   Greenawalt, R. Kent.   "The Unresolved Problems of Re-
            verse Discrimination."   Pp. 87-130.

            Examines the Supreme Court Bakke decision including the
            problems of statutory interpretation of Title VI faced by
            the Court and the merits of constitutional arguments.
            Concludes that the soundest and most viable constitutional
            standard for race-conscious classifications is taken by
            Justices Brennan, White, Marshall, and Blackmun.

235.   Henkin, Louis.   "What of the Right to Practice a Profes-
            sion?"   Pp. 131-141.

            Explains why the Supreme Court should have discussed in
            their decision on Bakke the constitutional issues arising
            from university policies on professional school admissions
            within the larger context of societal policies about entry
            into the professions.   Concludes that within constitutional
            limits, states ought to consider the professions in broad
            societal terms, and fit the qualifications for admission
            and the size of professional schools to that conception.
            The states, under pressure and scrutiny from the courts,
            ought to reexamine all state policies which lead to the
            exclusion of minorities from the professions.

236.   O'Neil, Robert M.   "Bakke in Balance: Some Preliminary
            Thoughts."   Pp. 143-170.

            Argues that while constitutional scholars may find the Su-
            preme Court ruling in Bakke unsatisfactory, the decision
            offers university administrators, foundations, and other
            higher education policymakers opportunities for "enlight-

ened experimentation" in future admissions policies and programs. Author focuses upon Justice Powell's opinion and the guidance it offers in the use of racial classifications in higher education, including financial aid.

237.   Posner, Richard A. "The Bakke Case and the Future of Affirmative Action." Pp. 171-189.

Explains why the court failed to vindicate affirmative action programs in higher education.

238.   "Symposium: The Quest for Equality." Washington University Law Quarterly. Volume 1979 (Winter).

This symposium is the third in a series on "The Quest for Equality." The sections relevant to the Bakke case, both in its legal and philosophical implications are the following:

239.   Foreward: "Equality, the Elusive Value," by Robert G. Dixon, Jr. Pp. 5-10.

240.   Philosophy of Equality: "The Philosophy of Equality," by Paul A. Freund. Pp. 11-23.

241.   Commentary: "The Meaning of Equality," by Thomas Nagel. Pp. 25-31.
Panel Discussion. Pp. 33-34.

242.   Racial Preferences and Scarce Resources: Implications of the Bakke Case: "The Bakke Problem--Allocation of Scarce Resources in Education and Other Areas," by Erwin N. Griswold. Pp. 55-80.

243.   Commentary: "Concealing Our Meaning from Ourselves: The Forgotten History of Discrimination," by Drew S. Days, III. Pp. 81-91.

244.   Commentary: "A Viable Compromise on Minority Admissions," by Nathan Glazer. Pp. 93-104.
Panel Discussion. Pp. 107-112.

245.   Equal Employment Opportunity: "Preferential Remedies and Affirmative Action in Employment in the Wake of Bakke," by Harry T. Edwards. Pp. 113-136.

246.   Commentary: "The Need for Self-Imposed Quotas in Academic Employment," by Herma Hill Kay. Pp. 137-146.

247.   Commentary: "The Disease as Cure: 'In Order to Get Beyond Racism, We Must First Take Account of Race," by Antonin Scalia. Pp. 147-158.
Panel Discussion. Pp. 159-161.

Other sections on "The Quest for Equality" include topics on "Sexual Equality Under the Fourteenth and Equal Rights Amendments, " "Public School Desegregation, " and "Equality in Basic Needs and Services: Constitutional Right to Subsidy and Sharing. "

248.   Tollett, Kenneth S.   "What Led to Bakke. "   Center Magazine.   11 (January-February, 1978), 2-10.

Briefly reviews the Bakke case and similar related cases; states their implications for higher education of minorities; defends special minority admissions programs; and argues that opposition to such programs probably conceals hostility to blacks.

249.   Tribe, Laurence H.   "Perspective on Bakke: Equal Protection, Procedural Fairness, or Structural Justice?"   Harvard Law Review.   92 (February, 1979), 864-877.

Examines the Bakke case from the perspective of broad doctrinal themes in constitutional law, specifically in the area of equal protection, idea of procedural fairness as distinct from accuracy of result, and the notion of structural justice.

250.   U. S. Commission on Civil Rights.   Statement on Affirmative Action.   Washington, D. C., October, 1977.   19 p. (ERIC ED 146 310)   CR 1. 10:54

Explains why the Commission considers the setting of affirmative action goals, including the use of numerically based, racially sensitive remedies for past discrimination, to be in the national interest.

251.   _____ .   Toward an Understanding of Bakke.   Washington, D. C., May, 1979.   189 p.
                                        CR 1. 10:58

Includes the complete text of the U. S. Supreme Court decision of Regents of the University of California v. Bakke; Equal Employment Opportunity Commission's Affirmative Action Guidelines; Statement by The U. S. Commission on Civil Rights on Affirmative Action (issued on July 1, 1978); Presidential Memorandum on Affirmative Action Programs (issued on July 20, 1978); and the U. S. Commission on Civil Rights, Statement on Affirmative Action (published in October, 1977).

252.   "U. S. Rights Aide Says Bakke Ruling Permits a Vigorous Drive on Bias. "   The New York Times, June 30, 1978, p. 1.

Drew S. Days III, Assistant Attorney General, says federal agencies will be able to continue vigorous enforcement of antidiscrimination laws in the wake of the Bakke Supreme Court decision, but that agency rule-making and enforcement of civil rights would have to be focused now on real causes and remedies for discrimination.

253. U. S. Supreme Court, Washington, D. C. The Regents of the University of California v. Allan Bakke. Petition for a Writ of Certiorari to the Supreme Court of the State of California. December, 1976. 35 p.

The question addressed in this petition for a writ of certiorari is "When only a small fraction of thousands of applicants can be admitted, does the equal protection clause forbid a state university professional school faculty from voluntarily seeking to counteract effects of generations of pervasive discrimination against discrete and insular minorities by establishing a limited special admissions program that increases opportunities for well-qualified members of such racial and ethnic minorities?" Appendices include the trial court opinion, findings and judgment.

254. _____. The Regents of the University of California, Petitioner, v. Allan Bakke, Respondent. On Writ of Certiorari to the Supreme Court of California. October, 1977. 73 p. (ERIC ED 151 482)

Case description which reviews the admissions criteria of the University of California medical school at Davis, Bakke's interview and rating, and the special admissions program. Also included are the proceedings of the trial and appellate courts, and the decision and supporting arguments of the California Supreme Court.

255. _____. The Regents of the University of California, Petitioner, v. Allan Bakke, Respondent. On Writ of Certiorari in the Supreme Court of the State of California. Brief for Petitioner. October, 1977. 101 p. (ERIC ED 154 073)

The University of California presents its case for special admissions programs for minority group members, which includes the history of racial discrimination in medical schools, the characteristics and purposes of special admissions programs, and relevant concerns in the utilization of racial criteria for remedial purposes in admissions.

256. _____. The Regents of the University of California, Petitioner, v. Allan Bakke, Respondent. On Writ of Certiorari to the Supreme Court of the State of California. Brief for Petitioner. October, 1977. 25 p. (ERIC ED 154 074)

Regents of the University of California defend their medical school admission policy at the Davis campus.

257.   . The Regents of the University of California, Petitioner, v. Allan Bakke, Respondent. On Writ of Certiorari
to the Supreme Court of the State of California. Supplemental Brief for Petitioner. October, 1977. 112 p.
(ERIC ED 154 075)

Regents of the University of California defend their special
admissions program on the Davis campus, emphasizing the
constitutionality of the program under Title VI of the Civil
Rights Act of 1964.

258. Van Alstyne, William. "Preliminary Report on the Bakke
Case. " AAUP Bulletin. 64 (December, 1978), 286-297.

Discusses the principal points in the Bakke Supreme Court
decision, including its immediate implications for the academic community, the instability of the decision, two counter-
vailing possibilities, and the constitutionality of racial quotas.

259. Van Dyke, Jon. "Bakke v. The Regents of the University
of California. " Hastings Constitutional Law Quarterly. 3
(Fall, 1976), 891-898.

Criticizes the California Supreme Court's Bakke decision for
its striking down of racially-based affirmative action programs. Cites some Supreme Court cases and interpretations
in the law which uphold such programs. Concentrates upon
the importance of such programs to create a pluralistic environment within institutions of higher education. Increased
minority admissions, the author believes, will meet the
commitment of professional schools to a pluralistic society
in which all people have equal access to positions of leadership.

260. Vieira, Norman. "Permissible Classification by Race and
the Bakke Case. " Idaho Law Review. 14 (Fall, 1977), 1-
19.

Author discusses early Supreme Court rulings on permissible
classification by race, reviews the use of racial criteria in
school desegregation, voting, and employment, and analyzes
general policy matters concerning racially differentiated treatment and alternatives to such treatment. All of the previous
Supreme Court decisions are examined for any light they may
shed on the pending Bakke case.

261. Voros, J. F. , Jr. "Three Views of Equal Protection: A
Backdrop to Bakke. " Brigham Young University Law Review.
Vol. 1979, pp. 25-78.

262. Walsh, John. "Bakke Case: Question of Special Minority
Admissions Programs. " Science. 197 (July 1, 1977),
25-27.

Discusses the sharp increase in medical school competition, history of special admissions programs, the arguments for and against special admissions, and the significance of the outcome. Concludes that the case is a "conflict of imperatives. "

263.   Watson, Denton L.   "In the Wake of Bakke. " Crisis.   86 (February, 1979), 51-61.

Reviews several court cases concerning affirmative action programs both in education and employment, focusing upon Titles VI and VII of the Civil Rights Act of 1964.   Discusses implications of past court decisions and possible future decisions.

264.   Watts, Barbara G.   "Bakke v. Regents of the University of California. "   University of Cincinnati Law Review.   46 (1977), 254-266.

Compares the California Supreme Court ruling in the Bakke case with several appellate court decisions upholding preferences for racial minorities.   Suggests the adoption of the strict scrutiny test to racial classifications and believes that such a test is consistent with legislative mandates to adopt workable affirmative action programs.

265.   Westerfield, Louis.   "Differential Admission Policies in Higher Education: The Proper Standards of Constitutional Review. "   Southern University Law Review.   3 (Spring, 1977), 147-188.

The purpose of the article is to analyze the nature of the California Supreme Court holding in the Bakke case, demonstrate the errors in the logic, and expose the potentially catastrophic results should the decision be upheld.   Concludes that the proper standard of review should have been the substantial interest test and that special admissions programs are harmonious with the spirit of the Fourteenth Amendment.

266.   "What Rights for Whites?" Time.   110 (October 24, 1977), 95-99.

Describes the oral arguments of the Bakke case before the U. S. Supreme Court.

267.   White, David M.   "Pride, Prejudice and Prediction: From Brown to Bakke and Beyond. "   Howard Law Journal.   22 (1979), 375-397.

Describes the Supreme Court Bakke decision as marking the first significant departure from the Court's commitment to desegregated education announced in Brown v. Board of Edu-

cation. Author particularly focuses upon the social assumption that certain races and ethnic groups are inherently inferior, and relates that assumption to the Bakke case.

268.   Young, R. L. "Year Ahead: Bakke Case Looms on the
Supreme Court Docket. " American Bar Association Journal.
63 (November, 1977), 1551-1557.

Explains the issues involved in the Bakke case pending before the U. S. Supreme Court.

269.   Zimmer, Michael J. "'Reverse' Discrimination: Will the
Court Act to End the Second Reconstruction?" Arkansas
Law Review. 31 (Fall, 1977), 370-419.

Presents the thesis that the history of the Fourteenth Amendment demonstrates two thrusts: the reduction of direct Supreme Court activism under the equal protection clause and
stringently limiting executive and legislative efforts to promote racial integration. Author uses the model of state
operated professional schools to discuss these two thrusts.
Traces recent Supreme Court retrenchment of equal protection available to minorities to challenge laws and practices
which impact more heavily on minority group members than
on the majority. Considers minority group challenges to the
allocation of scarce resources, such as medical and law
schools. Discusses the DeFunis and Bakke cases and others
related to preferential admissions.

ERIC RESOURCES

Bakke v. The Regents of the University of California

270.   Adamson, Bill. The Bakke Case and Special Admissions
Programs: A Case for Concern. 1978. 31 p.
ED 160 011

Explains how the Bakke decision and affirmative action programs are incompatible and that the surface of the case
hides a modified Darwinian principle of the survival of the
fittest and slickest.

271.   Asian and Pacific American Federal Employee Council,
Washington, D. C. The Bakke Case and Asian/Pacific Amer-
icans. 1977. 7 p.
ED 154 057

Criticizes the U. S. Department of Justice amicus curiae
brief in the Supreme Court on behalf of the special minority
admissions program at the University of California Medical
School at Davis. The government has become the first par-
ticipant to challenge the participation of Asian Americans in
a minority program.

272.   Aspen Institute for Humanistic Studies, Palo Alto, California.
        Bakke and Beyond. A Report of the Education Commission
        of the States and the Justice Program of the Aspen Institute.
        Report No. 112. Denver: Education Commission of the
        States, 1978. 45 p.
        ED 163 127

        Papers presented at a 1978 conference on the implications
        of the Supreme Court's ruling on the Bakke cases are re-
        printed. Discusses the constitutionality of special admis-
        sions programs and related policy problems facing educators;
        the future of admissions programs and the creation of poli-
        cies for professional school admissions; questions of educa-
        tional due process; the validity of test scores as a measure
        of merit; the socioeconomic biases of the admissions selec-
        tion systems; and the Bakke case explained from an histori-
        cal perspective.

273.   Association of American Colleges, Washington, D. C. Pro-
        ject on the Status and Education of Women. The Bakke
        Case: Implications for Women in Education. Washington,
        D. C.: Association of American Colleges, 1978. 4 p.
        ED 163 101

        Analyzes the U. S. Supreme Court's ruling in the Bakke case,
        particularly as it relates to women's admissions at institu-
        tions of higher education, quotas in student programs, volun-
        tary affirmative action, and employment. The Court implied
        that it does not extend the same equal protection of the law
        to women as it does to racial and ethnic groups.

274.   Blackwell, James E. In Support of Preferential Admissions
        and Affirmative Action in Higher Education: Pre- and Post-
        Bakke Considerations. 1977. 229 p.
        ED 139 351

        Explains why affirmative action is needed in higher educa-
        tion, particularly in graduate and professional study.

275.   New York State Library, Albany. Legislative and Govern-
        ment Services. Regents of the University of California v.
        Bakke. No. 76-811, in the Supreme Court of the United
        States. Albany: New York State Library, 1978. 160 p.
        ED 165 623

        Background information provided on the case before the Cali-
        fornia courts and the U. S. Supreme Court, and the ruling by
        the federal court explained in detail.

276.   Poindexter, Paula M. and Stroman, Carolyn A. The Black
        Press and the Bakke Case: An Analysis of Coverage.
        21 p.
        ED 165 169

Examines the contents of four black newspapers to determine how they covered the Bakke case. Cities for the newspapers include New York, Los Angeles, Atlanta, and Chicago. Suggests that the black press is a chronicler, rather than an interpreter, of issues affecting the black community.

277. United States. Supreme Court. The Regents of the University of California, Petitioner, v. Allan Bakke, Respondent. On Writ of Certiorari to the Supreme Court of California. October, 1977. 73 p.
ED 151 482

Case description which reviews the admissions criteria of the University of California medical school at Davis, Bakke's interview and rating, and the special admissions program. Also included are the proceedings in the trial court, and appeal, and the decision and supporting arguments of the California Supreme Court.

278. _____. The Regents of the University of California, Petitioner, v. Allan Bakke, Respondent. On Writ of Certiorari in the Supreme Court of the State of California. Brief for Petitioner. October, 1977. 101 p.
ED 154 073

The University of California presents its case for special admissions programs for minority group members, which includes the history of racial discrimination in medical schools, the characteristics and purposes of special admissions programs, and relevant concerns in the utilization of racial criteria for remedial purposes in admissions.

279. _____. The Regents of the University of California, Petitioner, v. Allan Bakke, Respondent. On Writ of Certiorari to the Supreme Court of the State of California. Brief for Petitioner. October, 1977. 25 p.
ED 154 074

Regents of the University of California defend their medical school admissions policy at the Davis campus.

280. _____. The Regents of the University of California, Petitioner, v. Allan Bakke, Respondent. On Writ of Certiorari to the Supreme Court of the State of California. Supplemental Brief for Petitioner. October, 1977. 112 p.
ED 154 075

Regents of the University of California defend their special admissions program, emphasizing the constitutionality of the program under Title VI of the Civil Rights Act of 1964.

Marco DeFunis v. Charles Odegaard

82 Wash. 2d 11; 507 P. 2d 1169 (1973)
40 L Ed. 2d 164
416 US 312
94 S Ct 1704
Argued before U.S. Supreme Court: February 26, 1974
Decided April 23, 1974: Vacated as moot

281.   "Ameliorative Racial Classification Under the Equal Protec-
        tion Clause: DeFunis v. Odegaard." Duke Law Journal.
        Vol. 1973, 1126-1152, 1973.

        The purpose of this note is to examine the Washington State
        Supreme Court's opinion in the DeFunis case to determine
        whether that court applied the appropriate standard or review
        to the law school's preferential admissions program and
        whether the U.S. Supreme Court should adopt a similar ap-
        proach.   Concludes that the federal court should acknowledge
        changes in race relations by recognizing the difference be-
        tween traditional racial classifications which sought to per-
        petrate Jim Crow, and those like the University of Washing-
        ton law school's which seek to lay Jim Crow in his grave.

282.   Baeza, Mario. "Efficiency, Equality and Justice in Admis-
        sions Procedures to Higher Education: A Constitutional
        Model for Resolving Conflicting Goals and Competing Claims."
        Black Law Journal. 3 (1973), 132-161.

        Analyzes the conceptual rules to enforce legitimate demands
        of racial justice. Focuses on the question: in the absence
        of a discriminatory motive of previous history of de jure
        segregation, can the state through the use of standardized
        tests and other admissions procedures neutral on their face,
        select applicants for college or graduate study in a manner
        which has a discriminatory impact upon a suspect classifica-
        tion?

283.   Baldwin, Fletcher N., Jr. "DeFunis v. Odegaard, the Su-
        preme Court and Preferential Law School Admissions:
        Discretion Is Sometimes Not the Better of Valor." Univer-
        sity of Florida Law Review. 27 (Winter, 1975), 343-360.

        Reviews the U.S. Supreme Court's decision in DeFunis, ex-
        amines the issues of compensatory programs as they affect
        legal education, and explains why the Court's refusal to hear
        the case is an avoidance of its responsibility authoritatively
        to legitimatize affirmative state programs designed to com-
        pensate for past segregationist policies.

284.   Bell, Derrick A. "In Defense of Minority Admissions Pro-
        grams: A Response to Professor Graglia." Black Law
        Journal. 3 (1973), 241-244.

Refutes Lino Graglia's arguments opposing minority group
admissions to law schools.   Criticizes Graglia for invalid
assertions (e. g. , unqualified minority students being admitted), inaccurate legal and educational conclusions, and
misguided asserted moral concern for racial injustice.

285.   Bickel, Alexander and Kurland, Philip.   "Brief of Anti-
Defamation League of B'Nai B'rith as Amicus Curiae in
DeFunis v. Odegaard. "

Most quoted of the briefs in DeFunis v. Odegaard.   In supporting DeFunis, authors claim that it is wrong to employ
or admit unqualified people solely because of race.   The
lesson of contemporary history that discrimination on the
basis of race is wrong, illegal, immoral and unconstitutional
is now to be unlearned and "those for whom racial equality
was demanded are now to be more equal than others. "

286.   Breland, Hunter M.   DeFunis Revisited: A Psychometric
View.   Princeton, New Jersey: Educational Testing Service,
1976.

Case is reviewed from a psychometric perspective.   Data
from DeFunis are analyzed by applying one of the latest
models of selection fairness.

287.   Cohen,   Carl.   "DeFunis Case: Race & the Constitution. "
Nation.   220 (February 8, 1975), 135-145.

Explores the issue of preferential treatment of minority
groups in admission to professional schools, with particular
emphasis upon the DeFunis case.   Reconstructs the arguments in favor of preferential admissions as enumerated by
the Washington State Supreme Court, gives counterarguments
to that decision, and explains why the court argument fails.
Concludes that racial classifications are always invidious,
stigmatizing, and hence unconstitutional, and that compensation is only justifiable as a response to specific wrongs done
to specific persons.

288.   Cox, Archibald.   "Harvard College Amicus Curiae DeFunis
v. Odegaard, U. S. Supreme Court October Term 1973. "
In Reverse Discrimination.   Edited by Barry R. Gross.
New York: Prometheus, 1977.

Reviews the issues raised by the case, the general policy of
law school and college admissions criteria.   Argues that
quotas are not the issue but rather the desirability of using
race as a criteria for admission.   The Equal Protection
Clause does not prohibit all racially conscious government
activity.   Intellectual capacity is only one criteria for admission; other criteria are necessary to meet the problems
of racial and ethnic inequalities. -

289. _____. The Role of the Supreme Court in American Gov-
      ernment. New York: Oxford University Press, 1976. 118 p.

      Book originated as four lectures at All Souls College, Ox-
      ford, in 1975. Chapter 3 deals with DeFunis v. Odegaard.
      Cox analyzes the application of the equal protection clause
      to the case and explains why the "time for a rigid constitu-
      tional rule has not yet come, " on the question of preferential
      admission to professional schools. Examines the validity of
      tests, whether academic performance is the best indicator
      of professional competence, whether benign racial discrimi-
      nation is socially divisive and substitutes concepts of group
      entitlement based upon numbers instead of individual merit.

290. DeFunis Versus Odegaard and the University Admissions
      Case, The Record. Edited by Ann F. Ginger. Dobbs Fer-
      ry: Oceana, 1974. 3 vols.

      Contains briefs, pleadings in the trial court, excerpts from
      the transcripts of the trial, the state court and the U. S.
      Supreme Court opinions.

291. "DeFunis Symposium, Involving 'Benign Discrimination' in
      Favor of Minority Group Applicants for Admission to the
      University of Washington's Law School. " Columbia Law Re-
      view. 75 (April, 1975), 483-602.

292. Greenawalt, Kent. "Judicial Scrutiny of 'Benign' Racial
      Preference in Law School Admissions. " Pp. 559-602.

      Considers issues of DeFunis v. Odegaard, discusses levels
      of review under the equal protection clause and 'benign'
      racial classifications, as well as the constitutional evalu-
      ation of justification for preferential admissions policies.
      The latter topic concerns compensatory and distributive
      justice, injustices that the government may constitution-
      ally redress, preferential admissions, and value of diver-
      sity. Argues for a third standard of judicial review:
      the substantial interest test.

293. Griswold, Erwin N. "Some Observations on the DeFunis
      Case. " Pp. 512-519.

      Notes that the Supreme Court was wise to decline any de-
      cision in the case because of the inadequate record, no
      full development of constitutionally important factors when
      the case was tried in the Washington State courts. Dis-
      cusses the factors favoring minority admissions programs,
      including that of diversity in the law school student body,
      and outlines the problem of admission criteria.

294. Lavinsky, Larry M. "DeFunis v. Odegaard: The 'Non-
      Decision' with a Message. " Pp. 520-533.

Addresses the question of whether racial preference and
quotas to advance the educational opportunities of racial
and ethnic minorities are compatible with the equal protection clause.   Concludes that the legitimate aspirations
of minority groups should be realized through the application of racially neutral criteria for admission.

295.   Nickel, James W.   "Preferential Policies in Hiring and
         Admissions: A Jurisprudential Approach. "   Pp. 534-558.

         Presents a framework for analyzing preferential policies
         that use racial, ethnic, or sexual classifications.   Dis-
         cusses arguments for and against preferential treatment,
         including the use of goals and quotas.

296.   Pollak, Louis H.   "DeFunis Non Est Disputandum. "   Pp.
         495-511.

         Reviews the DeFunis case in the Washington State courts
         and the U. S. Supreme Court.   Argues that the latter was
         right in not making a decision in that it lacked a "fully
         developed factual record with sharply defined and fully
         canvassed legal issues. "

297.   DeFunis; The Road Not Taken: A Symposium. "   Virginia
         Law Review.   69 (October, 1974), 917-1011.

298.   Gelhorn, Ernest and Hornby, D. Brock.   "Constitutional
         Limitations on Admissions Procedures and Standards. "
         Pp. 975-1011.

         Authors summarize the basic constitutional framework ap-
         plicable to the distribution of government benefits, based
         upon due process and equal protection principles; focus
         upon judicial treatment of educational administration and
         identifies those situations where more or less discretion
         is allowed administrators in education; define the scope
         of the constitutional duty owed by selective educational
         institutions to applicants and outline some minimum sub-
         stantive and judicial standards for the law school admis-
         sions process, and by inference for state colleges and
         universities generally.

299.   Karst, Kenneth L. and Horowitz, Harold W.   "Affirmative
         Action and Equal Protection. "   Pp. 955-974.

         Authors discuss the constitutional attacks on government-
         sponsored affirmative action programs in education and
         employment and focus upon these arguments: (1) affirma-
         tive action is unconstitutional because it submerges the
         principle of individual merit in favor of the "irrelevant"
         criterion of race; and (2) argument that quotas and pref-
         erences are constitutionally permissible, if ever, only

when designed to remedy past discrimination. Authors respond that "individual merit" is an artificial concept, concealing the facts that an individual's claim to equality is necessarily made as a member of a group and that the content of "merit" is necessarily defined by reference to community needs. Authors also discuss some recent employment decisions upholding affirmative action programs and argue that their holdings are justified by the community need to achieve rapid integration. Authors then apply their analysis to the DeFunis case.

300.   O'Neil, Robert M. "Racial Preference and Higher Education: The Larger Context. " Pp. 925-954.

Author explores the central legal issues raised by the DeFunis case, with particular attention to the preferential admissions question, but with an awareness of the larger context of a judicial ruling on the validity of preferential admissions as it will affect the allocation of financial aid, special preparatory programs for minority students, and affirmative action. Discusses the proper constitutional standard of review to judge racial classification and explains governmental compelling interests in granting preferential admissions: promotion of minority representation in the student body and the profession; correction of the discriminatory effects of traditional entrance criteria; correction of the effects of past segregation and discrimination; fulfillment of legal obligations imposed by federal and state affirmative action programs; and representation of a cross-section of society in institutions of higher education.

301.   "DeFunis v. Odegaard. " United States Law Week. 42 (March 5, 1974), 4578-4589.

Excellent editorial summary of the oral arguments before the U.S. Supreme Court.

302.   Douglas, Justice William O. "DeFunis v. Odegaard, Dissenting Opinion. " (April 23, 1974), U.S. Supreme Court, 416 U.S. 312 (1974).

Argues that the Court should have decided the DeFunis case on its merits. Believes that the key to the problem is considering all applications in a racially neutral way. Concludes that "so far as race is concerned, any state sponsored preference to one race over another in ... competition [at professional levels] is ... invidious and violative of the Equal Protection Clause. "

303.   Dworkin, Ronald. "The DeFunis Case: The Right to Go to Law School. " The New York Review of Books. 23 (February 5, 1976), 29-33.

Makes a distinction between equality as a policy and as a
right. DeFunis was treated as an equal and therefore he
cannot claim that all racial classifications are illegal. Suggests that fairness and constitutionality of any admissions
program is justified if it serves a plausible policy that respects the right of all members of the community to be
treated as equals, but not otherwise.

304. _____. "Reverse Discrimination." In Taking Rights
Seriously. Cambridge: Harvard University Press. Pp.
223-240.

Reprint of the original article which appeared above in the
New York Review of Books on the DeFunis case.

305. Fischer, Thomas C. "DeFunis in the Supreme Court: Is
That All There Is?" Journal of Law and Education. 4
(July, 1975), 487-509.

Discusses the consequences of the DeFunis ruling on higher
education institutions, the difficulties of deciding who should
be admitted to law schools, and the possible criteria to use
in admissions. Author perceives the major problem in reconciling the principles of affirmative action and equal protection.

306. Flaherty, James T. and Sheard, Kevin. "DeFunis, The
Equal Protection Dilemma: Affirmative Action and Quotas."
Duquesne Law Review. 12 (Summer, 1974), 745-792.

Discusses whether "reverse discrimination" as exemplified
in the DeFunis case, is contrary to the Brown decision or
whether it is merely an appropriate implementation of Brown.
Holding in DeFunis, author asserts, is that discrimination
against whites is permissible as long as it is in favor of the
"official" designated priority groups.

307. Freedman, Warren. "Is Race Relevant? Discrimination in
Education Today." New York State Bar Journal. 48 (April,
1976), 170-173, 216-218.

Reviews the DeFunis case, criticizes the use of quotas in
law school admissions, and suggests an affirmative action
program which seeks to expand educational opportunity to all
groups, and not particular groups of people.

308. Gillespie, John F. "Constitutional Law--Preferential Admissions Plan and Equal Protection." Toledo Law Review. 5
(Fall, 1973), 160-170.

Analyzes the Washington State Supreme Court's decision in
the DeFunis case and acknowledges that the court used a
double standard interpretation of equal protection in approving

the law school's admissions policy. A pro-minority double standard, author believes, appears necessary to offset the overwhelming effects of the anti-minority double standards that have previously existed in America.

309.   Graglia, Lino A. "Special Admission of the 'Culturally De-
         prived' to Law School." Black Law Journal. 3 (1973),
         232-240.

         Argues against special admissions programs for the cultur-
         ally deprived to law schools on the basis that the principle
         involved is objectionable and the factual premises question-
         able. The Special Admissions programs for blacks dis-
         serves the cause of Negro equality, impairs educational
         quality, and results in the deviation of schools from their
         educational function. Societal racial discrimination under-
         mines the basic ideal that individual merit and individual
         need should be the only relevant considerations for societally
         distributed rewards and benefits.

310.   Hayes, Robert E. "Equality and 'Reverse Discrimination':
         DeFunis v. Odegaard." New York State Bar Journal. 47
         (August, 1975), 378-380, 400-401.

         Affirmative action programs of the Federal government, cor-
         rectly administered, author believes, are fully consistent
         with the paramount objectives of non-discrimination and
         equality. But the Washington State Supreme Court's ruling
         in DeFunis, which upheld the minority admissions program,
         is harmful, unnecessary, and translates into equality re-
         quires inequality, integration requires discrimination, and
         justice for some requires injustice for others.

311.   Kirp, David L. and Yudof, Mark G. "DeFunis and Beyond."
         Change. 6 (November, 1974), 22-26.

         Two legal scholars examine the difficult problem of admis-
         sions based upon race in the wake of the Supreme Court de-
         cision in the DeFunis case.

312.   Landmark Briefs and Arguments of the Supreme Court of the
         United States: Constitutional Law. 1974 Term Supplement.
         (DeFunis v. Odegaard.) Vol. 80. Edited by Philip B. Kur-
         land and Gerhard Casper. Washington, D.C.: University
         Publications of America, Inc., 1974.

         Presents arguments of both sides in the controversy and
         briefs from the American Bar Association, Anti-Defamation
         League of B'nai B'rith, Association of American Law
         Schools, Center for Law and Education of Harvard Univer-
         sity, Group of Law School Deans, Lawyers Committee for
         Civil Rights Under Law, U.S. Equal Employment Opportunity
         Commission, NAACP Legal Defense and Educational Fund,

President and Fellows of Harvard College, and briefs against
some of above Amicus Curiae briefs.

313.   Leonard, Walter J.   "DeFunis v. Odegaard: An Invitation
        To Look Backward. "   Black Law Journal.   3 (Winter, 1974),
        224-231.

        Author analyzes and then rejects the contentions of DeFunis
        that preferential treatment of minority applicants and racial
        identity is violative of the Equal Protection Clause and that
        the LSAT and undergraduate grade point average should be
        the sole criterion for admissions to law schools.   Asserts
        that the issue raised by DeFunis case is, in narrow sense,
        the responsibility of a law school to help compensate for
        past racial injustices; and in the broad sense, the issue is
        the obligation of American society to make up for its cen-
        turies of assault on educational opportunity for Black citizens.

314.   Martin, Charles A.   "DeFunis v. Odegaard and the Holmes
        Memorandum: The Practice of Contemporary Racism. "
        Journal of Negro Education.   44 (Spring, 1975), 109-112.

        Suggests that the Supreme Court's resolution of the DeFunis
        case and memorandum from Peter Holmes, Director of the
        Civil Rights Office of the Department of Health, Education
        and Welfare, could mark the beginning of undeclared period
        of retrenchment in areas of minority group rights.   Effective
        strategies need to be formulated to develop reactive affirma-
        tive action policy and to monitor implementation of that poli-
        cy.

315.   Morris, Arval A.   "Equal Educational Opportunity, Consti-
        tutional Uniformity, and the 'DeFunis' Remand. "   Washington
        Law Review.   50 (June, 1975), 565-595.

        Analyzes competing definitions of equal educational opportun-
        ity and determines that some state courts required to give
        affirmative content to the term but the Fourteenth Amend-
        ment is interpreted only as a limit on state action.   Relates
        above argument to the DeFunis case.

316.   _____.   "Equal Protection, Affirmative Action and Racial
        Preferences in Law Admission: DeFunis v. Odegaard. "
        Washington Law Review.   49 (November, 1973), 1-53.

        Explores the constitutional dimensions of the equal protection
        problem presented by a law school's voluntary adoption of
        racial classifications in admissions, and focuses upon the
        DeFunis case.   Concludes that under current equal protection
        precedents a state law school constitutionally can award a
        racially conditioned preference in law admissions so long as
        it does so within a carefully constructed and openly adminis-
        tered affirmative action program.   The compelling justifica-

tion for using racial classifications would exist if institutions function to deny a racial group equal opportunity for a legal education.

317.   O'Neil, Robert M.   "After DeFunis: Filling the Constitution-al Vacuum. "   University of Florida Law Review.   27 (Win-ter, 1975), 315-342.

Argues that the Supreme Court was correct in ruling the DeFunis case moot and deferring decision until a better case is presented to the Court for decision, analyzes four com-pelling state interests which uphold the constitutionality of preferential admissions, and concludes that there are at present no racially neutral alternatives to increasing minority representation in law schools.

318.   _____.   Discriminating Against Discrimination: Prefer-ential Admissions and the DeFunis Case.   Bloomington: Indiana University Press, 1976.   271 p.

Author wrote and filed briefs in support of the University of Washington's position in the DeFunis case.   Chapters include the background of the case, the state courts' decisions, and the U. S. Supreme Court's non-decision, the practices of preferential admissions on nonracial grounds in higher edu-cation, the Constitution and racial preferences case for and against preferential admissions, the nonracial alternatives, and the policy implications of preferential admissions.   The Appendix includes the texts of the Washington Supreme Court and the U. S. Supreme Court decisions in the DeFunis case. Author favors preferential admissions on a "compelling in-terest" basis.

319.   Posner, Richard A.   "The DeFunis Case and the Constitu-tionality of Preferential Treatment of Minorities. "   Supreme Court Review, 1974.   Chicago: University of Chicago Press, 1974, pp. 1-32.

Discusses the background of the DeFunis case, whether the Supreme Court decision on mootness was correct, how the Court should have decided the constitutional issue if it had reached a decision.   Contains a section on the reasonable-ness of reverse discrimination (culturally biased exams, race as a surrogate for other, nonracial characteristics, racial proportional representation, and the need to appease militant minorities by preferential treatment).   Suggests that the preferred groups could be redefined as the underprivi-leged, which would avoid a racial or ethnic basis.

320.   Redish, Martin A.   Preferential Law School Admissions and the Equal Protection Clause: An Analysis of the Competing Arguments.   Princeton, New Jersey: Educational Testing Service, 1976.

Analyzes competing arguments from the DeFunis case in an effort to define the issues underlying the question of the legality of preferential minority applicants.

321.   . "Preferential Law School Admissions and the Equal Protection Clause: An Analysis of the Competing Arguments." UCLA Law Review. 22 (December, 1974), 343-400.

Examines the DeFunis case and preferential admissions policies, the standard of review in testing these programs under the equal protection clause, the relevance of the educational setting to the scope of judicial review, the goals offered to justify preferential admissions and possible alternative means of accomplishing equal opportunity.

322.   Riley, Robert J. "Constitutional Law--Fourteenth Amendment--Equal Protection--Racial Classifications for Law School Admissions Constitutionally Permissible." Journal of Urban Law. 51 (1973), 117-125.

Discusses the Washington State Supreme Court's ruling in the DeFunis case and the arguments which have been raised in support and opposition to preferential admissions for minority group members.

323.   Schmidtman, Kirk A. "DeFunis v. Odegaard--Reverse Discrimination in Law School Admissions." Willamette Law Journal. 11 (Winter, 1974), 134-142.

Analyzes the DeFunis case, with emphasis upon the standard of review used in preferential admissions cases. Concludes that the strict scrutiny test appears to provide the most workable solution and that the courts are likely to rule in support of preferential admissions programs in any future litigation.

324.   Spencer, Beverly Anita. "DeFunis v. Odegaard--The Aftermath and Effects of an Unresolved Issue." Howard Law Journal. 18 (1975), 783-807.

Describes various Supreme Court decisions relating to the constitutionality of racially preferential programs in education and employment, and compares these rulings to the DeFunis case. Author favors benign racial classifications in the light of the history of racial discrimination in America.

325.   Wilson, James B. "DeFunis--What Now?" Journal of College and University Law. 2 (February, 1974), 83-97.

Analyzes the Supreme Court decision in DeFunis and how it affects preferential special admissions programs for minorities in higher education.

326.   Zimmer, Michael J.   "Beyond DeFunis: Disproportionate Im-
        pact Analysis and Mandated 'Preferences' in Law School. "
        North Carolina Law Review.   42 (February, 1976), 317-388.

        Suggests that preferential admissions for minorities are not
        only permissible but mandated when there has been a failure
        to promote racial integration.

Additional Legal Sources

327. Alexander, Elaine A. and Alexander, Lawrence A. "The New Racism: An Analysis of the Use of Racial and Ethnic Criteria in Decision-Making." San Diego Law Review. 9 (1972), 190-263.

Explores general relationship between justice and use of group criteria, examines and criticizes the arguments most frequently advanced by proponents of such programs.

328. American Association of Law Schools. Section on Minority Groups. Proceedings. Black Law Journal. 4 (1975), 453-560.

Includes discussions and papers on varied subjects, among which is the DeFunis case, legal education of minority students, minority faculty, and biases in the California bar exam.

329. Askin, Frank. "The Case for Compensatory Treatment." Rutgers Law Review. 24 (1969), 65-79.

The author is one of the initiators of the Minority Student Program at Rutgers Law School which established a minimum quota for black and other minority students. Author states the legal justifications for this type of "reverse discrimination" and suggests that such affirmative action not only is permissible but may be even constitutionally required.

330. Association of American Colleges. Project on the Status and Education of Women. Federal Laws and Regulations Concerning Sex Discrimination in Educational Institutions. Rev. ed. Washington, D. C.: Association of American Colleges, June, 1977.

Chart of major federal laws, Executive Orders, and regulations on sex discrimination including what institutions are covered, affirmative action requirements (if any), what is prohibited, complaint procedures, and enforcement power and sanctions.

331. Babcock, Barbara. Sex Discrimination and the Law: Causes and Remedies. Boston: Little, Brown and Co., 1975.

This is a rich source-casebook on sex discrimination. Discusses issues of conditions that cause sex discrimination, legislation and executive orders that prohibit it, and legal remedies to prevent such discrimination.

332.   Bartnoff, Judith.   "Title VII and Employment Discrimination in 'Upper Level' Jobs. "   Columbia Law Review.   73 (December, 1973), 1614-1640.

Provides framework to assess the legal problems of discrimination in upper level employment, including higher education, and focusing primarily upon discrimination in hiring and promotion.   Concludes that Title VII of the Civil Rights Act of 1964 and other discriminatory laws applied by the courts, condemn not merely overtly discriminatory practices but also practices that result in unjustifiable adverse differential impact on women and minority groups.

333.   Baugh, James R.   "The Federal Legislation on Equal Educational Opportunity for the Handicapped. "   Idaho Law Review.   15 (Fall, 1978), 65-87.

Deals with the constitutional guarantee of equal educational opportunity and describes the federal statutes that form the core of a growing body of civil rights legislation on behalf of handicapped people's rights to appropriate and equal education.

334.   Bell, Derrick A.   "Black Students in White Law Schools: The Ordeal and the Opportunity. "   Toledo Law Review.   Vol. 1970, (Spring-Summer, 1970), 539-558.

Considers the early development of legal education for blacks, examines the types of black students that are currently being admitted to law school and concludes that their psychological and sociological experience makes the study of law extremely difficult for them.

335.   Belton, Robert.   "Title VII of the Civil Rights Act of 1964: A Decade of Private Enforcement and Judicial Developments. " Saint Louis University Law Journal.   20 (1976), 225-307.

Overview of the judicial developments under Title VII during the first decade.   Considers employment discrimination, establishing the unlawful employment practice, formulating effective relief, and the Equal Employment Opportunity Act.

336.   Bender, Louis W.   Federal Regulation and Higher Education. ERIC/Higher Education Research Report No. 1.   Washington, D. C.:   American Association for Higher Education.   March, 1977.   88 p.
       (ERIC ED 135 323)

Explores the nature of regulatory practices to determine if
federal regulations have altered governance patterns or infringed on institutional autonomy. Affirmative action regulations are included. Discusses how regulations are written,
federal accountability versus institutional autonomy, recommendations for reform, costs to institutions, resultant program changes, and implications of federal regulations on
higher education in the future. Includes an extensive bibliography.

337.   Bickel, Alexander M. "The Original Understanding and the
        Segregation Decision." Harvard Law Review. 68 (November,
        1955), 1-65.

Discusses the legislative history of the Fourteenth Amendment. Concludes that the Radical leadership deliberately obtained a provision whose future effect was left to future
determination.

338.   Bloom, Judith. "Constitutional Law--Equal Protection--'Be-
        nign' Descrimination--Minority Admissions Programs--Su-
        preme Court's Response to Preferential Treatment." Loyola
        of Los Angeles Law Review. 8 (February, 1975), 191-211.

Examines three U. S. Supreme Court's decisions on minority
preference (DeFunis v. Odegaard, Kahn v. Shevin (1974);
Morton v. Mancari (1974)). Concludes that the unpredict-
ability of the Court casts doubts on the validity of minority
preference and that special consideration be given in a racially neutral manner.

339.   Blumrosen, Alfred. "Quotas, Common Sense, and Law in
        Labor Relations: Three Dimensions of Equal Opportunity."
        Rutgers Law Review. 27 (Spring, 1974), 675-703.

Traces the history of efforts to achieve equal employment
opportunity without the use of numerical standards, the con-
sequent need for the use of numerical standards, limitations
on the use of such standards, and how such limitations make
numerical standards desirable and compatible with constitutional and statutory provisions.

340.   Bracy, Warren D. "The Questionable Legality of Affirma-
        tive Action: A Response to the Rejoinder [by Howard
        Sherain]." Journal of Urban Law. 42 (November, 1974),
        273-276.

Argues that the legality of Executive Order 11246 which requires affirmative action in employment, is legal and there
is no evidence that affirmative action leads to the hiring of
unqualified blacks and women.

341.   Brown, Frank. "Reverse Discrimination in Professional
        Schools' Admissions and in Employment." NOLPE School
        Law Journal. 8 (1979), 193-209.

        Discusses equal opportunity in America, antecedents of pres-
        ent reverse discrimination cases, discrimination in profes-
        sional schools' admissions, and reverse discrimination in
        employment. Also briefly discusses the Bakke case.

342.   Bryan, Karen Smith. "Recovery of Back Pay Under Execu-
        tive Order 11, 246." Southern California Law Review. 52
        (March, 1979), 767-803.

        Note examines whether the Executive may lawfully require
        contractors to give back pay to victims of discrimination.
        Reviews in detail a series of regulations of the concept of
        back pay as an aspect of affirmative action.

343.   Buckley, Mert. "Reverse Discrimination--A Summary of
        the Arguments with Further Consideration of Its Stigmatizing
        Effect." Washburn Law Journal. 16 (Winter, 1977), 421-
        438.

        Note summarizes arguments for and against reverse dis-
        crimination and presents standards to test the constitutional
        validity of the policy. Focuses upon argument that prefer-
        ential treatment for minorities tends to stigmatize them as
        inferior, thereby perpetuating prevailing stereotypes and
        prejudices.

344.   Buckner, Adair Melinsky. "Title VII and Preferential Treat-
        ment: The Compliance Dilemma." Texas Tech Law Review.
        7 (Spring, 1976), 671-701.

        Points out the inconsistencies in the language of Title VII,
        in governmental orders and regulations, and in court deci-
        sions which create problems for Title VII organizations in
        decision-making.

345.   Buek, Alexander and Orleans, Jeffrey. "Sex Discrimination
        --A Bar to a Democratic Education: Overview of Title IX
        of the Educational Amendments of 1972." Connecticut Law
        Review. 6 (Fall, 1973), 1-27.

        Section by section analysis of Title IX and a suggested legal
        framework in which to evaluate separate or different treat-
        ment of the sexes in educational activity.

346.   Bureau of National Affairs. The Civil Rights Act of 1964
        Text, Analysis, Legislative History; What It Means to Em-
        ployers, Businessmen, Unions, Employees, Minority Groups.
        Washington, D. C.: Bureau of National Affairs, 1964. 424 p.

Operations manual which explains the background, meaning, and effect of Titles II, VI, and VII of the Civil Rights Act of 1964.

347.   _____. The Equal Employment Opportunity Act of 1972: Editorial Analysis, Discussion of Court Decisions Under the 1964 Act, Text of Amended Act, Congressional Reports, Legislative History ... Washington, D. C.: Bureau of National Affairs, 1973. 423 p.

Contains sections pertaining to employment in higher education.

348.   "CLEO Symposium." Howard Law Journal. 22 (1979), 297-495.

Symposium includes the activities, effectiveness, and future prospects of the Council on Legal Education Opportunity, which assists minorities and the disadvantaged in obtaining a legal education. Symposium held at Howard University School of Law on October 6-7, 1979.

349.   Cadei, Raymond M. "Hiring Goals, California State Government and Title VII: Is This Numbers Game Legal?" Pacific Law Journal. 8 (January, 1977), 49-71.

This comment outlines the limitations imposed on the use of hiring plans by Title VII of the Civil Rights Act of 1964, with focus upon the legality of the numerical hiring plan utilized by the California State Government and Assembly Bill 4170. Discusses also court reaction to such hiring plans and general guidelines derived from federal case law which are helpful to organizations seeking to use numerical hiring plans within the limits outlined by the courts.

350.   Casetta, William M. and Quaglia, Paul L., Jr. "Reverse Discrimination--The Assault Against Affirmative Action." Detroit College of Law Review. 1979 (Spring, 1979), 89-122.

Examines two cases (Bakke and Detroit Police Officers Association v. Young), affirmative action programs, reverse discrimination, and the use of 'benign' classifications in light of the Fourteenth Amendment and the United States Code.

351.   Charlton, Edward J. and Heideck, Robert E. "Preferential Admissions to Professional Schools: The Equal Protection Challenge." Villanova Law Review. 22 (August, 1977), 983-1021.

Analyzes the major questions and problems presented by preferential admissions programs in professional schools to equal protection challenges; reviews past cases involving equal protection and the constitutional tests developed therein; discusses recent cases involving equal protection challenges to preferential admissions; sets forth the possible standards for reviewing preferential admissions programs; and analyzes the ends and means problems involved in a constitutional decision on preferential admissions.

352. Cohen, Carl. "Race and the Equal Protection of the Laws." Lincoln Law Review. 10 (1977), 117-158.

Discusses affirmative action within the context of what we may justly do to correct long-standing racial injustice, which categories may or may not be used, and how the courts should apply them. Discusses the issue and principles of affirmative action, focusing upon three cases: Bakke (before the California Supreme Court); DeFunis; Alevy v. Downstate Medical Center of the State of New York (1976).

353. Cohen, David M. "An End to Affirmative Action?" Labor Law Journal. 28 (April, 1977), 218-229.

Examines six cases in 1976 dealing with challenges to affirmative action plans or quotas. These decisions cast doubt upon the continued validity of affirmative action plans, at least when the defendant may not have been found guilty of past discrimination. Bakke case, college scholarship aid, and faculty "reverse discrimination" are three of the case topics cited.

354. Condon, James P. "Beyond Strict Scrutiny: The Limits of Congressional Power to Use Racial Classifications." Northwestern University Law Review. 74 (November, 1979), 617-645.

Author focuses upon Congressional affirmative action programs, as distinguished from court-ordered affirmative action and voluntary affirmative action. Discusses the grounds for granting special constitutional leeway to the congressional use of benign racial classifications. Suggests that the major check on any broad use of congressional power in this area should be judicial review of federal legislation that excessively burdens individuals disfavored because of their race in reversing past discrimination.

355. Connolly, Walter B., Jr. Practical Guide to Equal Employment Opportunity: Law, Principles, and Practices. New York: Law Journal Press, 1975. 2 vols.

Reviews the law, regulations of various federal agencies, including discrimination cases. Volume 2 is Appendix.

356. Consalus, Charles E. "The Law School Admission Test and the Minority Student." Toledo Law Review. Vol. 1970 (Spring-Summer, 1970), 501-525.

Claims that if minority group and disadvantaged students are being denied access to legal education because of the Law School Admission Test, the bias is only a measure of that demanded by our society and specifically by the law schools. The LSAT is an accurate predictor of success.

357.   Davidson, Kenneth M.   "Preferential Treatment and Equal Opportunity. "   Oregon Law Review.   55 (1976), 53-83.

Examines the definition of preferential treatment, legal constraints on its use, and factors making its use permissible.

358.   Divine, Thomas M.   "Women in the Academy: Sex Discrimination in University Faculty Hiring and Promotion. "   Journal of Law and Education.   5 (October, 1976), 429-451.

Cites evidence of sex discrimination in university hiring and promotion; argues that employers should not be permitted to defend hiring judgments by claiming that they hired the "best available candidate"; offers an alternative view of hiring, the "ordinal model" which clarifies the defenses which can be validly imposed by a defendant university.

359.   Dixon, Robert G., Jr.   "The Supreme Court and Equality: Legislative Classifications, Desegregation, and Reverse Discrimination. "   Cornell Law Review.   62 (March, 1977), 494-562.

Discusses two equal protection issues likely to be at the forefront of future litigation: use of equal protection clause to nullify legislation on a fairly large scale and continuing developments of equal protection theory in volatile areas such as desegregation and "reverse discrimination. " Discusses racial preference cases in higher education: DeFunis, Bakke, and Alevy v. Downstate Medical Center. Discusses also the changing interpretations of the equal protection clause: from negating governmental action limiting governmental imposition of "inequalities" through such policies as race preferences and reverse discrimination.

360.   Duncan-Peters, Stephanie.   "How Far Can Affirmative Action Go Before It Becomes Reverse Discrimination?"   Catholic University Law Review.   26 (Spring, 1977), 513-546.

Examines U.S. Supreme Court and appellate court decisions on the question of the use of quotas-type affirmative action programs in employment. Briefly discusses remedies other than quotas to eliminate discrimination in employment practices.

361.   Dunkle, Margaret and Sandler, Bernice.   "Sex Discrimination Against Students: Implications of Title IX of the Education Amendments of 1972. "   Inequality of Education.   No. 18, October, 1974, pp. 12-35.

Discusses the overall implications of Title IX as well as specific issues which affect schools and colleges.

362.   "E. E. O. C. Symposium: Equality in America: A Color-Blind Constitution?" Howard Law Journal. 21 (1978), 481-605.

Speeches presented at the second annual Equal Employment Opportunity Conference held at Howard University School of Law. Contents include:

Color Consciousness: A Historical, Legal and Philosophical Perspective.

363.   The Legal Precedents, William B. Gould.   Pp. 485-493

364.   The Historical Roots, Norman Hodges.   Pp. 495-503

365.   The Economic Basis, Barbara Jones.   Pp. 505-512

366.   The Moral Dilemma, James W. Nickel.   Pp. 513-517

367.   The Socio-Economic Question, Orlando H. Patterson. Pp. 519-527

368.   Affirmative Action Guideposts to Remedial Relief, Daniel E. Leach.   Pp. 529-537

Taking Race, National Origin and Sex into Account: Some Specific Circumstances

369.   University and Professional School Admissions and Hiring, Oscar Garcia-Rivera.   Pp. 539-543

370.   University and Professional School Admissions and Hiring, Walter Williams.   Pp. 545-557

371.   Employment, Hyman Bookbinder.   Pp. 559-563

372.   Employment, U. W. Clemon.   Pp. 565-571

Some Practical Problems

373.   Trying a "Reverse Discrimination" Case, Daniel Steiner. Pp. 573-577

374.   Trying a "Reverse Discrimination" Case, James B. Wilson.   Pp. 579-584

375.   Developing an Affirmative Action Plan, Martin Gerry. Pp. 585-592

376.   Developing an Affirmative Action Plan, Michael Gottesman.
        Pp. 593-598

377.   Developing an Affirmative Action Plan, Ralph Smith.   Pp.
        599-605

378.   "Education Amendments of 1972 (Public Law 92-318). " Con-
        gressional Quarterly Almanac, 1972.   Vol. 28, pp. 385-398.

        Useful discussion on the provisions of the bill, background,
        Senate and House action, discrimination amendment, and the
        debate.

379.   Education Commission of the States.   Digest of Federal
        Laws: Equal Rights for Women in Education.   ECS Report
        No. 61.   Denver: Education Commission of the States,
        1975.   40 p.
        (ERIC ED 109 738)

        An analysis of the federal statutory scheme dealing with
        equal rights for women in education.   Analysis of Title VII
        of the Civil Rights Act of 1964, Equal Pay Act of 1963
        amended in 1972, Title IX of the Education Amendments of
        1972, and Titles VII and VIII of the Public Health Service
        Act as amended.   Tabular description provided of substantive
        areas of federal concern, relevant provisions, sources, and
        coverage.

380.   _____ .   A Handbook of State Laws and Policies Affecting
        Equal Rights for Women in Education.   Report No. 62.
        Prepared by Jessica Pearson.   Denver: Education Com-
        mission of the States, 1975.   125 p.
        (ERIC ED 109 808)

        Presents state-by-state description of laws, executive orders,
        regulations, guidelines, administrative structure, and proce-
        dures dealing with equal rights of women in education.   Laws
        are organized by labor, fair employment practices, legisla-
        tion, status of the equal rights amendment, and the State
        Commissions on the Status of Women.

381.   _____ .   An Overview of Federal Court Decisions Affect-
        ing Equal Rights of Women in Education.   ECS Report No.
        70.   Prepared by William Pearson.   Denver: Education
        Commission of the States, 1975.   185 p.

        Chapters include the Fourteenth Amendment, post-Civil War
        Civil Rights Acts, Title VII of the Civil Rights Act of 1964,
        sex discrimination in employment, in educational employ-
        ment, in education (in admissions, athletics, rules affecting
        students), Executive Order 11246, the Equal Pay Act of
        1963, Title IX of the Education Amendments of 1972, Health
        Manpower Training Act.

382.   Edwards, Harry T. and Zaretsky, Barry L.   "Preferential
        Remedies for Employment Discrimination."   Michigan Law
        Review.   74 (November, 1975), 1-47.

        Presents overview of problems of preferential remedies to
        achieve equal employment opportunity for women and minor-
        ities.   Contends "color blindness" would not end discrimina-
        tion but some form of "color conscious" affirmative action
        must be employed.   Temporary preferential treatment is
        justified, by the Constitution and statutory provisions.

383.   Elden, Gary.   "'Forty Acres and a Mule' with Interest: The
        Constitutionality of Black Capitalism, Benign School Quotas,
        and Other Statutory Racial Classifications."   Journal of Ur-
        ban Law.   47 (1969-70), 591-652.

        Traces growth, assesses contemporary patterns and conse-
        quences of discrimination against blacks.   Contends that pub-
        lic policies are designed to support "black capitalism" and
        implement school racial quotas, and are not only legal but
        necessary.

384.   Elliot, Robert M.   "Reverse Discrimination: The Balancing
        of Human Rights."   Industrial Relations Law Digest.   9
        (Spring, 1977), 57-78.

        Explores reverse discrimination, focuses on preferential hir-
        ing practices, and those which have been contested in circuit
        courts.   Special emphasis is placed upon the quota system.
        Includes section on the factors to be considered in the bal-
        ancing of interests.

385.   Ely, John Hart.   "The Constitutionality of Reverse Racial
        Discrimination."   The University of Chicago Law Review.
        41 (Summer, 1974), 723-741.

        Discusses the DeFunis case and busing issues in relation to
        reverse race discrimination.   Concludes that measures which
        favor racial minorities pose a difficult moral question that
        should be left to the states.   Argues that reverse discrimi-
        nation can be constitutional and that it is not "suspect" in a
        constitutional sense for a majority to discriminate against
        itself in favor of a minority.

386/87 "Employment Discrimination and Title VII of the Civil
        Rights Act of 1964."   Harvard Law Review.   84 (March,
        1971), 1109-1316.

        Discusses permissible standards for hiring, firing, and pro-
        motion; sex discrimination; procedure under Title VII; and
        the Executive Order program.   Section included on affirma-
        tive action and its conflict with Title VII.

388. Evans, Franklin R. Applications and Admissions to ABA
      Accredited Law Schools: An Analysis of National Data for
      the Class Entering in the Fall of 1976. Princeton, New
      Jersey: Educational Testing Service, 1977.

      Data for over 76,000 applicants to 146 of the 157 ABA ac-
      credited law schools are analyzed collectively. Acceptance
      rates for applicants with each level of LSAT score and un-
      der-graduate record are presented for the total pool and
      separately for males, females, and several minority groups.
      The impact of a policy prohibiting the use of ethnic identity
      in making admissions is explored.

389. Ewald, Linda. "Sex Discrimination in Higher Education:
      Constitutional Equality for Women?" Journal of Family
      Law. 10 (1971), 327-343.

      Discusses how opportunity should be equally available to all
      persons. The equal protection clause of the Fourteenth
      Amendment believed to be the primary source of protection
      against discriminatory practices based on sex. Considers
      cases which involve both racial and sex segregation in higher
      education.

390. Feld, Lipman G. "Equal Pay Benefits for Women Profes-
      sors, Academic Administrators, Professionals." Journal of
      the Missouri Bar. (September-October, 1973), 455+

391. Fishel, Andrew and Pottker, Janice. National Politics and
      Sex Discrimination in Education. Lexington, Mass.: Lexing-
      ton Books, 1977. 159 p.

      Relevant chapters include:
      Sex Discrimination in Education Becomes a Public Policy Issue
      Sex Discrimination and Bureaucratic Politics: The U.S. Of-
          fice of Education's Task Force on Women's Education
      Sex Discrimination and the Legislative Process: The Enact-
          ment of the Women's Educational Equity Act
      Sex Discrimination and the Administrative Rule-Making
          Process: The Development of the Title IX Regulations
      Sex Discrimination in Education and the National Political
          Process

392. Fiss, Owen M. "The Fate of an Idea Whose Time Has
      Come: Antidiscrimination Law in the Second Decade After
      Brown v. Board of Education." The University of Chicago
      Law Review. 41 (Summer, 1974), 742-773.

      Discusses the second post-Brown decade with changes that
      the period 1964-1974 worked in federal anti-discrimination
      laws: in extending their reach, in devising new techniques
      to enforce them, including the achievement of certain eco-
      nomic and social goals for the protected group.

393. Fleming, Macklin and Pollak, Louis. "The Black Quota at
      Yale Law School: An Exchange of Letters. " Public Interest.
      No. 19 (Spring, 1970), 44-52.

      Debate between Fleming, Justice of the Court of Appeal,
      State of California at Los Angeles and Pollak, Dean of the
      Yale Law School. Fleming argues that quota of unqualified
      blacks perpetuates the ideas and prejudices it is designed to
      overcome, substitutes group membership for individual merit.
      Pollak replies that all applicants must measure up to a sin-
      gle standard of professional excellence and that the LSAT
      and grade scores are not highly predictive of successful per-
      formance, and that leadership and training of black lawyers
      is essential.

394. Fredericks, Albert G. "Civil Rights--Employment Discrimi-
      nation--Preferential Minority Treatment as an Appropriate
      Remedy Under Section 703(j) of Title VII. " Tennessee Law
      Review.   42 (Winter, 1975), 397-405.

      Reviews court decisions under Title VII of the Civil Rights
      Act of 1964 which despite section 703(j), prescribe a numeri-
      cal formula to improve minority employment opportunity.
      Concludes that pattern will continue until Congress or the
      Supreme Court clarifies the subject of preferential minority
      treatment.

395. Frohnmayer, David B. "Current Developments in Federal
      Law Affecting Equal Employment Opportunity in Higher Edu-
      cation. " Journal of College and University Law.   1 (Fall,
      1973), 1-15.

      Describes the Executive Orders, regulations requiring af-
      firmative action in higher education.

396.   . "Title IX, Education Amendments of 1972. "
      Journal of College and University Law.   2 (Fall, 1974), 49-
      64.

      Author reviews the questions posed by draft guidelines is-
      sued in June, 1976 by the Department of Health, Education
      and Welfare implementing provisions of Title IX.

397. Fuerst, J. S. and Petty, Roy. "The Supreme Court and
      Quotas. " The Christian Century.   94 (October 19, 1977),
      948-952.

      Predicts that the U. S. Supreme Court will reject Bakke's
      claim.   Examines some of the Court's recent decisions deal-
      ing with the issue of race in various fields, concludes that
      the court has firmly upheld the constitutionality of a state's
      right to impose racial quotas.

398.   Getman, Julius G.   "Emerging Constitutional Principle of
        Sexual Equality. " Supreme Court Review, 1972.   Chicago:
        University of Chicago Press, 1972.   Pp. 157-180.

        Includes a section on affirmative action programs and appli-
        cable considerations for such programs.

399.   Glickstein, Howard A.   "Equal Educational Opportunity:
        The State of the Law. " Howard Law Journal.   20 (1977),
        100-127.

        Prepared for ERIC Clearinghouse on Urban Education, Teach-
        ers College, Columbia University and published as part of
        the ERIC/CUE Urban Disadvantaged Series.   Addresses the
        state of the law, including the major legislation of the 1970's.
        Also discusses affirmative action.

400.   Gluckman, Ivan B.   "Affirmative Action: Is It Really Dis-
        crimination in Reverse?" NOLPE School Law Journal.   6
        (1976), 155-166.

        The purpose of the article is to clarify the meaning of "af-
        firmative action, " explore some of its applications, and
        determine its legal and constitutional adequacy.

401.   Goldberg, Seth A.   "A Proposal for Reconciling Affirmative
        Action with Nondiscrimination Under the Contractor Antidis-
        crimination Program. " Stanford Law Review.   30 (April,
        1978), 803-833.

        Author focuses on the labor market for college and univer-
        sity faculty to illustrate the problems in the implementation
        of the Executive Order Program concerning affirmative ac-
        tion.   Illustrates the present confusion concerning the proper
        point of termination of preferred status for a particular
        group and the difficulties contractors encounter in negotiating
        the narrow path between legitimate progress toward numeri-
        cal goals and illegal reverse discrimination.   Discusses the
        factors to be considered in properly resolving these issues
        and a solution offered that is consistent with the perceived
        goals of the Program.

402.   Goldman, Roger L.   "The Next Ten Years: Title VII Con-
        fronts the Constitution. " Saint Louis University Law Jour-
        nal.   20 (1976), 308-345.

        Discusses the Supreme Court's decisions in Title VII and re-
        lated cases, including some unresolved employment discrim-
        ination issues that raise difficult statutory and constitutional
        questions.   Both constitutional and nonconstitutional methods
        for resolving these issues are presented.

403.   Goodman, Carl F.   "Equal Employment Opportunity: Prefer-
       ential Quotas and Unrepresented Third Parties. "   George
       Washington Law Review.   44 (May, 1976), 483-515.

       Discusses the implications of quotas and examines whether
       the courts may properly order preferential employment plans
       where beneficiaries have not shown particularized injury
       from discrimination and where individuals disadvantaged by
       the plans are not represented in court.

404.   Gould, William B. , and others.   "Color Consciousness: A
       Historical, Legal and Philosophical Perspective. "   Howard
       Law Journal, 21 (1978), 485-537.

       Described in this collection of symposium papers are the
       historical development of "color-consciousness" in American
       society and its impact on American economics, educational
       and intellectual history, and employment.   The need for af-
       firmative action remedies is discussed along with suggestions
       for their implementation.

405.   Graglia, Lino A.   "Racially Discriminatory Admission to
       Public Institutions of Higher Education. "   Southwestern Uni-
       versity Law Review.   9 (1977), 583-596.

       Considers and then rejects arguments made in favor of racial
       preferences (e. g. , the need for a diverse student body, re-
       duction of racial and ethnic stereotypes).   Attacks racial
       preference for its denial of the principle that no person
       should be disadvantaged by governmental action because of
       race.

406.   Graham, Hugh Davis.   "Equality in the Academy. "   Center
       Magazine.   10 (September, 1977), 68-72.

       Author relates his role as defendant in the case of United
       States of America v. University of Maryland (1977), the first
       case in U. S. history in which the federal government has
       bought suit against a state university on charges of racially
       discriminating against an individual (a black female history
       professor who was denied tenure).   Author comments on fed-
       eral involvement in affirmative action programs in higher
       education.

407.   Gross, Barry R. , ed.   Reverse Discrimination.   New York:
       Prometheus, 1977.   401 p.

       Compilation of the pros and cons of reverse discrimination
       in education and employment.   Selections reprinted from
       various sources, and divided into three sections: the facts,
       the law, and value.   Excellent bibliography included.   Law
       selections include:

408.   Black, Virginia. "The Erosion of Legal Principles in the Creation of Legal Policies."

409.   Cox, Archibald. "Harvard College Amicus Curiae, DeFunis v. Odegaard, Supreme Court of the United States/October Term, 1973."

410.   Douglas, Justice William O. "DeFunis v. Odegaard, Dissenting Opinion (April 23, 1974)."

411.   Ely, John Hart. "The Constitutionality of Reverse Racial Discrimination."

412.   Greenawalt, Kent. "Judicial Scrutiny of 'Benign' Racial Preference in Law School Admissions."

413.   Sandalow, Terrance. "Racial Preferences in Higher Education: Political Responsibility and the Judicial Role."

414.   Hallam, Charlotte B. "Legal Tools to Fight Sex Discrimination." Labor Law Journal. 24 (December, 1973), 803-809.

        Discusses Title IX of the Education Amendments, Title VII of the Civil Rights Act of 1964; Executive Orders 11246 and 11375 as they apply to sex discrimination in higher education. Includes a section on how to eliminate discriminatory practices.

415.   Harkins, M. J. III. "Affirmative Action: The Constitution, Jurisprudence and the Formulation of Policy." Kansas Law Review. 26 (Fall, 1977), 85-103.

        Discusses how affirmative action conflicts with the principles of individualism and reward of individual merit.

416.   Holland, Theresa M. "Executive Order 11246: Problems and Implications on Sex Discrimination in Higher Education." Albany Law Review. 37 (1973), 810-828.

        Examines Executive Order 11246 in detail and its present application to sex discrimination in higher education. Examines the status of women in higher education and concludes that contract compliance requirements are but the first step toward the elimination of sex discrimination.

417.   Hughes, Graham. "Reparations for Blacks?" New York University Law Review. 43 (December, 1968), 1063-1074.

        Examines the possibilities and necessities of sacrifices on the part of the more affluent white majority in order to eliminate both the disrespect and the poor economic standards of its black brethren. While admitting that utilitarian considerations may dictate against such sacrifices by whites, author strongly urges that such considerations must yield to the demands of justice. If they do not yield and if the lot of the disadvantaged minority is not improved, demands for black separatism will be justified.

418. _____. "The Right to Special Treatment." The Rights of Americans: What They Are, What They Should Be. Edited by Norman Dorsen. New York: Random House, 1970. Pp. 94-109.

419. Husak, Douglas N. "Preferential Hiring and Reverse Discrimination in Favor of Blacks: A Moral Analysis." American Journal of Jurisprudence. 1978, pp. 143-168.

Outlines a broad and general defense of the constitutionality of some kinds of preferential admissions and hiring programs in favor of Blacks by constructing a moral justification of these practices.

420. Ijalaye, D. A. "Concessional Admission of Underprivileged Students in Law School." Buffalo Law Review. 20 (Winter, 1971), 435-446.

Discusses the issue of admission of students from underprivileged areas or classes without regard to grades and admission of minority students with good grades but who, as a result of family obligations, do not have the privilege or opportunity to pursue regular day courses.

421. "Implementing Title IX: The HEW Regulations." University of Pennsylvania Law Review. 124 (January, 1976), 806-842.

Legislative history and executive and judicial interpretation of Title VI and Title VII of the Civil Rights Act of 1964 are examined as a background for Title IX of the Education Amendments of 1972 prohibiting sex discrimination in education. HEW regulations implementing Title IX are evaluated and found to adhere fairly closely to legislative intention.

422. Jackson, Diane P. "Update on Handicapped Discrimination." Personnel Journal. 57 (September, 1978), 488-491.

Presents guidelines for federal contractors in complying with the Rehabilitation Act of 1973, in view of stepped-up government enforcement activities. Describes provisions of the Act, some complaints filed under the affirmative action section, and personnel practices that contractors may use in compliance with federal law.

423. Jacobs, Roger B. "New Rights for the Handicapped: The Rehabilitation Act and the 1978 Amendments." Civil Rights Digest. 11 (Spring, 1979), 22-27.

Describes the significant changes and clarifications of the
1973 act, including affirmative action requirements.

424.   Jones, James E., Jr.   "The Bugaboo of Employment Quotas. "
       Wisconsin Law Review.   Vol. 1970, pp. 341-403.

       Explores the development, theory, and design of the revised
       Philadelphia plan, analyzes the attacks against the quota is-
       sue, identifies current arguments against the legality of the
       plan and presents arguments supporting it.

425.   _____.   "The Development of Modern Equal Employment
       Opportunity and Affirmative Action Law: A Brief Chronolog-
       ical Overview. "   Howard Law Journal.   20 (1977), 74-99.

       Sketches, in chronological order, the major events and de-
       velopments leading up to the Civil Rights Act of 1964, com-
       ments upon selected legal developments of the first decade
       under Title VII, discusses highlights of equal employment
       cases in the Supreme Court in 1976, and future developments
       in affirmative action law.

426.   _____.   "Employment Discrimination, Minority Faculty
       and the Predominantly White Law School--Some Observations. "
       Black Law Journal.   4 (1974), 488-494.

       Focuses upon factors which impede remedies in the hiring
       of minority teachers in law schools.   Describes the strate-
       gies for increased minority hiring and how organizations such
       as the American Association of Law Schools are remedying
       the problem.

427.   Joyner, Nancy D.   "'Reverse' Discrimination in Student Fi-
       nancial Aid for Higher Education: The Flanagan [Flanagan
       v. President and Directors of Georgetown College, Civil Ac-
       tion No. 75-1500, U. S. Dist. Ct. D. C. (Memorandum Brief,
       July 25, 1976)] Case in Perspective. "   Journal of Law and
       Education.   6 (July, 1977), 327-348.

       The Flanagan case revolves around the issue of "reverse"
       discrimination in student financial aid.   Analyzes the legal
       issues in conflict, what constitutes discrimination in educa-
       tion under the law, the legal issues contending "reverse"
       discrimination in higher education, the Georgetown Law
       School's dilemma in the dispute, and some guidelines for the
       non-discriminatory allocation of increasingly scarce financial
       resources for students seeking degrees in graduate school.

428.   Kadzielski, Mark A.   "Postsecondary Athletics in an Era of
       Equality: An Appraisal of the Effect of Title IX. "   The
       Journal of College and University Law.   5 (1978-79), 123-141.

       Considers the use, meaning and constitutional validity of
       "separate but equal" concept employed in Title IX of the

Education Amendments of 1972 concerning athletics in post-secondary institutions. Discusses the standard of review in sex discrimination cases, relevant case law from federal and state jurisdictions, and examines general applicability of Title IX to athletic programs, especially to those programs which are revenue producing.

429. Kaplan, John. "Equal Justice in an Unequal World: Equality for the Negro--the Problem of Special Treatment." Northwestern University Law Review. 61 (July-August, 1966), 363-410.

Analyzes the appropriateness of preferential treatment for blacks, including the moral, political, and economic problems resulting from governmental action on their behalf. Two such problems discussed are the weakening of government as an educative force and societal divisiveness. Author focuses upon preference in employment, benign quotas in housing and measures to reduce de facto segregation in education.

430. Katzner, Louis J. "Is Favoring Women and Blacks in Employment and Educational Opportunities Justified?" In Philosophy of Law. Edited by Joel Feinberg and Hyman Gross. New York: Dickinson Publishing Co., 1975.

431. Kendrigan, G. M. "Reverse Sex Discrimination--The Horns of the Dilemma." Trial. 13 (July, 1977), 28-30.

Cramer v. Virginia Commonwealth University; EEOC v. American Telephone and Telegraph Co.; and McAllen v. American Telephone and Telegraph Co. Concludes that "a strong core of resistance to the basic concept of equality still remains."

432. Kilberg, William J. "Application of Equal Employment Laws to Higher Education." Journal of the College and University Personnel Association. 27 (April-May, 1976), 28-32.

Kilberg, Solicitor General of the U.S. Department of Labor, responds to critics in the higher education community who deny the applicability of equal employment laws to academia. Points out the reality of salary differentials between men and women faculty, the exaggerated debate over goals and timetables, and that the goal is equality of opportunity and not equality of result.

433. Kirp, David L. "Law, Politics, and Equal Educational Opportunity: The Limits of Judicial Involvement." Harvard Educational Review. 47 (May, 1977), 117-137.

Discusses how the Equal Protection Clause during the 1960's was widely seen as a primary instrument for attaining dis-

tributive justice and the courts perceived as the most important branch in bringing about a fairer social order. Recently
the courts have become more restrained from making new
constitutional law, relying instead on the political process to
resolve questions of distributive justice as these affect the
allocation of particular goods such as education. Concludes
that questions concerning the allocation of goods seem best
fit for joint resolution, the courts initially defining minimal
constitutional guarantees, the legislative enactments giving
substance to these definitions, and the courts clarifying am-
biguities in the law.

434.   Lange, Richard and Pollak, Frederick. "Equal Protection
        and Benign Racial Classification: A Challenge to the Law
        Schools. " American University Law Review. 21 (Septem-
        ber, 1972), 736-757.

        Concludes that in the DeFunis case, the trial courts' asser-
        tion that racial classifications are violative of the equal pro-
        tection clause is inconsistent with Supreme Court decisions
        which permit racial classifications under the Fourteenth
        Amendment. Claims that the Supreme Court has not explicit-
        ly resolved the question of which standard of review should
        be employed when dealing with benign racial classification.
        Although the strict scrutiny approach is not the valid test
        which should be applied; if it were, the compelling state in-
        terests at issue would render constitutionally valid the use
        of preferential minority admissions standard.

435.   LaNoue, George R. "Tenure and Title VII. " Journal of
        College and University Law. 1 (Spring, 1974), 206-221.

        Asserts that tenure may violate Title VII of the Civil Rights
        Act of 1964 and more general affirmative action concepts.

436.   Larson, E. R. "The Development of Section 1981 as a
        Remedy for Racial Discrimination in Private Employment. "
        Harvard Civil Rights-Civil Liberties Law Review. 7 (Janu-
        ary, 1972), 56-102.

        Pertains to third parties seeking redress against discrimina-
        tion, and private institutions of higher education as defendants
        in discrimination cases.

437.   Leach, Daniel E. "Affirmative Action Guidelines: An Ap-
        propriate Response. " Labor Law Journal. 29 (September,
        1978), 555-561.

        Explains how the forthcoming Equal Employment Opportunity
        Commission affirmative action guidelines are designed to en-
        courage voluntary compliance. They seek to establish a ra-
        tional system designed to identify the effects of discrimina-
        tion in employment. Suggests that case law focuses upon
        work force analysis as a base for government approved action.

438. Lepper, Mary. "The Continuing Struggle for Equal Opportun-
      ity." Phi Delta Kappan. 57 (December, 1975), 246-250.

      Reviews the prime statutes and executive orders requiring
      equal employment opportunity and affirmative action. Dis-
      tinguishes between nondiscrimination and affirmative action
      with each requiring different compliance enforcement proce-
      dures. Describes the difficulties universities have expressed
      with meeting compliance regulations, with suggestions by
      critics concerning their enforcement. Author is Special As-
      sistant to the Director, Office for Civil Rights, the Depart-
      ment of Health, Education and Welfare.

439. Lichtman, Richard. "The Ethics of Compensatory Justice."
      Law in Transition Quarterly. 1 (Spring, 1964), 76-103.

      Discusses the blacks' right to preferential treatment in rela-
      tion to the Fourteenth Amendment. Analyzes the reparative
      aspect of compensation through the use of benign quotas and
      preferential treatment, such treatment justified because it
      removes an unfair advantage to whites to which they are not
      entitled.

440. Lieb, Carol A. "Affirmative Action: A Delicate Balance in
      Employment and Education." Hofstra Law Review. 5
      (Spring, 1977), 581-607.

      Examines the period from October, 1975 to June, 1976 when
      the Supreme Court considered cases on affirmative action.
      Judicial treatment of the competing interests of protected
      and unprotected group members is also studied. Presents
      the historical and conceptual background of affirmative action
      programs, major decisions imposing or denying such pro-
      grams, with an emphasis upon the quota system, and allega-
      tions of reverse discrimination, particularly with regard to
      preferential admissions programs in various medical and law
      schools.

441. Maize, Kennedy P. and Stencel, Sandra. "Affirmative Ac-
      tion Under Attack." Editorial Research Reports. (March
      30, 1979), 227-244.

      Discusses challenges to job programs, including law suits,
      legislation upholding equal employment and affirmative action,
      and obstacles to full job equality.

442. Malloy, Michele. "The Regulation of Title IX: Sex Dis-
      crimination in Student Affairs." Houston Law Review. 13
      (May, 1976), 734-752.

      Focuses upon aspects of student affairs covered by Title IX
      and the final regulations, with the regulations examined for
      accomplishments, exemptions, oversights, and effects.

443/44 Martin, William.   "Equal Employment Opportunities and
        Government Contracting: Three Theories for Obtaining Judi-
        cial Review of Executive Order No. 11246. " Wisconsin Law
        Review.   Volume 1972, 133-152.

        Analyzes three different legal bases upon which private liti-
        gants should be able to achieve enforcement of the Executive
        Order in the federal courts: 1) a constitutional argument
        based on the Fifth Amendment; 2) a statutory argument aris-
        ing from the implications of a private cause of action under
        the Executive Order; and 3) an administrative review argu-
        ment based on the Administrative Procedure Act.   Concludes
        that the Executive Order 11246 can be a very effective remedy
        against employment discrimination.

445.   Moeller, James L.   "Executive Order No. 11, 246:   Presi-
        dential Power to Regulate Employment Discrimination. "
        Missouri Law Review.   43 (Summer, 1978), 451-502.

        Describes the history and operation of Executive Order
        11, 246, which prohibits racial discrimination by employers
        who are federal contractors.   Examines the fundamental con-
        stitutional issues raised in recent decisions regarding the
        Executive Order.   Topics include obligations imposed by the
        Order, penalties for noncompliance, and validity of the re-
        quirement for affirmative action.

446.   Nash, Peter G.   "Affirmative Action Under Executive Order
        11246. " New York University Law Review.   46 (April, 1971),
        225-261.

        Describes Executive Order 11246, as amended, as the latest
        in a long series of Executive Orders designed to make equal
        employment opportunity a reality for present and potential
        employees of government contractors and subcontractors, in
        that it requires government contractors to take "affirmative
        action" to ensure that hiring and promotion of employees be
        on a nondiscriminatory basis.   The vagueness of the affirma-
        tive action requirement has led to confusion among govern-
        ment contractors and a generally low level of compliance.
        Author describes the Office for Federal Contract Compli-
        ance's efforts to give the affirmative action obligation speci-
        fic content and at the same time to avoid the pitfall of re-
        verse discrimination.

447.   Nisenbaum, Steven.   "Race Quotas. " Harvard Civil Rights
        Law Review.   8 (January, 1973), 128-180.

        Discusses case histories of racial quotas in school desegre-
        gation and employment.   Concludes that such quotas offer
        one constitutionally acceptable, sometimes constitutionally
        required, method for eliminating the adverse effects of past
        discrimination.

448. Northrup, James. <u>Old Age, Handicapped and Vietnam-Era</u>
      <u>Antidiscrimination Legislation.</u> Labor Relations and Public
      Policy Series No. 14. Philadelphia: University of Pennsyl-
      vania, Wharton School of Finance and Commerce, 1977. 234 p.

      Book brings together materials, cases, and opinions regard-
      ing the Age Discrimination in Employment Act of 1967, the
      Rehabilitation Act of 1973, and the Vietnam Era Veterans'
      Readjustment Act of 1974. These laws represent a relative-
      ly underdeveloped but potentially highly significant aspect of
      a continuing and expanding public policy of creating an ever-
      increasing number of protected groups that already comprise
      a majority of the labor force. Laws that deal with affirma-
      tive action and these protected groups are discussed.

449. O'Neil, Robert M. "God and Government at Yale: The
      Limits of Federal Regulation of Higher Education. " <u>Cin-</u>
      <u>cinnati Law Review.</u> 44 (1975), 525-547.

      Presents a preliminary overview of constitutional issues in
      the relationship between higher education and federal regula-
      tion or control. Reference is made to the Dartmouth Col-
      lege case and views of Yale President Kingman Brewster,
      and the implications of Title IX regulations.

450. _____. "Preferential Admissions: Equalizing Access to
      <u>Legal Education. " Toledo Law Review.</u> Vol. 1970 (Spring-
      Summer, 1970), 281-320.

      Author explores the constitutional ramifications of prefer-
      ential treatment programs for minority students, including
      the basic problems involved in defining the various classes
      of persons eligible for preferential treatment and the degree
      to which compensation should be afforded.

451. _____. "Preferential Admissions: Equalizing the Access
      of Minority Groups to Higher Education. " <u>Yale Law Journal.</u>
      80 (March, 1971), 699-767.

      Discusses three options open to a court on a case involving
      preferential admissions standards. Presents detailed argu-
      ments for and against preferential admissions, and alterna-
      tives to such preferences. Concludes that there is no effec-
      tive substitute for the explicit use of race as a preferential
      criterion for most colleges.

452. Perhacs, Richard W. "But Some Animals Are More Equal
      than Others: A Look at the Equal Protection Argument
      Against Minority Preferences. " <u>Duquesne Law Review.</u> 12
      (Spring, 1974), 580-602.

      Examines court cases dealing with affirmative action pro-
      grams within the context of the question: How strong is the

argument that certain types of government programs which
result in preferential treatment of deprived groups are a
violation of the Fifth and Fourteenth Amendments?

453.   Petersen, John D.   "Constitutional Law: Affirmative Action
        --Does It Afford Equal Protection Under the Law?"   Wash-
        burn Law Journal.   16 (Fall, 1976), 190-196.

        Analyzes Alevy v. Downstate Medical Center of the State of
        New York (1976), a case involving the issue of "reverse dis-
        crimination" in state financial aid in higher education.   Fo-
        cuses upon the substantial state interest test as the standard
        of review in racial classifications cases.   Author sees this
        standard of review as playing a role in the development of
        constitutional interpretations of affirmative action programs.

454.   Pinderhughes, Charles A.   "Increasing Minority Group Stu-
        dents in Law Schools: The Rationale and the Critical Is-
        sues."   Buffalo Law Review.   20 (Winter, 1971), 447-457.

        Author focuses upon the responsibility of law schools to de-
        velop lawyers to serve the many people who are deprived of
        legal services.   In devising constructive models for recruit-
        ment and training programs, law schools should bear in mind
        the lack of group experience of blacks and the overall his-
        torical context and background of the black experience in
        America.

455.   Plessy v. Ferguson.   163 U.S. 537 (1896).   Justice Harlan,
        Dissenting.

        Contains famous quotation that the "Constitution is color-
        blind."   Harlan went on to explain that "all citizens are
        equal before the law" and "takes no account of his surround-
        ings or of his color when his civil rights as guaranteed by
        the supreme law of the land are involved."

456.   Powers, Jan.   "Constitutional and Statutory Limitations on
        Preaward Denial of Government Contracts under Executive
        Order 11, 246."   Southern California Law Review.   52
        (March, 1979), 973-998.

        Note examines the existing procedures for enforcement of the
        equal opportunity provisions of Executive Order 11, 246 and
        regulations pursuant thereto.   Analyzes the adequacy of these
        enforcement procedures, the constitutional due process chal-
        lenges to the procedures in terms of two issues: whether
        the government's action constitutes a deprivation of property,
        and, if so, whether the contractor has been afforded suffi-
        cient "opportunity" to be heard.   Author proposes new com-
        pliance hearing procedures in preaward situations to accommo-
        date competing due process and nondiscrimination concerns.

457.   "Preferential Admissions in Higher Education: Should We
        Support or Condemn It?   Debate between Frank Askin, 'sup-
        port, ' and Carl Cohen, 'condemn. '"   Civil Liberties Review.
        2 (Spring, 1975), 95-116.

        Debate between two civil libertarians.   Askin argues that
        racial group identification is permissible grounds for giving
        preference to qualified minority applicants in order to foster
        racial harmony, promote racial integration, and to eliminate
        racial stigmas.   In a non-democratic society that is racist,
        it is irrelevant to argue that a democratic society ought to
        be completely color-blind.   Cohen replies that honorable
        ends do not justify wrongful means; reverse racial prefer-
        ence betrays constitutional principles and civil libertarian
        commitments; preference by race is malign, stigmatizing,
        and disintegrates rather than integrates the races.

458.   Pressman, Steven.   "The Confused Legal State of Affirmative
        Action Programs. "   California Journal.   10 (March, 1979),
        106-108.

        Comments on recent court decisions in various California
        cases on the legality of affirmative action programs.

459.   Ratterman, David B.   "Fourteenth Amendment Practice in
        Sex Discrimination Cases. "   Journal of Family Law.   14
        (1975-76), 435-463.

        Traces the history of the Equal Protection Clause as inter-
        preted in sex discrimination cases; analyzes current Supreme
        Court application of the "rational relationship" and "strict
        scrutiny" tests of equal protection to sex discrimination
        cases; and presents some contemporary problems with the
        Supreme Court application.   Also discusses "benign dis-
        crimination. "

460.   Reidhaar, Donald L.   "Minority Preference in Student Ad-
        missions. "   Journal of College and University Law.   2
        (Spring, 1975), 197-209.

        Overviews current and recent preferential admissions cases,
        particularly the Bakke case, pointing up major issues in
        preferential admissions.   Concludes that schools, not the
        courts, must fashion and apply admissions policies respon-
        sive to educational objectives and needs.

461.   Remmert, James E.   "Executive Order 11246:   Executive
        Encroachment. "   American Bar Association Journal.   55
        (November, 1969), 1037-1040.

        Reviews the Executive Order, discusses the substantive and
        procedural contents, and points up the dangerous encroachment
        of the Executive upon the powers of the legislative branch.

462. Renfrew, Charles B. "Affirmative Action: A Plea for a
      Rectification Principle. " Southwestern University Law Re-
      view. 9 (1977), 597-611.

      Suggests that preferential minority admissions programs can
      be legally justified by the rectification principle whereby
      reparations in the form of preferential admissions be granted
      to racial minorities.   The conditions which must be met for
      such a principle to operate include: minority status must be
      paired with history of pervasive discrimination by the major-
      ity, and it must be satisfactorily proven that the effect of the
      discrimination is an underrepresentation in a particular field
      (i. e., there must be a demonstrable current social problem
      caused by historical injustice).

463. "Report of the Boalt Hall Asian American Special Admissions
      Research Project.   Asian American Law School Students'
      Association. " Amerasia. 5 (February, 1978), 21-37.

      Edited excerpts are taken from a report written by Asian
      American students at the University of California at Berkeley
      Law School in 1975 in response to the faculty's proposal to
      eliminate or reduce the special admission program or reduce
      the special admissions program for Asians on the grounds
      that they have "made it" in American society.

464. 'Reverse Discrimination' and the Supreme Court: A Micro-
      fiche Collection of the Records and Briefs Concerning the
      General Issues of 'Equal Opportunity' and 'Affirmative Ac-
      tion' Submitted to the Supreme Court of the United States in
      the Following Cases: DeFunis v. Odegaard; McDonald v.
      Santa Fe Trail Transportation Co. ; Regents of the University
      of California v. Bakke. Microfiche. (loose-leaf) Englewood,
      Colo.: Information Handling Services, 1978.

      Microfiche edition of the records and briefs on equal oppor-
      tunity and affirmative action, with the Bakke and DeFunis
      cases relevant to higher education.

465. Roberts, Steven V. "Temple Law School Offers Unusual Af-
      firmative Action Plan for Deprived Students. " The New
      York Times, February 7, 1978, p. 25.

      Discusses the school's Special Admissions and Curriculum
      Experiments Program, which reserves one quarter of its
      enrollment for the disadvantaged, whatever their color or
      ethnic background, who show exceptional promise.

466. Rosen, Sanford J. "Equalizing Access to Legal Education:
      Special Programs for Law Students Who Are Not Admissible
      by Traditional Criteria. " Toledo Law Review. Vol. 1970
      (Spring-Summer, 1970), 321-376.

Author critically examines present attempts at compensatory
education in legal education in light of their avowed purpose
and evaluates their success in meeting their goals. Believes
that the duration of present programs and the scope of future
trends in solving problems caused by the racial basis for unequal allocation of resources necessarily depends upon the nature of future society, whether culturally homogeneous or
pluralistic.

467.   Rosenberg, Donald J. "Racial Classifications in Law School
        Admissions. " Catholic Lawyer. 20 (Summer, 1974), 254-
        286.

        Analyzes three theories for handling reverse discrimination
        cases: 1) concept of equal treatment for all races; 2) com-
        pelling state interest used to justify preferential treatment
        of minority members; 3) use of racial classifications but
        disallowance of preferential treatment for members of one
        race over better qualified members of another. Examines
        the justifications and weaknesses of the three theories, with
        particular attention upon the DeFunis case.

468.   Rosenbloom, David H.   Federal Equal Employment Opportun-
        ity: Politics and Public Personnel Administration. New
        York: Praeger, 1977. 184 p.

        Case study of public policy making in the national bureau-
        cratic arena. Study focuses on the politics of the Federal
        Equal Employment Opportunity Program, and how the pro-
        gram is dominated by a contest between those who seek to
        maintain the merit system as it has traditionally existed,
        and those who seek a more representative federal service.

469.   Ruben, Alan Miles and Willis, Betty J. "Discrimination
        Against Women in Employment in Higher Education. " Cleve-
        land State Law Review. 20 (September, 1971), 472-491.

        Cites evidence of the underrepresentation of women as uni-
        versity and college faculty, in numbers, academic ranking,
        and salaries. Explores three possible remedies to end sex
        discrimination on campus: Title VII of the Civil Rights Act
        of 1964; the Fourteenth Amendment and state fair employment
        practices legislation; and the federal contract compliance pro-
        gram.

470.   Saario, Terry. "Title IX: Now What?" Policy Issues in
        Education. Edited by Allan C. Ornstein and Steven I. Mul-
        ler. Lexington, Mass.: D. C. Heath, 1976.

        Discusses the provisions of Title IX of the Education Amend-
        ments of 1972, efforts to bring a variety of educational insti-
        tutions and agencies into full compliance with the law, and
        what political, social, and economic constraints are likely
        to affect these efforts.

471.   St. Antoine, Theodore J.   "Affirmative Action: Hypocritical
       Euphemism or Noble Mandate?"   Journal of Law Reform.
       10 (Fall, 1976), 28-43.

       Author focuses upon the nature and legality of affirmative ac-
       tion programs.   Sections deal with affirmative action as a
       remedy for discriminatory conduct and as a condition of
       federal contracts.   Concludes that affirmative action and
       preferential treatment, despite their very real risks, remain
       the best hope for employment equality.

472.   Salomone, Rosemary C.   "Enforcing Educational Rights
       Through Private Action: One Step Beyond Bakke. "   NOLPE
       School Law Journal.   8 (1978), 76-100.

       Describes the Bakke case as the first case to raise the is-
       sue of the private right of action under Title VI of the Civil
       Rights Act of 1964, since the early days of civil rights liti-
       gation.   Author focuses upon the private right of action un-
       der Title VI, Title IX, and Section 504.   Concludes that pri-
       vate litigants in educational discrimination cases may seek
       judicial redress of institutional wrongs, subject to certain
       limitations.

473.   San Jose State University, San Jose, Calif.   Office of the
       President.   Affirmative Action Plan.   June, 1975.   i-xiv,
       36 ℓ.

       Parts deal with equal employment opportunity policy; internal
       audit and reporting system; required analyses and methodol-
       ogies for the identification of problem areas; identification
       of problem areas; and miscellaneous programs supportive of
       affirmative action.

474.   Sandalow, Terrance.   "Judicial Protection of Minorities. "
       Michigan Law Review.   75 (April-May, 1977), 1162-1195.

       Explores the two versions of the argument that courts have
       a special responsibility to protect minorities.   Last section
       sketches an alternative conception of the court's role which
       permits them to protect minorities against the most serious
       threats to their interests and yet would respect the repre-
       sentative institutions as the ultimate authority to determine
       the values to be expressed by law.

475.   _____ .   "Racial Preferences in Higher Education: Poli-
       tical Responsibility and the Judicial Role. "   The University
       of Chicago Law Review.   42 (Summer, 1975), 653-703.

       In the DeFunis and like cases, the question is whether pref-
       erential admissions policies are valid when adopted by a
       university without explicit legislative sanction.   Asserts that
       there are good reasons for sustaining such policies but that
       they are less compelling in the absence of explicit legal

mandates. Gives a legislative history of the equal protection
clause, and analyzes the arguments for and against minority
preference in law school admissions.

476.   Sandler, Bernice. "Sex Discrimination, Educational Institu-
         tions, and the Law: A New Issue on Campus. " Journal of
         Law and Education. 2 (October, 1973), 613-635.

         Summarizes the federal laws and regulations on sex discrim-
         ination in educational institutions. Subjects include the dif-
         ference between quotas and goals; the unwritten but function-
         ally effective "affirmative action" plan for white males under
         which the university has traditionally operated, the possibility
         of upgrading the quality of education under civil rights laws,
         retirement benefits, and discrimination against students.
         Also includes where one can obtain the implementing regula-
         tions and guidelines for laws concerning sex discrimination
         in higher education.

477.   _____. "Title IX: Antisexism's Big Legal Stick. " Amer-
         ican Education. 13 (May, 1977), 6-9.

         Discusses the provisions of Title IX of the Education Amend-
         ments of 1972, which went into effect July 21, 1975. An-
         swers such questions as what institutions are covered, what
         constitutes discrimination, Title IX regulations, and a brief
         comparison with Title VII of the Civil Rights Act of 1964.

478.   Sape, George C. and Hart, Thomas J. "Title VII Recon-
         sidered: The Equal Employment Opportunity Act of 1972. "
         George Washington Law Review. 40 (July, 1972), 824-889.

         Analyzes the principles and provisions of the act and presents
         the historical development of the acceptance of federal re-
         sponsibility in this area.

479.   Scanlan, John A., Jr. "Racially-Preferential Policies in In-
         stitutions of Higher Education: State Action Limitations on
         42 U.S.C. Section 1983 Complaints. " Notre Dame Lawyer.
         52 (June, 1977), 882-924.

         Analyzes the state action doctrine in relation to a "reverse
         discrimination" claim against a private institution of higher
         education.

480.   Schaffrau, Andrew J. "Title VII and Preferential Treatment:
         Response to EEOC Affirmative Action Guidelines. " George-
         town Law Journal. 67 (February, 1979), 855-878.

         Argues that Title VII prohibits preferential treatment of any
         group unless ordered by a court pursuant to a finding of un-
         lawful discrimination and unless the preferential treatment is
         limited to providing relief to judicially identified victims of
         that discrimination.

481.   "Sex Discrimination and Intercollegiate Athletics: Putting
        Some Muscle on Title IX. "   Yale Law Journal.   88 (May,
        1979), 254-279.

        Argues that the general language of Title IX of the Education
        Amendments of 1972, together with certain specific features
        of it, strongly suggests that the Department of Health, Edu-
        cation, and Welfare should develop more stringent and de-
        manding regulations, and that HEW should look to social
        policy considerations concerning sex discrimination in inter-
        collegiate sports.

482.   "Sex Discrimination--The Enforcement Provisions for Title
        IX of the Education Amendments of 1972 Can Be Strengthened
        to Make the Title IX Regulations More Effective. "   Temple
        Law Quarterly.   49 (Fall, 1975), 207-222.

        Examines the provisions of Title IX, contrasting the existing
        and proposed procedural rules, and delineating the strengths
        of each.   Discusses the enforcement effort under identical
        or similar procedural rules by the Office for Civil Rights to
        predict the effectiveness of Title IX regulations, and presents
        recommendations concerning the retention of specific provi-
        sions of the existing and proposed rules, and the measures
        necessary for a more productive enforcement effort.

483.   Shaffer, Butler D. and Chapman, J. Brad.   "Hiring Quotas--
        Will They Work?"   Labor Law Journal.   26 (March, 1975),
        152-162.

        Discusses the legal background for hiring quotas, reverse
        discrimination, whether hiring quotas reinforce prejudices,
        and the DeFunis case.   Concludes that the quota system
        threatens a shift from a system of individual rights to one
        based upon group privilege.

484.   Shaman, Jeffrey M.   "College Admissions Policies Based on
        Sex and the Equal Protection Clause. "   Buffalo Law Review.
        20 (Spring, 1971), 609-623.

        Focuses on the issue of whether it is a violation of the equal
        protection clause for colleges and universities to exclude stu-
        dents on the basis of sex.   Examines Supreme Court cases
        dealing with this issue and rationales offered for discrimina-
        tion in admissions.   Concludes that an admissions policy
        which uses sex as a criterion for exclusion violates the equal
        protection clause.

485.   Sherain, Howard.   "The Questionable Legality of Affirmative
        Action. "   Journal of Urban Law.   51 (1974), 25-47.

        Author's theses are that affirmative action is not yet re-
        quired by law; as American constitutional law stands today,
        there are grave doubts that Affirmative Action in hiring

could be required by law; and even if these legal doubts
could be resolved, it is not certain that Affirmative Action
is desirable.

486.   Shulman, Carol H.   Federal Laws: Nondiscrimination and
        Faculty Employment.   Prepared by ERIC Clearinghouse on
        Higher Education, George Washington University.   Washing-
        ton, D. C.:   American Association for Higher Education,
        1975.   63 p.
        (ERIC ED 109 979)

        Describes the federal laws that apply to faculty employment.
        Laws include Title VII of the Civil Rights Act of 1964, Exe-
        cutive Order 11246, post-Civil War Rights laws, Equal Pay
        Act of 1963, and Title IX of the Education Amendments of
        1972.   Regulations implementing these laws are examined
        and the policies and practices that have developed from inter-
        pretive case law are explored.   Report reviews the impact
        of these laws on university personnel policies and the impli-
        · cations of the laws for future changes in faculty employment.

487.   Sloan, Allan.   "An Analysis of Uniform Guidelines in Em-
        ployee Selection Procedures. "   Employee Relations Law
        Journal.   4 (Winter, 1978-79), 346-356.

        Author explains that while the new federal Uniform Guidelines
        on Employee Selection Procedures, which becomes effective
        on September 25, 1978, attempt to clarify two conflicting
        sets of rules, they also impose new burdens on public and
        private employers.

488.   Solmon, Lewis D. and Heeter, Judith S.   "Affirmative Ac-
        tion in Higher Education: Towards a Rationale for Prefer-
        ence. "   Notre Dame Lawyer.   52 (October, 1976), 41-76.

        Discusses the conditions which led to the promulgation of
        guidelines for employing minorities and women, and the re-
        quirements they impose in the name of equal opportunity in
        colleges and universities.

489.   Squires, Gregory D.   Affirmative Action: A Guide for the
        Perplexed.   East Lansing: Michigan State University.   In-
        stitute for Community Development Continuing Education Serv-
        ice, 1977.   204 p.

        Summary of major U. S. legislation, court decisions, execu-
        tive orders, and implementing regulations relating to af-
        firmative action.   Includes a directory of federal organiza-
        tions involved in enforcement, research, advocacy, or other
        civil rights related activities.

490.   _____.   "Rising Above the Numbers Game: Long-Term
        Solutions to Discrimination. "   Civil Rights Digest.   10
        (Summer, 1978), 28-34.

Argues that the status of minorities and women can be mar-
ginally improved if the government implements more effective
enforcement procedures and if more employers are persuaded
to implement voluntarily affirmative action programs.   But
to realize long-term improvements, we must examine the
assumptions on which affirmative action was founded.

491.   Steinbach, Sheldon E.   "Equal Employment and Equal Pay =
Multiple Problems for Colleges and Universities. " Journal
of College and University Law.   2 (Fall, 1974), 25-48.

Discusses the issues involved in government regulation of
university employment practices, including pregnancy as a
disability, alleged discrimination in benefits, tests and other
employment criteria, reverse discrimination, use of statistics
for determination of discrimination, and the Equal Pay Act.

492.   Stencel, Sandra.   "Reverse Discrimination. "   Editorial Research Reports.   11 (August 6, 1976), 561-580.

Useful overview of issues dealing with reverse discrimination.
Sections on debate over remedies for past bias, development
of affirmative action regulations and programs, controversy
over seniority rights, and the leading court decisions on the
subject, including the DeFunis case.

493.   Stewart, Shirley E.   "The Myth of Reverse Race Discrimination: An Historical Perspective. "   Cleveland State Law Review.   23 (Spring, 1974), 319-336.

Analyzes the competing considerations in the struggle for true
equality for all persons.   Areas covered include seniority,
testing, qualifications, affirmative action, and admissions.

494.   Stitt, Robert B. and Limitone, Anthony P. , Jr.   "University
Fair Employment Practices: Litigation Strategy and Tactics. "
Journal of College and University Law.   1 (Fall, 1973), 20-
31.

Purpose of the article is to discuss tactics and techniques
found to be productive in defending a variety of claims including allegations of unequal pay, wrongful termination, refusal to hire, violations of the employer's affirmative action
plan and a refusal to grant admission to specialized or remedial programs.   Three special problems are also discussed: multi-forum litigation, preliminary injunctions and
debarment from federal contract funds.

495.   Summers, Clyde W.   "Preferential Admissions: An Unreal
Solution to a Real Problem. "   Toledo Law Review.   Vol.
1970 (Spring-Summer, 1970), 377-402.

Author suggests that preferential admissions do not increase
the opportunities for legal education of minority students, but

instead create handicaps to professional training.   It has also
led to a wasteful use of financial aid so as to reduce the
total number of needy minority students who can go to law
school.   Suggests a massive cooperative effort of all law
schools to pool resources to meet more effectively the need
for more minority lawyers.

496.   Sundram, Clarence J.   "Increasing Minority Admissions in
Law Schools--Reverse Discrimination. "   Buffalo Law Review.
20 (Winter, 1971), 473-486.

Examines the constitutional questions involved in affirmative
action programs within the framework of a hypothetical fact
situation: Can a state law school create racial classifications or must it be strictly neutral and color-blind in its
approach?   Author suggests that law schools can grant preferential admissions to minority members to meet the needs
of the minority community in providing legal help.

497.   "Title VI of the Civil Rights Act of 1964--Implementation and
Impact. "   George Washington Law Review.   36 (May, 1968),
824-842.

Attempts to ascertain the manner in which the government
has responded to the congressional mandate to prohibit discrimination in programs financed with federal funds and the
effect of that mandate on federal programs.

498.   Todorovich, Miro and Glickstein, Howard.   "Discrimination
in Higher Education: A Debate. "   Civil Rights Digest.   7
(Spring, 1975), 3-21.

Exchange of letters which focus on affirmative action, special admissions in higher education.   Todorovich is the Co-
ordinator of the Committee on Academic Non-Discrimination
and Integrity; Glickstein is the Director of the Center for
Civil Rights of the University of Notre Dame, formerly staff
director of the U. S. Commission on Civil Rights.

499.   Van Alstyne, William.   "Rites of Passage: Race, the Supreme Court, and the Constitution. "   The University of Chicago Law Review.   46 (Summer, 1979), 775-810.

Discusses the regulation and allocation of rights according to
race in American history and how the U. S. Supreme Court
has gone through two distinct rites of passage in ruling upon
the question: what is the extent to which government may
regulate or allocate by race.   The Supreme Court is now
considering a third rite of passage, as exemplified in the
Bakke case and the pending "minority contractors" case, the
latter involves the constitutionality of a law setting aside 10
per cent of federal public works grants to minority business
enterprises.   Author suggests that the Court is being asked

to permit not racial rectification (in reviving the licitness
of race as an explicit device of government) but racial repet-
ition, whereby the legitimate use of race in allocating rights
will bring about racism, racial spoils systems, racial competition, and racial odium, which will be fixtures of government in America even into the twenty-first century.

500.   Vieira, Norman.   "Racial Imbalance, Black Separatism and
        Permissible Classification by Race. "   Michigan Law Review.
        67 (June, 1969), 1553-1626.

        Examines court decision to determine the constitutionality of
        racial classifications.   Assumes that racial classification
        cannot be resolved on a result-oriented basis.   Discusses
        racially differentiated treatment as "benign" treatment one
        year, invidious the next.   Cautions against special treatment
        based upon race and quotas because they operate at the ex-
        pense of other groups which have essentially the same needs
        and also that such treatment is highly divisive.

501.   Wasserstrom, Richard A.   "Racism, Sexism, and Prefer-
        ential Treatment: An Approach to the Topics. "   UCLA Law
        Review.   24 (February, 1977), 581-622.

        Addresses the issues of racism, sexism, and preferential
        treatment not from the constitutional perspective but from
        the broader questions concerning a number of moral, con-
        ceptual, and methodological issues: what is true of the
        culture, the social realities, why things ought to be, means
        by which the ideal may be achieved.   Argues that much of
        the opposition to affirmative action and preferential treatment
        is not justifiable.   It rests upon confusion in thinking about
        relevant issues and upon the failure to perceive and appre-
        ciate some of the ways our society is racist and sexist.

502.   Weber, David A.   "Note: Racial Bias and the LSAT: A
        New Approach to the Defense of Preferential Admissions. "
        Buffalo Law Review.   24 (Winter, 1975), 439-462.

        Explores the issues and implications of whether the criteria
        used for the allocation of the scarce benefit of legal educa-
        tion is racially biased.   Focuses upon the possibility of ra-
        cial bias in the law school admissions process, particularly
        the use of the LSAT.

503.   Weitzman, Lenore J.   "Legal Requirements, Structures, and
        Strategies for Eliminating Sex Discrimination in Academe. "
        In Women in Academia.   Edited by Elga Wasserman and
        others.   New York: Praeger, 1975. Pp. 45-81.

        Includes the legally required components of an affirmative
        action plan; structural pitfalls, specific action programs, the
        problems of implementation and unconscious bias, action
        strategies for academic women, and notes on sources.

504.   Wilkinson, J. Harvie.   From Brown to Bakke: The Supreme
        Court and School Integration, 1954-1978.   New York: Oxford
        University Press, 1979.   368 p.

        Presents a history of the U. S. Supreme Court's role in pub-
        lic school integration in the quarter century since Brown v.
        Board of Education (1954).   Includes four sections: Brown;
        Southern school desegregation, 1955-1970; busing: urban
        school desegregation in the 1970's; and Bakke.

505.   Willey, Robert J.   "The Case for Preferential Admissions. "
        Howard Law Journal.   21 (1978),   174-244.

        The author's purpose is to present the arguments relied upon
        in the various briefs in support of the Regents of the Univer-
        sity of California in the Bakke case, and to further support
        these arguments by referring to the success of the Cleveland
        State College of Law program, initiated in 1970, revised in
        light of De Funis, and in anticipation of the Bakke ruling.
        Author once served as chairman of the Admissions Commit-
        tee at the above law school.

506.   Wilson, James B.   "Admissions and Preferences: Sequel
        to De Funis. "   Journal of College and University Law.   1
        (February, 1973), 38-45.

        Examines three unresolved affirmative action admissions
        problems: role of the student in admissions decisions, valid-
        ity of racial quotas, and to what extent applicants are en-
        titled to due process protection of the Fourteenth Amendment.
        Includes a synopsis of the De Funis case.

507.   Young, D. Parker.   "Affirmative Action Admissions Programs
        in Urban Higher Education--Constitutional or Reverse Dis-
        crimination?"   NOLPE School Law Journal.   6 (1976),   23-28.

        States the constitutional issue as whether a program that em-
        bodies some form of preferential treatment of selected
        groups resulting in possible quotas constitutes reverse dis-
        crimination in violation of basic constitutional rights?   Pres-
        ents cases which attempt to resolve this issue (De Funis,
        Alevy, Bakke, and Henson v. the University of Arkansas).

                            ERIC RESOURCES

508.   Biehl, G. Richard.   Guide to the Section 504 Self-Evaluation
        for Colleges and Universities.   Washington, D. C.:   National
        Association of Colleges and University Business Officers,
        1978.   132 p.
        ED 152 208

Discusses Section 504 of the Rehabilitation Act of 1973 which
mandates equal opportunity for qualified handicapped persons
in education programs.

509.   California State Commission on the Status of Women, Sacra-
        mento. California Women. Special Edition: Title IX.
        Sacramento, California State Commission on the Status of
        Women, 1977. 21 p.
        ED 141 945

        Lists California and federal laws relating to Title IX and in-
        cludes reports on the state-wide task force monitoring the
        implementation of Title IX.

510.   California State Legislature. Assembly. Permanent Sub-
        committee on Postsecondary Education. Unequal Access to
        College. Postsecondary Opportunities and Choices of High
        School Graduates. Staff Report. Sacramento: State Print-
        ing Office, 1975. 33 p.
        ED 116 589

        Report discusses why access to college for ethnic minorities
        and the poor remain very limited and steps to overcome
        educational inequities are presented.

511.   California State Legislature. Joint Committee on the Master
        Plan for Higher Education. Blacks and Public Higher Edu-
        cation in California. Prepared by Robert Singleton and
        Ralph Dawson. Sacramento, 1973. 120 p.
        ED 177 316

        Reviews the present status of black students in California
        higher education and makes recommendations for the formu-
        lation of the Master Plan for California pertaining to the ac-
        cess, retention, and graduate education for blacks.

512.   California State Postsecondary Education Commission, Sacra-
        mento. Equal Educational Opportunity in California Postsec-
        ondary Education. Part I. Commission Report 76-6.
        Sacramento, 1976. 26 p.
        ED 175 295

        Reports California's progress towards the equitable partici-
        pation of ethnic minorities and women in the admission and
        retention of postsecondary education students. Parts include
        background and summary of the California student affirma-
        tive action program; student body composition by ethnicity
        and sex; development of comparison bases for universities
        and colleges; California Community Colleges' response to the
        affirmative action program; report submitted by California
        State Universities and Colleges; progress made toward the

development of a comprehensive plan for student affirmative action by the University of California; five obstacles to equal educational opportunity and recommendations for achieving this goal.   Appendix included.

513.   _____ . Equal Educational Opportunity in California Post-
secondary Education.   Part II.   Commission Report 77-4.
Sacramento, 1977.   263 p.
ED 143 290

Discusses ways to expand opportunities for ethnic minorities, women, and low-income students in postsecondary educational institutions.   Discusses barriers to equal educational opportunity, student affirmative action programs, and the Bakke decision, among other topics.

514.   _____ . Planning for Postsecondary Education in California: A Five-Year Plan Update, 1977-1982.   Sacramento,
1977.   222 p.
ED 139 337

Update of the first five-year plan for postsecondary education in California, adopted in 1976.   Discusses in part equal educational opportunities for minorities, women, and the handicapped.

515.   _____ . Planning for Postsecondary Education in California: A Five-Year Plan Update, 1978.   Sacramento, 1978.
108 p.
ED 105 928

Includes a section on equal educational opportunity for minorities, women, and the handicapped in California.

516.   Days, Drew S. , III.   Language Lacking Discrimination.
Remarks by Drew S. Days, III, Before the International Association of Official Human Rights Agencies at the Washington Plaza Hotel, Seattle, Washington, July 17, 1978.   14 p.
ED 157 987

Assistant Attorney General, Civil Rights Division, Department of Justice, analyzes euphemistic terms such as "reverse discrimination" and "affirmative action" which fail to remind Americans that present discrimination must be eradicated in words and fact.   Discusses how such cases as Bakke obscure the problems of the cumulative effect of racism and discrimination against minorities.

517.   Lopez, Ronald W. and Enos, Darryl D.   Chicanos and Public Higher Education in California.   Sacramento: California State Legislature.   Joint Committee on the Master Plan for Higher Education, 1972.   211 p.
ED 071 627

Describes the characteristics of Chicanos in higher education and makes recommendations for increasing Chicano enrollment.

518.   Pottinger, J. Stanley. Administrating a Solution--Goals Versus Quotas. Washington, D. C.: U. S. Office for Civil Rights, 1974. 16 p.
ED 100 246

Director of the Office for Civil Rights (HEW) clarifies the difference between goals and quotas and discusses two appellate court decisions related to affirmative hiring.

519.   _____. Affirmative Action in Higher Education. Washington, D. C.: U. S. Office for Civil Rights, 1976. 17 p.
ED 132 904

Director of the Office for Civil Rights (HEW) discusses why more and more cases of race and sex discrimination are going to court. Emphasizes the need for a balance between objective criteria and subjective decisions regarding hiring, promotion, and firing.

520.   Redden, Martha Ross, and others. Recruitment, Admissions, and Handicapped Students. A Guide for Compliance with Section 504 of the Rehabilitation Act of 1973. Washington, D. C.: American Association of Collegiate Registrars and Admissions Officers, 1978. 59 p.
ED 156 042

Focuses upon how the Rehabilitation Act affects the recruitment and admissions policies and practices of colleges and universities.

521.   Sandler, Bernice. Admissions and the Law. Washington, D. C.: Association of American Colleges. Project on the Status and Education of Women, 1974. 8 p.
ED 091 971

Discusses admissions and Title IX provisions, types of discrimination in admissions, legality of affirmative recruiting and what needs to be done to end discrimination in admissions.

522.   Smith, Robert E. [Remarks on Non-Discriminating Hiring Practices in Higher Education.] Washington, D. C.: Office for Civil Rights, March, 1972. 18 p.
ED 077 402

Director of the Office for Civil Rights analyzes the steps that colleges and universities must take to comply with Executive Order 11246 and affirmative action requirements in the hiring and promotion policies for faculty and staff.

523.   Taylor, Emily and Shavlik, Donna.   Institutional Self-Evalu-
        ation: The Title IX Requirement.   Washington, D. C.:
        American Council on Education.   Office of Women in Higher
        Education.   1975.   47 p.
        ED 122 714

        Outlines a general procedure for self-evaluation by education-
        al institutions with specific suggestions made for major ar-
        eas of institutional operation.

524.   Verheyden-Hilliard, Mary Ellen.   Title IX of the Education
        Amendments of 1972--Its Enforcement and Implementation:
        A Progress Assessment Memorandum.   Final Report.   1977.
        146 p.
        ED 157 155

        Focuses upon the Office for Civil Rights (HEW) enforcement
        of Title IX provisions.

Late Additions

524A.   Bakke, Weber, and Affirmative Action: A Rockefeller
        Foundation Conference, July 12-13, 1979.   New York: The
        Foundation, 1979.   251 p.

524B.   California.   Department of Education.   Office of Intergroup
        Relations.   Guidelines for Affirmative Action Employment
        Programs.   Sacramento, 1979.   19 p.

        The purpose of the guidelines is to assist governing boards
        of school districts, county offices of education, and other
        educational agencies to carry out the requirements of the
        California laws on affirmative action employment.   Includes
        recommendations on the essential elements of affirmative
        action plans and techniques for its implementation.

524C.   U. S. Department of Health, Education, and Welfare.   Office
        for Civil Rights.   Nondiscrimination in Federal Assisted
        Programs: Title VI of the Civil Rights Act of 1964; Policy
        Interpretation.   Washington, D. C.:   Office for Civil Rights,
        October, 1979.   11 p.
        (ERIC ED 178 661)

        The policy interpretation encourages institutions of higher
        education to continue to expand voluntary affirmative action
        programs to increase minority student enrollment and to at-
        tain a diverse student body.   Identifies permissible techniques
        to achieve these objectives consistent with Title VI and the
        Bakke Supreme Court decision.

PART TWO:

THE ACADEMIC COMMUNITY RESPONSE

An Analysis of the Academic Community Response to Affirmative

Action and Preferential Admissions in Higher Education

The controversy over affirmative action and preferential admissions in higher education has produced acrimonious and often rhetorical debate within the academic community and in the larger American society. But behind the verbal barrage of "quotas, " "debasement of academic standards, " "racist heritage" and "meritorcratic myth" fundamental issues are being raised concerning the purposes of a university, the relationship between meritocratic and egalitarian values, and government regulation of higher education.

The academic community response to these issues reveal deep-seated differences in the meaning, purposes, and desirability of affirmative action and preferential admissions. The purpose of this introduction is to present the background for this controversy within the academic community and to summarize the conflicting viewpoints as found in the vast literature on affirmative action and preferential admissions.

Considerable controversy revolves around the questions of whether affirmative action in higher education is necessary, legitimate, and meets the high standards of academic excellence expected in colleges and universities. Much of the debate focuses on the federal government's methods to determine the "underutilization" of women and minorities in the academic and nonacademic workforce and how to overcome that underutilization.

As explained in Part One of this bibliography, the Office for Civil Rights (HEW) issued Higher Education Guidelines, Executive Order 11246 in October, 1972. Under these affirmative action guidelines, colleges and universities receiving federal contracts are required "to make additional efforts to recruit, employ and promote qualified members of groups formerly excluded, even if that exclusion cannot be traced to particular discriminatory actions on the part of the employer. " Institutions of higher education are also required to:

> determine whether women and minorities are "underutilized" in its employee work force and, if that is the case, to develop as a part of its affirmative action program specific goals and timetables designed to overcome that underutilization. Underutilization is defined in the regulations as "having fewer women or minorities in a particular job than would reasonably be expected by their availability. "[1]

Goals are defined as "projected levels of achievement resulting from an analysis by the contractor of its deficiencies, and of
what it can reasonably do to remedy them, given the availability of
qualified minorities and women. "[2]

The Department of Labor developed a clarification memorandum on the technical requirements for affirmative action plans in
August, 1975 and transmitted them to the Office for Civil Rights.
The memorandum, entitled, "Format for Development of an Affirmative Action Plan by Institutions of Higher Education, " makes opera-
tional the concepts of "utilization analysis, " "goals and timetables, "
and "good faith. " Details are provided on how to conduct workforce
analyses, availability and utilization analyses. Whenever the percentage for women or for each minority in the workforce unit is
less than the corresponding ratio in the availability estimate, the
university's affirmative action plan is required to state that underutilization exists in that group and to make every good faith effort
to overcome that underutilization. [3]

Despite repeated "clarifications" of what is required of colleges and universities, regulations on affirmative action cause considerable confusion in the nation's campuses. Even neutral observ-
ers point up the complexity of making utilization analyses, ascer-
taining goals and timetables, and measuring the availability of qualified women and minorities. For example, the National Board on
Graduate Education conducted a survey of the 56-member Institutions
of the Association of American Universities to ascertain the institutions' affirmative action employment targets for minority faculty in
tenure-track positions for a three-year period (1974-1977). [4] The
results demonstrate a great diversity in responses to affirmative
action requirements--in attitudes, perceptions, methodologies, utilization analyses, and calculating goals and timetables.

It was evident from the furor within the academic community
over affirmative action that the issue most in need of "clarification"
was the meaning and intent of "goals and timetables. " The Office
for Civil Rights was compelled to deny repeatedly that numerical
goals were actually quotas that universities and colleges were required to meet or face the loss of federal funds. One clarifying
memorandum was issued by Peter E. Holmes, Director of the Office for Civil Rights, in December, 1974. Holmes distinguished
between goals and quotas and denied that women and minorities were
to be hired by colleges and universities regardless of their qualifications.

> Goals are good faith estimates of the expected numerical
> results which will flow from specific affirmative actions
> taken by a college or university to eliminate and/or coun-
> teract factors in the university's employment process
> which have contributed to underutilization of minorities
> and women ... They are not rigid and inflexible quotas
> which must be met. Nor should a university strive to
> achieve goals as ends in themselves.

Colleges and universities are entitled to select the most
qualified candidate, without regard to race, sex, or ethnicity, for any position.   The College or university, not
the federal government, is to say what constitutes qualification for any particular position. [5]

In a separate article, Peter Holmes repeated the concepts
behind affirmative action in higher education--that qualified women
and minorities are available for faculty positions and that, as federal contractors, colleges and universities must give them an equal
opportunity to compete for positions "by eliminating practices which
realistically have foreclosed their candidature in significant numbers
in the past. " Moreover, it is "not sustainable" to impart a "stigma
of professional inferiority" to qualified potential applicants by concluding that affirmative action represents an assault on merit.   The
concept of "good faith" means nothing more than that "the university
define and justify the standards it applies and the decisions that are
reached as a consequence. "[6]

J. Stanley Pottinger, Holmes' predecessor as Director of the
Office for Civil Rights, also denied that goals were quotas.   Universities were required, however, to take "defined, specific steps" to
bring the institutions into contact with qualified women and minorities who then, in the selection process, "will be judged fairly on
the basis of their capabilities. " Pottinger further denied the frequent charge by college officials that there are virtually no qualified
women or minorities who are currently unemployed or unpromoted
or that affirmative action infringes upon academic freedom. [7]

But despite official disclaimers by the federal government
that it had no intention of interfering with the autonomy and academic standards of colleges and universities, federal affirmative action regulations have been greeted with bitter criticism within the
academic community, and there is increasing evidence that the criticism is "heating up. " Federal officials are again appearing on
campuses conducting "on-site reviews" to determine whether colleges and universities are complying with civil-rights laws and affirmative action regulations.   Increased investigations by the Office
for Civil Rights are brought about by an agreement that the OCR
negotiated with several civil-rights groups in 1977 to settle lawsuits
charging that that agency had failed to enforce federal anti-bias
laws.   That agreement committed the OCR to significantly increase
its investigations of how higher education institutions were complying
with equal opportunity regulations. [8]

Further evidence that the federal government is tightening up
on enforcing affirmative action regulations on college campuses is
the issuance of new guidelines in March, 1978, for the Office for
Civil Rights to follow.   The issuing agency was the Department of
Labor's Office of Federal Compliance Programs, who, it will be
recalled, had only delegated to the Office for Civil Rights of HEW
the responsibility for enforcing Executive Order 11246 and subsequent affirmative action regulations.   In March, the Department of

Labor rejected the four conciliation agreements the OCR had negotiated with the University of Michigan, Ohio State University, Purdue
University, and the University of Wisconsin.   Weldon J. Rougeau,
Director of the Labor Department's Office of Federal Compliance
Programs, informed the OCR of the rejection and included 11 pages
of guidelines OCR was to follow in future analyses of affirmative
action plans in higher education.   The guidelines called for the OCR
to conduct on-site reviews and statistical analyses of the academic
workforce rather than rely upon statistics furnished by the individual
universities themselves to determine whether, if any, discrimination
exists.   The guidelines further provided that conciliation agreements
will be unacceptable if they only commit the contractor to prospective development of sufficient workforce analysis, utilization analysis, or goals and timetables.   Each part of the affirmative action
regulations were to be in place to be in compliance.   Part of the
compliance review involved multiple regression analyses to determine any salary discrimination. [9]

     Academic response to these new guidelines was swift to fol-
low and indicated the kind of concerns college officials had been
making since the inception of affirmative action regulations.   Sheldon
Steinbach, staff counsel of the American Council on Education, and
Susan Fratkin, director of special programs at the National Association of State Universities and Land-Grant Colleges, raised a number of issues in a memorandum to the Labor Department and the
Office for Civil Rights.   The issues revolve around the following:

     1)   O. C. R. regional investigators give little advanced no-
          tice that they will be coming to a university for a
          compliance review and they ask for huge amounts of
          material and documents in a hasty attempt to conduct
          pre-award clearances.
     2)   O. C. R. investigators give little information to univer-
          sities about the procedures and policies to be followed
          in the reviews.
     3)   There need to be uniform procedures for data collec-
          tion and analysis to achieve consistent policies in the
          conduct of compliance reviews throughout the U. S.
     4)   There need to be safeguards to limit investigators'
          access to personnel files in order to protect employ-
          ees' right to privacy. [10]

     The authority of federal investigators to inspect personnel
files has been fiercely contested by universities, the latest being
the University of California at Berkeley.   At Berkeley, some $55
million in federal grants were jeopardized when investigators required officials to let them see letters of recommendation that were
submitted for unsuccessful applicants for positions in nine departments.   Two departments, Art History, and History, refused either
to let investigators see the letters or let them make copies of confidential files for fear that the material could become public under
the federal Freedom of Information Act.   Federal contracts to
Berkeley were eventually released but the prospect of opening up

confidential files to governmental investigators or private citizens remains a bitterly contested issue. 11

The Berkeley experience and the academic community response to the new guidelines issued by the Labor Department in
March, 1978 reveal the deep-seated conflicts between institutions of
higher education and the federal government.   The next section summarizes the major issues raised by the academic community concerning affirmative action.

Arguments Against Affirmative Action

By far the most frequent criticism of affirmative action regulations
in higher education is that they require the imposition of racial and
sexual quotas upon faculty hiring and student admissions.   The government, by equating statistical underrepresentation of minorities
and women with evidence of discrimination, compels colleges and
universities to hire and promote unqualified persons from these
groups or face the consequences of losing thousands, even millions
of dollars worth, of federal contracts.

The quota system (euphemistically called "numerical goals"
by federal officials) erodes standards of academic excellence by
substituting the ascriptive characteristics of race and sex over intellectual ability and performance as the criterion for faculty hiring
and admissions.

Affirmative action, moreover, is symptomatic of the drive
toward the "new equality" which is aimed at producing equality of
results--in income, status, and power--for all Americans.   Thus,
proportional group representation is replacing the traditional American value of equality of opportunity and advancement based upon individual merit. 12

Critics further charge that quota systems stigmatize women
and minorities by making it appear that group membership rather
than individual ability of persons within these groups accounts for
their being hired as faculty or admitted as students.   Preferential
treatment also contributes to racial and ethnic polarization and reinforces racial stereotypes.

Much wrath is aimed at the federal government's assumption
that underutilization of women and minorities means discrimination
and that by comparing these groups' actual number employed by universities with the number of Ph. D. 's available, underutilization is
proven.   Such a naive approach, critics explain, ignores the important differences in quality among individuals and that the university
wants to hire the "best qualified, " rather than the "qualified, " or
"qualifiable. "

The "best qualified, " moreover, involves more than the pos-
session of a Ph. D.   Institutions look for specialties within academic

fields and particular levels of scholarship not necessarily found in a general Ph. D. pool.

An additional fallacy is that "underutilization" may not be the result of institutional discrimination but be caused by individual choices such as female academics opting for home and family responsibilities rather than continuous academic employment.

Critics of affirmative action save their sharpest attacks for those unelected, unrepresentative federal bureaucrats whose primary interests are statistical body counts and rule by fiat. Officials from the Office for Civil Rights come in for particular criticism. Frequent charges include:

1) Investigators give little notice to institutions that compliance reviews are being undertaken, with the result that college officials are unable to take remedial action or defend themselves against charges of discrimination.

2) O. C. R. employs inconsistent policies and practices in various regions of the country.

3) Investigators practice invasion of the institutions' privacy by their insistence in getting access to personnel files and other confidential documents.

4) Investigators practice a violation of due process of law by assuming that institutions are guilty of discrimination if there is statistical underrepresentation of women and minorities. Colleges and universities are not presumed innocent until proven guilty.

5) O. C. R. investigators are poorly trained and have little knowledge or understanding of the complexities involved in faculty hiring.

6) H. E. W. makes excessive delays in processing compliance reviews and complaints and only a small number of affirmative action plans have received final approval. As a consequence, protracted negotiations between the government and universities extend over a period of years.

7) Exorbitant costs are involved in gathering data and processing the reams of paper statistics required by federal investigators.

As will be seen in the next section, both supporters and critics of affirmative action write about the same issues (e. g., "merit," "reverse discrimination," and "underutilization"), but come up with far different conclusions.

Arguments for Affirmative Action

Proponents of affirmative action argue that plans are necessary in academia to provide equal opportunities for women and minorities to compete fairly for faculty positions and student admissions. Affirmative action is an attempt to overcome past "reverse discrimination" when white males were the preferred groups in higher education.   As J. Stanley Pottinger explains, affirmative action means that "men will simply be asked by their universities to compete fairly on the basis of merit, not fraternity; on demonstrated capability, not assumed superiority."[13]

A representative sample of the kinds of concerns raised by supporters of affirmative action in higher education is found in the American Association of University Professors' Council Commission on Discrimination report, "Affirmative Action in Higher Education" (1973).   The idea of affirmative action, the report explains,

> is essentially the revision of standards and practices to assure that institutions are in fact drawing from the largest marketplace of human resources in staffing their faculties, and a critical review of appointment and advancement criteria to insure that they do not inadvertently foreclose consideration of the best qualified persons by untested presuppositions which operate to exclude women and minorities.[14]

Throughout the literature on affirmative action, its defenders consistently deny that such programs lower academic standards and compel universities to hire less qualified women and minorities when better qualified white males are available.   What women and minorities are asking for, supporters insist, is that the traditional recruiting practices in faculty hiring be reexamined to broaden and to include qualified people previously underrepresented.

The "traditional" recruitment pattern frequently attacked is the "old boy network"--that pattern of recruitment whereby members of one faculty make personal inquiries and references to their colleagues in other institutions regarding potential candidates for faculty appointment.   Critics charge that this informal referral system is rarely accessible to women and minorities.   What the government is asking for, supporters assert, is that colleges and universities are required to open up their recruitment process to a larger pool of qualified applicants, and to relate criteria for hiring, promotion, and salary increases to the job itself and be able to justify their personnel decisions on the basis of individual merit and not based on discriminatory practices.[15]

In exposing the "myth of reverse discrimination," affirmative action proponents point out that even with laws prohibiting sex and race bias in higher education, discrimination continues in faculty hiring, promotion, and salary with white males getting all the better of it.   Several studies focus on sex discrimination and provide evidence that women occupy the lower academic ranks, part-time, and non-tenured track positions, and are paid less than male academics of comparable rank and work.[16]

In addition to the "myths" of reverse discrimination and that women opt for family responsibilities over career advancement, sup-

porters of affirmative action refute the charge that there are few
qualified women and minorities available for faculty appointment and
promotions.   Particular emphasis is placed upon statistics contrast-
ing the availability of female Ph. D. 's with their actual employment
in higher education. [17]

While both sides of the affirmative action issue concede that
salary differentials exist between male and female academics, controversy rages over the cause of such differentials--whether actual
discrimination is evident, or whether salary structures represent
personal choices made by women in favor of family and home over
their career advancement. [18]

It can be seen from the opposing viewpoints concerning affirmative action in higher education that the academic community is
deeply split over the issue and cannot agree even on the meaning,
purposes, and legitimacy of affirmative action.   Without a consensus
in higher education, affirmative action will continue to divide the
academic community for years to come.

A Note on Preferential Admissions

The literature on the academic community response to affirmative
action focuses almost entirely on the issue of faculty hiring, promotion, and pay.   Articles on preferential admissions tend to
emerge primarily as a response to court cases challenging such admissions, particularly to professional schools.   Witness the furor
over the Marco DeFunis and Allan Bakke cases.   The relatively few
articles mentioned in this second bibliography tend to repeat the
kinds of arguments found in the first bibliography, namely, that intellectual merit should be the criteria for admissions rather than
race or sex.   Role models and the need for diversity in higher education are also mentioned, as well as the need to provide more
professionals within the minority community at large. [19]

References

1.   U. S. Department of Health, Education and Welfare.   Office of
       the Secretary.   Office for Civil Rights.   Higher Education
       Guidelines Executive Order 11246.   October 1, 1972, p. 3.
2.   Ibid.
3.   U. S. Department of Health, Education, and Welfare.   Office
       for Civil Rights.   "Format for Development of an Affirma-
       tive Action Plan by Institutions of Higher Education. "
       Federal Register, 40, August 25, 1975, 37064-37070.
4.   National Board on Graduate Education, Minority Group Partici-
       pation in Graduate Education (Washington, D. C. :   National
       Academy of Sciences, 1976), 116-124.
5.   U. S. Department of Health, Education, and Welfare.   Office
       for Civil Rights.   "Memorandum to College and University
       Presidents, " December 4, 1974, pp. 2, 4.

6. Peter E. Holmes, "Affirmative Action: Myth and Reality, " in
    Toward Affirmative Action, edited by Lucy W. Sells. (San
    Francisco: Jossey-Bass, 1974), pp. 42-43.
7. J. Stanley Pottinger, "Race, Sex, and Jobs: The Drive toward
    Equality, " Change, 4 (October, 1972), 27-28.
8. "Colleges Feeling Impact of New U.S. Civil-Rights Effort, "
    The Chronicle of Higher Education, 16 (February 27, 1978),
    7-8.
9. "New Guidelines Set for Affirmative-Action Negotiations, "
    The Chronicle of Higher Education, 16 (April 17, 1978), 15.
10. Ibid.
11. "Dispute Imperils Research Projects at Berkeley. The New
    York Times, April 25, 1978, p. 21; "U.S. Holds Up $1.5-
    Million Contract for Berkeley Lab; Layoffs Threatened, "
    The Chronicle of Higher Education, 16 (May 1, 1978), 4;
    "U.S. Approves Release of Contracts at Berkeley, " The
    Chronicle of Higher Education, 16 (May 8, 1978), 18;
    "Berkeley Moves to Avoid Cutoff of Federal Funds, " The
    Chronicle of Higher Education, 16 (July 24, 1978), 8.
        As recently as September, 1980, the dispute continues
between officials of the University of California at Berkeley
and federal civil-rights investigators over the right of these
investigators to copy confidential employment records in
their review of suspected discriminatory hiring practices
by the university.   On September 5, the Department of
Labor, under its Secretary Ray Marshall, announced that
it has given Berkeley 30 days to turn over confidential employment records to their investigators or face the loss of
$25-million in government contracts.   Regulations accom-
panying Executive Order 11246, Secretary Marshall explained, clearly required contractors to allow investigators
to copy "such books, records, accounts, and other material
as may be relevant to the matter under investigation" and
that such copies were necessary for investigators to assess
whether the documents indicated that discriminatory hiring
decisions had been made.   The Berkeley Chancellor, I.
Michael Heyman, responded that the university would probably go to court to challenge the Labor Secretary's order.
Copies of confidential documents, including letters of recommendation and evaluations by review committees, the
university pointed out, as it had previously, might be subject to public disclosure under the Freedom of Information
Act, if such copies entered government files.   "Berkeley
Faces Loss of $25-Million in Battle with U.S. over Job
Data, " The Chronicle of Higher Education, 21 (September
15, 1980), 15-16.   The two-year dispute over government
access to confidential employee documents was finally settled on September 3, 1980 the day before an order barring
the University of California from receiving federal contracts
was to go into effect.   The University and the Department
of Labor signed a consent decree whereby government officials, in their investigation of suspected bias in the recruitment, hiring, and promotion of faculty members, can copy

and remove confidential records from all nine campuses of
the University of California, including three major labora-
tories administered by the university. In return, Labor
Department officials gave assurances to preserve the con-
fidentiality of these documents and to return them to the
university after concluding their review of possible job bias.
The government further agreed that civil-rights investigators
could copy documents only after higher-level officials in
the Department of Labor determined that such documents
were essential to their investigations. Chancellor Heyman,
in announcing the settlement in a letter to Berkeley faculty
members on September 3rd, said that the settlement, he
believes, "will permit the Department of Labor to carry
out its federal law-enforcement responsibilities while pro-
tecting the interests of the university in assuring the continuing effectiveness of peer review in the academic personnel process." "Last-Minute Compromise with U. S. Averts
Berkeley's Loss of $25-Million," The Chronicle of Higher
Education, 21 (October 14, 1980), 21, 24.

12.   The most vocal and persistent critics of affirmative action,
but by no means the only critics, are the following persons:
Daniel Bell, John Bunzel, Sidney Hook, Richard Lester,
Allan Ornstein, George Roche, Paul Seabury, Malcolm
Sherman and Thomas Sowell.

13.   J. Stanley Pottinger, "Come Now, Professor Hook," The New
York Times, December 18, 1971, p. 29.

14.   "Affirmative Action in Higher Education: A Report by the
Council Commission on Discrimination." AAUP Bulletin,
59 (Summer, 1973), 178-183.

15.   For examples of the criticism of the "old-boy network," see
the articles by Gertrude Ezorsky, Bernice Sandler, Rose
Coser, and Judy Egelston.

16.   See, for example, the books and articles by Frances Barasch,
Alan Bayer and Helen Astin, Ann Harris, Emily Hoffman,
Suzanne Howard, Lionel Lewis, Bernice Sandler, and Carol
Van Alstyne.

17.   See, for example, the articles by Frances Barasch, Ann Harris, and Agnes Green.

18.   Articles dealing with salary differentials are by Julie Anderson
and Norman Murphy, the Carnegie Commission, Michael
Faia, Stephen Farber, Marianne Ferger and Jane Loeb,
Ferber and Anne Westmiller, Nancy Gordon, Thomas Mor-
ton, and Ina Braden, Ketayun Gould and Bok-lim Kim,
Ester Greenfield, Emily Hoffman, George Johnson and
Frank Stafford, David Katz, James Koch and John Chizmar,
Michael LaSorte, Richard Lester, Barbara Reagan and
Betty Maynard, and Myra Strober and Aline Quester.

19.   See, for example, the articles by Vernon Jordan and Richard
Wasserstrom and the Carnegie Council on Policy Studies in
Higher Education, Selective Admission in Higher Education
(1977).

BIBLIOGRAPHIES

526. Astin, Helen S. Women: A Bibliography on Their Education
and Careers; by Helen S. Astin and others. New York: Be-
havioral Publications, 1974. 243 p.

Includes more than 350 abstracts or annotations of books and
periodical articles, with the majority published after 1966.
Sections also on overview of findings, interpretations, and
implications for the future.

527. Brekke, Beverly. "Women in Higher Education: A Selected
Bibliography." Journal of Teaching and Learning. 3 (June,
1977), 9-13.

13 books annotated which provide a background for understanding equity issues in the academic community.

528. Forrest, Kathryn; Chang, Wendy; [and Faustina, Stephen],
comps. Affirmative Action & Equal Employment: A Bibliography. San Jose: San Jose State University, April, 1977.
19ℓ.

Contains listing of books, pamphlets, articles and speeches.
Arranged by year; within year, alphabetically.

529. Harmon, Linda H., comp. Status of Women in Higher Education: 1963-1972. A Selective Bibliography. Ames: Iowa
State University Library, 1972. 124 p. (Series in Bibliography no. 2)

Annotated bibliography on the status of women as faculty,
staff, administrators, librarians, and students, excluding
women in non-academic positions. Citations listed by author. Includes books, periodical articles, ERIC documents,
government publications, dissertations, and ephemera.

530. Haro, Robert P. Affirmative Action in Higher Education:
A Selected and Annotated Bibliography. Monticello, Ill.:
Council of Planning Librarians, 1977. 26 p. (Exchange
Bibliography #1229)

Bibliography includes topics on academic policy and affirmative action. Concentration is upon policy development of affirmative action in higher education. Includes books, articles, government publications, newspaper articles and editorials, and reports.

531.   Hull, W. Frank.   "The Black Student in Higher Education: A Bibliography." Journal of College Student Personnel.   11 (November, 1970), 423-425.

Selection of the most significant writings presented.

532.   _____ , and Davies, Marshall W.   "The Black Student in Higher Education: A Second Bibliography." Journal of College Student Personnel.   14 (July, 1977), 309-312.

Updated list of articles published since mid-1970.

533.   Kane, Rosalyn D.   Sex Discrimination in Education: A Study of Employment Practices Affecting Professional Personnel. Volume I: Study Report. Volume II: Annotated Bibliography. Washington, D. C.: National Center for Education Statistics, 1976. Volume 1, 321 p. Volume II, 258 p. (ED 132 743 and ED 132 744)

Contains abstracts of the major research studies, surveys, and expert analyses used in writing the Study Report. Material emphasizes publications within the last five years and primary sources presenting original research. Two bibliographical appendices include some studies of the status of women in various academic disciplines and at various postsecondary institutions.

534.   Mills, Gladys H. , comp.   Equal Rights for Women in Education. Seminar 6, a Bibliography. Denver: Education Commission of the States, 1973. 14 p. (ED 102 439)

Articles cover affirmative action, continuing education and counseling of women, employment profiles and opportunities, manpower research, sex discrimination, women's studies, and the status of women in higher education.

535.   Pemberton, S. Macpherson, comp.   Research Reports on Affirmative Action Programs in Colleges and Universities: An Annotated Bibliography. Washington, D. C.: U. S. Department of Health, Education, and Welfare, Office of Education, 1977. 16 p. (ED 147 247)

Includes annotations of 31 articles and books dealing with affirmative action in higher education that appeared between 1972 and 1977.

536.   Piesco, Judith and others.   Review of the Evaluative Litera-
       ture on Open Admissions at CUNY.   Office of Program and
       Policy Research, City University of New York.   New York,
       October, 1974.   70 p.
       (ED 097 816)

537.   Westervelt, Esther Manning and Fixter, Deborah A.   Wom-
       en's Higher and Continuing Education: An Annotated Bibliog-
       raphy with Selected References on Related Aspects of Wom-
       en's Lives.   Princeton, New Jersey: College Entrance Ex-
       amination Board, 1971.   67 p.

       Contains studies pertaining to women's status as college stu-
       dents, graduate students, and mature women.   Material and
       documents include women's social and cultural roles, re-
       search on feminine psychology and development, sex differ-
       ences in intellectual characteristics and academic perform-
       ance, continuing education, and women in the labor force.

BOOKS, PERIODICAL ARTICLES, AND NEWSPAPER ARTICLES

538.   AAUW Conference on Graduate and Professional Education of
       Women, Washington, D. C. , 1974.   Graduate and Professional
       Education of Women.   Proceedings of AAUW Conference held
       at the AAUW Educational Center May 9-10, 1974.   Washing-
       ton, D. C. :   American Association of University Women,
       1974.   94 p.

       Panel members discuss the law and women (including federal
       remedies for discrimination in universities, Office for Civil
       Rights and sex discrimination); academic admissions and the
       law; women in medicine; financial aid policies; social, struc-
       tural and institutional barriers; women graduate students;
       conference recommendations, and status of the graduate and
       professional education of women: a review of the literature.

539.   Abrams, Elliott.   "The Quota Commission. "   Commentary.
       54 (October, 1972), 54-57.

       Charges that the federal Equal Employment Opportunity Com-
       mission violates the law by insisting that employers follow
       a system of preferential treatment and proportional repre-
       sentation of non-whites and women.

540.   Abramson, Joan.   The Invisible Woman: Discrimination in
       the Academic Profession.   San Francisco: Jossey-Bass,
       1975.   248 p.

       Book divided into 4 parts: author's challenge of the Univer-
       sity of Hawaii's decision not to grant her tenure and her fil-
       ing a charge of sex discrimination; analysis of the academic
       setting, including myth that merit alone dictates academic

success, the male backlash and the role of academic committees in sex discrimination cases; exploration of the various
methods of appeal of sex discrimination complaints; and outline of the steps necessary to take for voluntary compliance
with the anti-discrimination laws.

541.   "Academicians at Meeting in Capital Voice Resentment Over
        Federal Regulation of Higher Education. " The New York
        Times. December 13, 1976, p. 23.

        The Conference, entitled: "The University and the State:
        The Proper Role of Government in Higher Education, " was
        sponsored by the University Centers for Rational Alterna-
        tives. Spokesman for the group charges that targets and
        goal quotas called for in affirmative action programs repre-
        sent reverse discrimination.

542.   Ackley, Sheldon. "To Overcome Discrimination Now. " Cur-
        rent. No. 129 (May, 1971), 35-38.

        Debates whether racial minorities should be granted prefer-
        ential treatment regarding entrance requirements and achieve-
        ment at college level. Presents a rationale which favors
        the proposal.

543.   Adams, Betty. "The Status of Affirmative Action. " Urban
        League Review. 2 (Summer, 1977), 6-8.

        Concludes that essential to the success of affirmative action
        is the understanding that it demands sensitive interpretation
        and broad based support as a concept and aggressive, un-
        compromising execution as a tool.

544.   Adams, Velma A. "'Affirmative Action' You Must Take. "
        College Management. 8 (February, 1973), 28-33, 40.

        Discusses the various federal laws and regulations relating
        to affirmative action, why a remedy for discrimination is
        necessary, semantic misunderstanding, writing an affirmative
        action plan, tests of good faith, equal pay is mandatory, and
        when the feds arrive.

545.   "Affirmative Action?" Journal of the National Association
        for Women Deans, Administrators, and Counselors. 39
        (Winter, 1976), 49-97.

        Entire issue is devoted to affirmative action. Contents in-
        clude:

546.   Jo Ann Fley, About This Issue

547.   Thomas G. Travis, Affirmative Action on Campus: How
        Firm the Foundation?

548.   Patricia Palmieri and Charol Smith Skakeshaft, Up the Front
        Staircase: A Proposal for Women to Achieve Parity with
        Men in the Field of Educational Administration

549.   Judy Cobb Egelston, Sex Bias in Publications and Grant
        Awards

550.   Ann H. Beuf, The Home of Whose Brave? Problems Con-
        fronting Native Americans in Education

551.   Diane W. Strommer, Whither Thou Goest: Feminism and
        the Education of Women

552.   Kathryn G. Heath, Our Heritage Speaks

553.   Margaret Fisher, Once Over Lightly

554.   Affirmative Action and Minority Student Development. Edited
        by Joseph L. Amprey. Washington, D. C.: ECCA Publica-
        tions, 1976.

555.   "Affirmative Action: Effects of De Funis Decision on Employ-
        ment. " Today's Education. 64 (March/April, 1975), 89-92,
        94-96.

        Several points of view on topics of affirmative action plans,
        reverse discrimination, and quotas in college admissions,
        employment, and promotion are presented.

556.   "Affirmative Action: Federal Policy. " Nations' Schools and
        Colleges. 2 (January, 1975), 34-35.

        Analysis of background of recent HEW memo to 2800 col-
        leges warning them not to practice reverse discrimination
        while trying to improve opportunities for minorities and wom-
        en.

557.   Affirmative Action Register. Edited by Warren H. Green.
        8356 Olive Blvd., St. Louis, Mo. 63132. 1971- . Monthly.

        Advertising service of job vacancies in institutions and cor-
        porations, including section on higher education openings.

558.   Albright, Robert L. "College and the Minority Student. "
        Journal of the National Association of College Admissions
        Counselors. 19 (July, 1974), 13-16.

        Crusade to recruit minority students has progressed far
        enough to draw some conclusions from the results. Article
        summarizes the minority student recruitment program in
        general and outlines some areas in need of revision.

559.   Alexis, Marcus. "The Case for Affirmative Action in Higher
        Education. " Urban League Review. 2 (Summer, 1977), 25-38.

Discusses the difficulty in assessing affirmative action performance of colleges and universities. Data on the availability of minority candidates with advanced degrees is poor.

560. American Historical Association. Report by the Ad Hoc Committee on the Status of Women Historians. Presented to the A.H.A. June 5, 1971, with summary in Newsletter of September, 1971.

Includes a view of the committee's work, its recommendations, and a summary of its findings. Shows concern with the overall status of women historians as deteriorating, especially in employment opportunities, particularly at the upper academic levels.

561. Anderson, Julie A., and Murphy, Norman C. "An Empirical Approach to Salary Discrimination: With Case Study of Sex Discrimination in Education." Educational Research Quarterly. 2 (Spring, 1977), 48-57.

562. Arce, Carlos H. "Chicanos in Higher Education." Integrated Education. 14 (May/June, 1976), 14-18.

Discusses academic colonialism as related to Chicanos in higher education. Gives an historical sketch, along with statistics, of Chicano faculty and students.

563. Association of American Colleges. Women in Higher Education Administration. Washington, D.C.: Association of American Colleges. Project on the Status and Education of Women, 1978. 8 p.
(ED 162 572)

Two papers are presented which examine the barriers to women in academic decision making and identify a variety of effective strategies for improving the status of women in higher education administration. Discusses also affirmative action hiring goals, search procedures, and development programs.

564. _____. Project on the Status and Education of Women. Summary of Issues Being Raised by Women's Groups Concerning the Proposed Regulations for Title IX of the Education Amendments of 1972. Washington, D.C.: Association of American Colleges, 1974.

Comments strongly criticize many provisions in the proposed regulations concerning employment and compliance procedures, including the lack of a clear requirement for affirmative action, record-keeping requirements, and the rights of complainants during compliance investigations.

565.   Association of American Medical Colleges. Medical School
       Admission Requirements, 1978/79. Washington, D. C.: As-
       sociation of American Medical Colleges, 1977. 349 p.

       This annual includes information on U. S. medical school ap-
       plications by race and by sex from 1970/71 to the present.
       Also includes information on trends on medical school appli-
       cations for first-year entering classes, 1971-78, AAMC
       statement on medical education of minority group students,
       and resolution on equal opportunity.

566.   Association of Research Libraries, Washington, D. C. ARL
       Annual Salary Survey, 1977-78. Compiled by Suzanne
       Frankie. Washington, D. C.: Association of Research Li-
       braries, 1978. 40 p.
       (ED 168 473)

       Survey includes tabulations of median and beginning profes-
       sional salaries in all Association of Research Libraries
       (ARL) member libraries. Cites evidence of the imbalances
       in the distribution of librarians by sex and position with men
       favored at the top administrative levels and women as depart-
       ment heads. Average salaries for men are higher than for
       women in the majority of categories, including minority li-
       brarians.

567.   Astin, Alexander W. "Equal Access to Postsecondary Edu-
       cation: Myth or Reality?" UCLA Educator. 19 (Spring,
       1977), 8-17.

       Argues that American higher education has evolved into a
       highly refined institutional-status hierarchy. Examines this
       hierarchy in public and private school systems, emphasizing
       the kinds of students attending these institutions.

568.   _____ . The Myth of Equal Access in Public Higher Edu-
       cation. Atlanta: Southern Education Foundation, 1975. 32 p.
       (ED 119 551)

       Concludes that the existing hierarchical public systems do
       not present a set of opportunities that are even remotely
       equal for all students.

569.   _____ . "Racial Considerations in Admissions in Amer-
       ica. " The Campus and the Racial Crisis. Edited by David
       C. Nichols and Olive Mills. Washington, D. C.: American
       Council on Education, 1970. Pp. 113-141.

       Examines alternative arguments concerning college admis-
       sions policies and racial problems. Explores some basic
       assumptions involved in the use of aptitude test scores and

high school grades in college admissions and presents recent empirical evidence concerning the relative usefulness of
these measures for students of different races.

570.   Astin, Helen S.   "Achieving Educational Equity for Women. "
       NASPA Journal.   14 (Summer, 1976), 15-24.

571.   _____, and Bayer, Alan E.   "Sex Discrimination in Aca-
       deme. "   Educational Record.   53 (Spring, 1972), 101-118.

       Analysis of data concerning discrimination, academic rank,
       tenure and salary differentials; includes recommendations for
       restructuring the system.   Sex is a better predictor of rank
       than are the number of years since completion of education,
       number of years employed at the present institution, or the
       number of books published.

572.   Bailey, Robert L. and Hafner, Anne L.   Minority Admis-
       sions.   Lexington, Mass.: Lexington Books, D. C. Heath
       and Co. , 1978.   213 p.

       Examines the challenging role of admission policies and prac-
       tices in higher education as they apply to minority access
       and admissibility.

573.   The Balancing Act: Quota Hiring in Higher Education, by
       George C. Roche III; Black Studies Revisited, by Ernest Van
       Den Haag and Alan Reynolds.   La Salle, Ill.:   Open Court
       Publishing Co. , 1974.   251 p.

       Roche criticizes Affirmative Action for substituting group
       rights over individual merit, government tyranny over higher
       education in its disregard for basic legal guarantees and its
       imposition of a quota system.

574.   Ballard, Allen B.   "Academia's Record of Benign Neglect. "
       Change.   5 (March, 1973), 27-33.

       Discusses the history of blacks in higher education.   Author
       is the Dean for Academic Development at City University of
       New York.

575.   _____ .   The Education of Black Folk: The Afro-American
       Struggle for Knowledge in White America.   New York: Harp-
       er & Row, 1973.   173 p.

       Argues for educational compensation for black Americans.

576.   Barasch, Frances.   "HEW, the University, & Women. "   Dis-
       sent.   20 (Summer, 1973), 333-339.

       Refutes argument that there are few qualified women to hire
       or promote in higher education.   Provides data on the large

pool of qualified women available for high positions. Women
presently concentrated at lower end of rank and salary, and
when high rank attained, it is in less prestigious departments. Affirmative action means that qualified women would
be given an equal chance to compete.

577. Bayer, Alan E. Teaching Faculty in Academe: 1972-1973.
      ACE Research Reports, vol. 8, no. 2. Washington, D. C.:
      American Council on Education, 1973.

      Study reveals that despite intensive efforts to increase num-
      bers of blacks and women on college faculties, gains have
      been negligible: proportion of black faculty members in-
      creased from 2. 2 per cent in 1969 to 2. 9 per cent in 1972,
      while proportion of women increased from 19. 1 per cent to
      20 per cent. Includes graphs on female and minority repre-
      sentations on college faculties from 1968 to 1973.

578. _____, and Astin, Helen S. "Sex Differentials in the
      Academic Reward System. " Science. 188 (May 23, 1975),
      796-802.

      Analyzed a random sampling of 5, 000 cases, approximately
      one-half female and one-half male, from a larger study un-
      dertaken by the American Council on Education. Concluded
      that the differences between males and females having the
      same academic background, professional activities, and work
      setting indicate the presence of sex bias. There has been
      a greater equality between males and females since the anti-
      bias regulations have been in effect. Total equality has not
      yet been achieved.

579. Beaumont, Marion S. "Efficiency and Equity: The Single
      Salary Schedule in Public Higher Education. " AAUP Bulletin.
      64 (March, 1978), 19-25.

      Study based on data collected at California State University,
      Long Beach, and describes a fixed schedule of salary steps
      within each academic rank and a normal time-in-step speci-
      fication for each salary step.

580. Belanger, Charles H. , and Coleman, Daniel K. "Strategies
      and Procedures Used in Developing Goals for an Equal Em-
      ployment Opportunity Affirmative Action Plan. " Journal of
      the College and University Personnel Association. 26 (Octo-
      ber-November, 1975), 15-25.

      Authors draw from their workshop experience to lay out the
      basic issues involved in the planning and implementation of
      an equal employment opportunity plan.

581. Bender, Louis W. Federal Regulation and Higher Education.
      ERIC/Higher Education Research Report Number 1. Wash-

ington, D. C.: American Association for Higher Education, 1977. 88 p. (ED 135 323)

Author explores the nature of regulatory practices to determine if federal regulations have changed governance patterns or infringed on institutional autonomy. Affirmative action regulations are discussed. Includes an extensive bibliography.

582. Benokraitis, Nijole V., and Feagin, Joe R. Affirmative Action and Equal Opportunity: Action, Inaction, Reaction. Boulder, Colo.: Westview Press, 1978. 255 p.

Focuses on affirmative action in employment and education. Chapters include Equal Opportunity and Affirmative Action: An Overview; The Labored Birth of Affirmative Action: A Focus on Employment; Government Employment and Affirmative Action; The Impact of Affirmative Action in Industry; Affirmative Action, Equal Employment Opportunity, and Higher Education; Public and Private Reactions to Organized Affirmative Action; and Affirmative Action: Reverse Discrimination or Equity? Contains a 33-page bibliography.

583. Bergmann, Barbara R., and Maxfield, Myles. "How to Analyze the Fairness of Faculty Women's Salaries on Your Own Campus." AAUP Bulletin. 61 (October, 1975), 262-265.

Analyzes the faculty salaries at the University of Maryland, and suggests that the methods used could serve as a model for groups on other campuses. Major ingredients are the raw data on individual salaries and on some of the characteristics of individual faculty members which might legitimately explain salary differences. Uses multiple regression computations.

584. Berwitz, Clement J. The Job Analysis Approach to Affirmative Action. New York: John Wiley & Sons, 1975. 327 p.

Provides conceptual guidelines and methods for implementing the job analysis approach to affirmative action plans. Model is based upon the Wagner College Affirmative Action Plan. The college is located in Staten Island, New York.

585. Bickel, Alexander. "More on Quotas." New Republic. 167 (October 28, 1972), 8-9.

Cautions against establishing a quota system, particularly for the professions, because it could lead to the appointment or hiring of less qualified candidates. Calls for the wider recruiting and training of the disadvantaged. Suggests that quotas would compromise and ruin "morally and practically,

the society that has wronged them in the past, as it earlier
wronged others. "

586.   Bickel, P. J. and others. "Sex Bias in Graduate Admis-
        sions: Data from Berkeley." Science. 187 (February 7,
        1975), 398-404.

        Discusses whether the decision to admit or deny admission
        was influenced by the sex of the applicant. Concluded that
        statistics show a clear but misleading pattern of bias against
        female applicants. Suggests that bias stems from prior
        screening at earlier levels of the educational system.

587.   Bierman, Leonard. "Affirmative Action: Where Are We?"
        Social Research Administrators Journal. 9 (Fall, 1977), 41-
        44.

        Article based on a conference paper and discusses federal
        contract compliance with respect to fair employment, with
        some emphasis on higher education.

588.   "Black Presence Grows in Higher Education." The New
        York Times. November 14, 1976, XII, p. 15.

        Describes current increase in number of blacks attending
        colleges and expectations for future enrollment growth; while
        percentage of blacks who go to college is the same as whites,
        the dropout rate for blacks and minorities is higher than for
        whites, making it unlikely that these groups will soon achieve
        parity in college attendance with whites.

589.   Blackwell, James E. Access of Black Students to Graduate
        and Professional Schools. Atlanta: Southern Education
        Foundation, 1975. 81 p.
        (ED 119 555)

        Discusses admissions policies, practices and results of mi-
        nority access, enrollment trends and patterns in graduate
        and professional schools, barriers to professional practices,
        and efforts to increase the number of blacks in graduate and
        professional schools throughout the U.S.

590.   Booth, Philip. "When Discrimination Is an Academic Ques-
        tion." The Chronicle of Higher Education. 13 (October 11,
        1976), 32.

        Chides academicians for abstractly sanctifying the word
        "equality" thus failing to discriminate between average and
        outstanding accomplishment by professors and students.
        Suggests that the ability to discriminate is a central value
        of education, including the ability to discriminate between
        social urgency and academic ability.

591. Borgatta, Edgar F.   "The Concept of Reverse Discrimination
      and Equality of Opportunity. " American Sociologist.   11
      (May, 1976), 62-72.

      In recent times, the bureaucratic interpretation by HEW and
      legal innovations in lower courts with consent decrees have
      led to the use of preference systems and quotas which con-
      stitute a new form of discrimination.   Emphasizes that im-
      plementation of the universalistic value of equality of oppor-
      tunity favors minorities if they are relatively disadvantaged.
      Statistical indicators suggest that in some important areas
      such as education, no great differences exist for current
      cohorts of persons classified by age, sex, or ethnic cate-
      gories.

592. _____.   "Rejoinder ... to Susan Keller's Reply.... "
      American Sociologist.   11 (May, 1976), 82-84.

      Comments on Keller's response and notes that concern about
      discrimination is not the issue, but recent developments and
      informal acceptance of benign quotas and preference as form
      of discrimination that is justified in the name of eliminating
      discrimination.

593. Boring, Phyllis Z.   "Affirmative Action and the Recruitment
      Process. " Association of Departments of Foreign Lan-
      guages.   Bulletin.   10 (November, 1978), 21-22.

      Suggests procedures for complying with affirmative action
      policies and for handling job applicants in the language pro-
      fession.

594. _____.   "Antibias Regulation of Universities: A Biased
      View?" AAUP Bulletin.   61 (October, 1975), 252-255.

      Reviews Richard Lester's Antibias Regulation of Universities:
      Faculty Problems and Their Solutions (1974).   Criticizes
      study for its lack of objectivity, shaky premises underlying
      analysis of the university situation, and refusal to acknowl-
      edge that the different treatment of women and minority fac-
      ulty could be the result of prejudice and not that groups are
      less meritorious than men.   Challenges Lester's basic as-
      sumptions of lack of progress relative to men because they
      have child-caring and housekeeping responsibilities, and that
      women are less meritorious because they teach lower level
      courses, publish less, and do less research.   Author criti-
      cizes "old-boy" network which extends to all aspects of aca-
      demic life, and maintains that without the potential clout of
      Uncle Sam in the background, women and minorities would
      still be where they were four or five years ago.

595. Boylan, Hunter R.   "Facilitating Minority Admissions: Some
      Legal Considerations. " College and University Journal.   48
      (Spring, 1973), 171-176.

Offers general legal guidelines to facilitate minority enrollment in higher education. Concludes that it is permissible
to identify potential students on the basis of race in an effort
to relieve racial imbalance and to modify admissions standards for such students, provided that such modification may
not restrict enrollment opportunities for non-minority students.

596.   Branan, Robert D. "Personnel Policies and Federal Con-
        cerns. " Journal of the College and University Personnel
        Association. 26 (October-November, 1975), 26-33.

Outlines the kinds of personnel policy questions an institutional manager needs to consider, and the kinds of questions
Federal monitors have been asking concerning anti-discrimination and affirmative action.

597.   Breiter, Toni. "Affirmative Action: Playing with Words,
        Masking the Problem. " Agenda. 7 (May-June, 1977), 20-22.

This article, the first of two, focuses on the historical background and the legal basis for affirmative action.

598.   Brickman, William W. "Quota System, Quality, and Equality
        in Education. " Intellect. 101 (December, 1972), 152-153.

Questions the use of quotas which raise group representation
above individual merit as the criteria for selection in higher
education.

599.   Brodbelt, S. S. "The Democratic Myth--Equality of Educa-
        tional Opportunity. " College Student Journal. 6 (November/
        December, 1972), 93-97.

Concludes that the only fool-proof method for achieving total
equality of education is to guarantee equality of end product.
School will not be an effective force in breaking the environ-
mental cycle of inequality unless and until concentrated effort
is made by all governmental agencies to equalize opportunities throughout society.

600.   Brown, Frank and Stent, Madelon D. Minorities in U. S. In-
        stitutions of Higher Education. New York: Praeger, 1977.
        178 p.

Presents data and analyses of the status of racial and ethnic
minorities enrolled in institutions of higher education. Chapters include the benefits of a college education, undergraduate enrollment, Bachelor's degrees earned, engineering and
pharmacy, graduate and professional school enrollment and
earned degrees, higher education enrollment in selected
states, economic indicators and the minority college student,
minority students on campus, summary and recommendations. Bibliography included.

601.   Bunzel, John H.   "Do Colleges Practice Reverse Bias?"
        Wall Street Journal.   180 (July 27, 1972), 8.

        Discusses federal affirmative action regulations, voices op-
        position to the use of any form of quota system which makes
        the exclusive criterion for faculty hiring a person's race or
        sex.   Giving preference in faculty hiring to certain groups
        on racial grounds undermines the fundamental precept of in-
        dividual merit and performance, and undermines the integrity
        of the university to control its own tenure, hiring, and pro-
        motions functions.   Governmental encouragement of prefer-
        ential hiring on racial classifications increases the impor-
        tance of race in an already race-ridden society.

602.   _____ .   "The Quota Mentality."   Freedom at Issue.   No.
        22 (November/December, 1973), 10-14.

        Responds to the following questions on discrimination in the
        academic community and alternatives to the quota mentality:
        Can quotas solve or help to solve the problem of discrimina-
        tion; is statistical underrepresentation on the faculty prima
        facie evidence of discrimination; and what recommendations
        can be made that will improve the present state of affairs?

603.   _____ .   "Race, Sex and Jobs: The Politics of Quotas."
        Change.   4 (October, 1972), 25, 30-35.

        Suggests that HEW regulations on affirmative action encour-
        ages race and sex rather than individual merit as the pre-
        dominant criterion for faculty hiring, that numerical goals
        are unsuitable to the academic world, and that preferential
        hiring, once institutionalized, is likely to set minority
        against minority, because it encourages irrational schemes
        of compensatory redress.   Concludes that higher education
        should undertake an unprecedented search for qualified wom-
        en and minorities and that increased opportunities must be
        provided at the graduate level to train women and minorities
        for the professions.

604.   Burke, Yvonne Brathwaite.   "Minority Admissions to Medical
        Schools: Problems and Opportunities."   Journal of Medical
        Education.   52 (September, 1977), 731-738.

        Discusses the progress made in the proportion of minority
        group students in M.D. programs.   Yet formidable barriers
        remain for prospective minority candidates.   Subtle discrim-
        inatory pressures exist and the concept of "reverse discrim-
        ination" poses a new political obstacle in the elimination of
        such pressures.

605.   Busi, Frederick.   "Admissions Policies After DeFunis."
        The Journal of Intergroup Relations.   3 (Fall, 1974), 13-18.

Argues that universities must modify the means and not the goals of recruitment policy before other cases, with more persuasive evidence, comes before the courts.

606.   Cain, Rudolph A.   "What's Happening to Black Ph. D. Applicants?"   Educational Forum.   37 (January, 1973), 225-228.

Black graduate students continue to face discrimination at the doctoral level because of widespread belief that black graduates are not research-oriented.

607.   Caliendo, Nate, and John K. Curtice.   "Title IX: A Guide for Financial Aid Administrators."   Journal of Student Financial Aid.   7 (May, 1977), 32-43.

"Title IX Self-Assessment Guide for Financial Aid Officers" developed by the authors to assure that sex is not a barrier to accessing campus based student aid.

608.   "Califano Says Quotas Are Necessary to Reduce Bias in Jobs and Schools."   The New York Times.   March 18, 1977, p. 1.

Secretary of HEW Joseph Califano believes that quotas can and do work in reversing patterns of job discrimination; statement comes in middle of national debate that has placed minorities and women in confrontation with white males who claim they are victims of reverse discrimination.

609.   California.   University.   Berkeley.   Affirmative Action Program and Related Documents.   2 vols.   February, 1975.

Includes a compilation of materials concerning the University's attempt to comply with affirmative action regulations.

610.   "Can All Americans Be Made 'Equal'?"   U. S. News & World Report.   74 (April 9, 1973), 39-44.

Discusses the deeply rooted conflict between equality of opportunity for all or preferential policies aimed at achieving equalization of socially and economically depressed segments of the population.

611.   Carnegie Commission on Higher Education.   Opportunities for Women in Higher Education: Their Current Participation, Prospects for the Future, and Recommendations for Action.   New York: McGraw-Hill, 1973.   282 p.

Comprehensive report on women and equality of opportunity in higher education.   Major chapters include women as undergraduates, in graduate and professional schools, women as faculty members and academic administrators, affirmative action (including legal background, some case histories, policy considerations, and recommendations) and suggestions for change in attitudes and policies.

612.   Carnegie Commission on the Future of Higher Education.   A
        Chance to Learn: An Action Agenda for Equal Opportunity in
        Higher Education: A Special Report and Recommendations.
        New York: McGraw-Hill, 1970.   31 p.

        Series of recommendations to increase educational opportun-
        ities in higher education for all qualified students.

613.   Carnegie Council on Policy Studies in Higher Education.
        Making Affirmative Action Work in Higher Education: An
        Analysis of Institutional and Federal Policies with Recom-
        mendations: A Report. . . .   San Francisco: Jossey-Bass
        Publishers, 1975.   272 p.

        Carnegie Council calls for major changes in government and
        institutional policies designed to end discrimination in hiring,
        promoting, and paying faculty and staff.   27 recommendations
        are made related to eleven major themes, including increas-
        ing the supply of qualified women and minorities for faculty
        hiring, and a better distribution of women and minorities
        among fields of academic specialization and academic ranks.
        Chapters include problems and viewpoints, women and minor-
        ities on faculties--recent changes, academic policies under
        the impact of affirmative action, background of federal poli-
        cies, goals and timetables, deficiencies in the administration
        of federal programs, grievances and enforcement procedures,
        and who should have what responsibilities.   Statistical tables
        and extensive bibliography included.

614.   _____. Selective Admission in Higher Education: Com-
        ment and Recommendations and Two Reports.   San Francisco:
        Jossey-Bass, 1977.

        Analysis of selective admissions policies, procedures, and
        programs.   The first of three parts includes a number of
        guidelines for public and academic policymakers in the na-
        tional debate over special admissions programs for minority
        groups.   The Council recommends that race should be con-
        sidered by professional schools in admitting students who have
        already met impartial academic standards.   The other two
        reports, by members of the Educational Testing Service,
        contain enrollment data on minority admissions, and the na-
        ture of selective admissions and policy issues at the root of
        reverse discrimination cases.

615.   Carroll, Mary Ann.   "Women in Administration in Higher
        Education. "   Contemporary Education.   43 (February, 1972),
        214-218.

        Explores why there are so few women administrators in high-
        er education and suggests what women should do to increase
        their numbers in educational administration.

616.   Cass, James.   "Affirmative Action in the Academy. "   Satur-
        day Review.   2 (February 8, 1973), 45.

        Discusses the opposing viewpoints of affirmative action in
        higher education, particularly the ideas of Derek Bok, Pre-
        sident of Harvard, and Sidney Hook of New York University.
        Author suggests that racial diversity among faculty and stu-
        dents prepares students to live in the contemporary world.

617.   Castro, Raymond E. and John Garcia.   "Admissions: Who
        Shall Occupy the Seats of Privilege? " Aztlan.   6 (Fall,
        1975), 363-377.

        Briefly discusses the Marco DeFunis and Allan Bakke cases
        on "reverse discrimination. " Argues for a pluralistic ap-
        proach to testing admissions to professional schools so that
        institutions can fairly meet their responsibility to all students
        and to society-at-large.

618.   Cebulski, Bonnie G.   Affirmative Action Versus Seniority--
        Is Conflict Inevitable? Monograph of the California Public
        Employee Relations Program.   California University, Berke-
        ley.   Institute of Industrial Relations, 1977.   58 p.

        Discusses the concept of affirmative action with reference to
        legislation and national policy and the interrelationship of af-
        firmative action to layoffs by seniority.   Discusses also case
        law on issues of seniority and affirmative action in the pri-
        vate and public sector and a case of layoffs in the public
        sector in California, with particular attention given to minor-
        ity layoffs.

619.   "Census Shows Blacks Are Falling Behind in College Enroll-
        ment. " The New York Times.   May 5, 1976, p. 51.

        Conferees at National Association for Equal Education in
        Higher Education conference notes blacks comprise only 2
        per cent of doctoral graduates in the country; advocate that
        attention be given to increasing this figure.

620.   Centra, John A.   Women, Men, and the Doctorate.   Prince-
        ton, New Jersey: Educational Testing Service, 1974.   214 p.

        First major national survey that compared the experiences
        of women and men who have earned Ph. D. 's or Ed. D. 's.
        Analyzed responses from 3, 658 women and men matched ac-
        cording to disciplines, the institutions they attended, and
        their year of graduation.   Author concludes that women have
        not reaped the rewards many of their male colleagues enjoy,
        although the situation is improving somewhat, probably due
        to the women's rights movement and Federally mandated Af-
        firmative Action programs.

621.   Chait, Richard, and Ford, Andrew.   "Can a College Have
        Tenure and Affirmative Action Too?"   The Chronicle of
        Higher Education.   8 (October 1, 1973), 16.

        Discusses why compliance with affirmative action regulations
        may well end, or at least drastically transform, academe's
        tenure practices.

622.   Chalmers, E. L., Jr.   "Achieving Equity for Women in
        Higher Education: Graduate Enrollment and Faculty Status."
        Journal of Higher Education.   43 (October, 1972), 517-524.

        Focuses upon three points where there exists the greatest
        difference in treatment between men and women: admissions
        to post-baccalaureate education, appointment to faculty posi-
        tions, and faculty advancement.   Suggestions for achieving
        equity included.

623.   Chicanos in Higher Education: Proceedings of a National In-
        stitute on Access to Higher Education for the Mexican Amer-
        ican.   Edited by Henry J. Casso and Gilbert D. Roman.
        Albuquerque: University of New Mexico Press, 1976.   177
        p.

        Conference was held to clarify the issues in higher education
        as they related to the Chicano, to identify the current trends,
        and to provide some direction for the future.   Includes ad-
        dresses by Roger Heyns, President of the American Council
        on Education on "Equality of Access to Postsecondary Educa-
        tion for Full Participation in American Society," and Peter
        Holmes, former Director, Office for Civil Rights, on "The
        Ineffective Mechanisms of Affirmative Action Plans in an
        Academic Setting."

624.   Cohen, Carl.   "Why Racial Preference Is Illegal and Im-
        moral."   Commentary.   67 (June, 1979), 40-52.

        Discusses racial preference within the context of underlying
        moral and legal premises, focusing particularly upon the
        Weber v. Kaiser Aluminum case, with brief allusions to the
        Bakke case.   Such preference violates the rights of individu-
        als to equal treatment under the law, produces racial dis-
        harmony, and fails to make the morally crucial distinctions
        between the blameworthy and the blameless, between the de-
        serving and the undeserving.

625.   Cole, Robert.   "Title IX: A Long Dazed Journey into
        Rights."   Phi Delta Kappan.   57 (May, 1976), 575-577, 586.

        Describes the attempts to clarify what is required by Title
        IX and to implement it (or not to implement it) and discusses
        the problems of enforcement.

626. "College Faculties: Over 40, White and Male. " The New
      York Times.   August 26, 1973, IV, p. 11.

      Describes in detail the study by Alan Bayer, for the Ameri-
      can Council on Education, Teaching Faculty in Academe,
      1972-1973.

627. "College Presidents React to AAUW Guidelines on Equality. "
      American Association of University Women.   Journal.   Janu-
      ary, 1972, p. 5.

      AAUW report "Campus 1970: Where Do Women Stand?" re-
      vealed that women on American campuses are underpaid at
      all levels.   NOW and WEAL have filed suits against more
      than 250 colleges and universities and all medical schools
      charging sex discrimination.

628. "Colleges Feeling Impact of New U. S. Civil-Rights Effort. "
      The Chronicle of Higher Education.   16 (February 27, 1978),
      7-8.

      University campuses have begun to feel the impact of a far-
      reaching agreement that the Office for Civil Rights (HEW)
      negotiated last year to settle lawsuits charging that it had
      failed to enforce federal antibias laws.   The settlement,
      worked out with several civil-rights groups, committed OCR
      to significantly step up its investigations of how institutions
      were complying with equal-opportunity regulations.   Most
      agreements require institutions to perform statistical analyses
      to determine whether women and members of minority groups
      are employed in lower numbers than their availability would
      suggest should be the case.   Includes criticisms of federal
      investigations intruding upon institutional autonomy.

629. "Colleges Given Antibias Guides. " The New York Times.
      October 5, 1972, p. 20.

      HEW issues on October 4, guidelines for colleges to follow
      in complying with Federal nondiscrimination orders on em-
      ployment of minorities and women, making clear that quotas
      are not required.

630. "Colleges Warned on Reverse Job Discrimination. " The New
      York Times.   December 13, 1974, p. 16.

      Office for Civil Rights Director, Peter Holmes, issues
      memorandum to college and university presidents stating that
      they may not discriminate against white males while trying
      to attract women or minority groups.   In pursuing affirma-
      tive action policies, institutions may not lower job standards
      or designate certain jobs on basis of race or sex to meet
      employment goal.   Memo issued after widespread misunder-

standing over enforcement of Federal executive order prohibiting discrimination by colleges holding Federal contracts.

631.   Commission on Discrimination.   "Affirmative Action in Higher Education: A Report by the Council Commission on Discrimination. "   AAUP Bulletin.   59 (Summer, 1973), 178-183.

Position paper on the role of affirmative action in the elimination of discriminatory practices in academic recruiting, appointment, and advancement.   The idea of affirmative action is the revision of practices and standards to assure that institutions draw from the largest market place of human resources.   Affirmative action is "wholly consistent with the highest aspirations" of university excellence and "outstanding quality" and should not be used as the very instrument of racial or sexual discrimination which it deplores.

632.   Connolly, H. X.   "Assessing Affirmative Action. "   Intellect. 106 (October, 1977), 134-136.

Discusses the economic background for affirmative action legislation.   Raises number of issues and obstacles to affirmative action advocates, including the resolution of the problem of how to balance individual, group, and social rights and responsibilities and needs.   Suggests that affirmative action, to be successful, must be placed within the more comprehensive framework of economic justice.

633.   Coser, Rose L.   "Affirmative Action: Letter to a Worried Colleague. "   Dissent.   No. 22 (Fall, 1975), 366-369.

Argues that numerical goals are not quotas, the former defined as hiring qualified women and minorities who otherwise would be excluded; universities use numerical considerations for admissions (e. g., offspring of alumni, regional representation); there is no evidence that numerical goals threaten standards, or evidence that hiring women and minorities over white males demonstrates lowered standards.   Affirmative action means "open search"--the application of objective and universalistic means for recruitment rather than the old-boys club network.

634.   "Court to Rule in College Admissions Case. "   The New York Times.   December 27, 1976, I, 18.

Gives background of Bakke reverse discrimination case, arguments for and against special admissions programs and outlook for such programs in future discussed.

635.   Cross, K. Patricia.   "Women Want Equality in Higher Education. "   Educational Horizons.   52 (Winter, 1973/74), 72-76.

Article investigates the inequality of opportunity for women in higher education.

636.   Crossland, Fred E. Minority Access to College: A Ford Foundation Report. New York: Schocken Books, 1971. 139 p.

Presents data on black students in higher education and barriers to their access. Efforts to lower these barriers discussed.

637.   Crowfoot, James E. and others. "Whatever Happened to Affirmative Action?" Integrated Education. 14 (November-December, 1976), 5-7.

Identifies five specific tactics for blunting affirmative action in universities: obliterate or contain responsibility, delay responsibility, develop and operate recruitment efforts designed to fail, recruit minorities and women so they will subsequently fail, and delegitimize applicants.

638.   Culliton, Barbara. "Weinberger on Affirmative Action. " Science. 189 (August 22, 1975), 618.

Secretary of HEW discusses affirmative action as applied to universities, its present "statistical and mechanistic" approach, and the pressures both to weaken and to strengthen the regulations. HEW wants universities "to broaden their base of recruiting, to make it national, " so people can have the opportunity to compete. Universities should appoint whom they think best, Weinberger concluded, having completed this process.

639.   Curiei, Ramon. "Avoiding the Pitfalls of Affirmative Action. " Association of Departments of Foreign Languages. Bulletin. 10 (November, 1978), 18-20.

Discusses the compliance regulations dealing with recruitment to postemployment practices in university language departments.

640.   Dancy, North Barry. "Affirmative Action in Labor Contracts: Some Implications for College and University Personnel. " Civil Rights Digest. 5 (October, 1972), 41-45.

Discusses legal theory and practical aspects of affirmative action plan, encouraging institutions to look at their histories of hiring practices, and to set goals that can be realistically met in expanding their hiring practices for minority groups.

641.   Darland, M. G. and others. "Applications of Multivariate Regression to Studies of Salary Differences Between Men and Women Faculty. " American Statistical Association. Proceedings, 1973. Pp. 120-130.

642.   Davis, Abraham L. and Hope, Corrie. "Some Notes on Re-
        verse Discrimination. " Review of Black Political Economy.
        9 (Winter, 1979), 199-207.

        The purpose of the article is to clarify some confusion that
        the term "reverse discrimination" has evoked. Author cites
        recent court cases on the subject, including the Bakke case,
        and refutes the argument that blacks are being favored over
        whites in higher education.

643.   Davis, Bernard D. , M. D. "[Academic Standards in Medical
        Schools.]" The New England Journal of Medicine. 294
        (May 13, 1976), 1118-1119.

        Harvard Medical School physician raises the question of bal-
        ancing medicine's obligation to promote social justice with
        the primary obligation to protect the public interest in pro-
        viding competent M. D. 's. Suggests that the quest for social
        justice has at times led to lowered standards in medical
        school admissions and grading.

644.   _____. "Minority Admissions: A Third Option. " Wall
        Street Journal. 189 (August 23, 1977), 16.

        Discusses the critical issue of how medical schools should
        balance their primary obligation to screen for the aptitude of
        their candidates and to ensure the competence of their gradu-
        ates with the more recently recognized obligation to help
        rectify past injustices and to help meet long ignored needs of
        underprivileged groups. Suggests a third option: to adjust,
        supplement, or stretch standards for judging minority group
        applicants, but only within limits of satisfactory performance.
        Adjusted standards would determine the numbers of minor-
        ities admitted, not vice versa.

645.   DeStefano, Johanna S. "Response to 'Return of Racial
        Quotas'" [by Ornstein, Allan C. November, 1975]. Educa-
        tional Forum. 40 (November, 1975), 114-117.

        Criticizes Ornstein for being biased and lacking in evidence
        to back up his objections to affirmative action and for as-
        suming that no qualified blacks exist for academic positions
        and if they are hired, they create mediocrity. Reverse dis-
        crimination is a red herring because affirmative action
        means equal opportunity for all people.

646.   Dickinson, Elizabeth. "Affirmative Action and American Li-
        brarianship. " In Advances in Librarianship. 1978. Vol.
        8. New York: Academic Press, 1978. Pp. 82-133.

        Presents an overview of the legal and socioeconomic aspects
        of affirmative action in general, librarianship in particular.
        Section includes section on affirmative action in academic
        libraries. Excellent bibliography included.

647/48.   Dinerman, Beatrice.   "Sex Discrimination in Academia. "
          Journal of Higher Education.   42 (April, 1971), 253-264.

          Refutes stereotype that women faculty members are inherent-
          ly inadequate in credibility, innovativeness, and productivity.
          Includes evidence of sex discrimination in academia which is
          facilitated by the absence of objective, empirical criteria by
          which to judge the quality of teaching performance.

649.   Divine, Thomas M.   "Women in the Academy: Sex Discrim-
          ination in University Faculty Hiring and Promotion. "   Journal
          of Law and Education.   5 (October, 1976), 429-451.

          Briefly reviews federal laws prohibiting sex discrimination in
          higher education, and the difficulties of enforcing anti-dis-
          crimination laws.   Distinguishes between two university hir-
          ing models: the ordinal model and the skill pool model.
          The former, which assumes that applicants can be ranked
          according to merit, violates the law and permits covert em-
          ployment discrimination and provides a ready justification
          for failure to meet affirmative action goals.   Advocates the
          implementation of a skill pool model composed of a number
          of individuals who are capable of performing a given job.

650.   Dorfman, Robert, and Cell, Donald C.   "Nearly Keeping Up:
          Report on the Economic Status of the Profession, 1975-76. "
          AAUP Bulletin.   62 (August, 1976), 195-207.

          Average faculty compensation at institutions reporting com-
          parable data both this year and last increased by 6. 4 per
          cent.   Related statistics presented on faculty status, fe-
          males, medical schools, librarians, and financial problems.

651.   Ducey, Walter J.   "Equal Employment Opportunity Comes
          to the Campus. "   The Journal of the College and University
          Personnel Association.   25 (January, 1974), 1-13.

          Presents informational background for college and university
          administrators who are shaping new programs necessary to
          meet broadened and strengthened Civil Rights Act.

652.   Dunkle, Margaret C.   "Title IX: New Rules for an Old
          Game. "   Teachers College Record.   76 (February, 1975),
          385-399.

          Outlines statutory provisions of Title IX of the Education
          Amendments of 1972, and examines a number of the student
          issues which have generated the most controversy, such as
          admission to schools, financial aid, competitive athletics,
          and discriminatory rules and regulations.

653.   Duster, Troy.   "The Structure of Privilege and Its Universe
          of Discourse. "   American Sociologist.   11 (May, 1976), 73-
          78.

Discusses the relationship between universalism and merit and the relationship between structure of privilege and its maintenance. Discusses the past century of affirmative action in favor of white gentile males in such areas as medical schools, sports, business and labor which has perpetuated social stratification based upon race and sex. Concludes that affirmative action programs are worthy of support when they are designed to break down the cycle of exclusion and privilege.

654.   Eckert, Ruth E.   "Academic Woman Revisited."   Liberal Education.   57 (December, 1971), 479-487.

Study of faculty members in Minnesota throws light on when and why women chose academic careers, how many had undergraduate achievements and assistantships, how female and male faculty compared in rank and research and scholarly writing. Major implications are that women undergraduates must be made acquainted with the opportunities of academic careers, financial support must be made available to all qualified candidates, and in-service education of women faculty demands attention.

655.   Eckess, Marie Conti.   "We Had to Hire a Woman Syndrome." Thrust for Educational Leadership.   6 (October, 1976), 22, 26.

Discusses five prevalent practices by those who want to defeat Title IX and kindle flames of resentment and discrimination between men and women faculty.

656.   "Education: The Wrong Affirmative Action."   The New York Times.   March 29, 1975, p. 22.

Six letters from professors who are members of the Committee of Academic Nondiscrimination and Integrity criticize full-page advertisement by the Committee for Affirmative Action in Universities advocating hiring of women and minorities; contends numerical goals suggested by such hiring practices cause less-qualified persons to be chosen; calls for outlawing all numerical goals and concentrating on positive affirmative action for development and enforcement of effective, nondiscriminatory hiring and promotion procedures.

657.   Egelston, Judy Cobb.   "Sex Bias in Publications and Grant Awards."   Journal of the National Association for Women Deans, Administrators, and Counselors.   38 (Winter, 1976), 66-69.

Discusses the reasons why women are underrepresented in the faculty of prestigious universities and do not publish as much as men do in academic journals. Evidence presented to suggest that anonymity for authors and their institutional

affiliation improves women's chances for more of their papers being published.

658.   Engineers Joint Council. Engineering Manpower Commission.
        Statistics on Women and Minority Students in Engineering.
        A Report by the Engineering Manpower Commission of Engi-
        neers Joint Council. New York: The Commission, 1974.
        21 p.

        Analysis of data on women and minority engineering students
        in higher education. Tables included on engineering field,
        by degree level of men and women, class standing of women
        and minority students, high school background, and financial
        support for these students.

659.   English, Richard A., and Settle, Theodore J. "Minority
        Students in Higher Education." Integrated Education. 14
        (May-June, 1976), 3-6.

        Advocates federal program of financial assistance for minor-
        ity students seeking graduate and professional education and
        direct financial support for graduate schools and universities
        to develop more effective delivery systems and to recruit
        and retain minorities. Provides statistics on participation
        of minorities in higher education, 1960-1974, distribution of
        minorities by field of study, and section on barriers to
        graduate and professional education.

660.   Epstein, Benjamin R. and Forster, Arnold. Preferential
        Treatment and Quotas. New York: B'nai B'rith Anti-De-
        famation League, 1974. 32 p.

        Criticizes federal government for failing to take action
        against preferential treatment and quota system in higher
        education admissions and hirings; argues that college admin-
        istrators, fearing loss of government funding, practice pref-
        erential treatment, which is leading to the polarization of
        society along racial, religious, and ethnic lines and to loss
        of those best qualified to serve it. Epstein is National Di-
        rector of B'nai B'rith Anti-Defamation League.

661.   "Evaluating the Impact of Affirmative Action: A Look at the
        Federal Contract Compliance Program: A Symposium."
        Industrial and Labor Relations Review. 29 (July, 1976),
        485-584.

        Contents include:

662.   Gregory J. Ahart. A Process Evaluation of the Contract
            Compliance Program in Nonconstruction Industry

663.   Robert J. Flanagan. Actual Versus Potential Impact of
            Government Antidiscrimination Programs

664.   Morris Goldstein and Robert S. Smith. The Estimated Im-
         pact of the Antidiscrimination Program Aimed at Federal
         Contractors

665.   James J. Heckman and Kenneth I. Wolpin. Does the Con-
         tract Compliance Program Work? An Analysis of Chicago
         Data

666.   George E. Johnson and Finis Welch. The Labor Market Im-
         plications of an Economy-wide Affirmative Action Program

         Includes comments by Glen G. Cain, Orley Ashenfelter, and
         James E. Jones, Jr.

667.   Evans, Doris A. and Jackson, Edgar B., Jr. "Deans of
         Minority Student Affairs in Medical Schools." Journal of
         Medical Education. 51 (March, 1976), 197-199.

         Rationale is presented for medical schools to hire deans who
         are members of a minority group, with special capabilities
         and responsibilities for representing the interests of minority
         students and for making opportunities available so that more
         minority students might enter medical school.

668.   Evans, Therman E. "Reverse Discrimination in Medical
         Education." Journal of Negro Education. 46 (Fall, 1977),
         373-379.

         Refutes argument that reverse discrimination exists in medi-
         cal school admissions, that admissions standards are low-
         ered for minority students, and that there is a lack of quali-
         fied minority candidates. Calls for the institutionalization
         of affirmative action which includes fairness, equity, and
         compensation.

669.   Ezorsky, Gertrude. "Exchange of Letters." The New York
         Review of Books. 21 (October 31, 1974), 44-46; 22 (April
         3, 1975), 36-38.

         Author responds to critics of her earlier article, "The Fight
         Over University Women."

670.   _____. "The Fight Over University Women." The New
         York Review of Books. 21 (May 16, 1974), 32-39.

         Discusses the gap which exists between women trained and
         women hired by major universities, and the general condition
         of sex discrimination which exists in most universities.
         Demonstrates that the actual hiring system is the "old buddy"
         system and that numerical goals are not quotas. Shows that
         some of the allegations made against HEW are deliberately
         misconstrued facts. HEW has never actually cancelled con-
         tracts to any university and has accepted the failure to reach

hiring goals when they felt the university involved acted in good faith.

671. _____. "Hiring Faculty Women. " The New York Times. October 11, 1976, p. 27.

Discusses why numerical hiring goals by HEW for women faculty members helps to extend impartiality in selection process. Defends HEW's goals system and explains why it is necessary.

672. _____. "Hiring Women Faculty. " Philosophy and Public Affairs. 7 (Fall, 1977), 82-91.

Distinguishes between two types of goals, impartial and preferential. Refutes idea that HEW imposes quotas on colleges.

673. "Faculties: For More Women and More Minorities. " The New York Times. April 2, 1972, IV, p. 9.

Article discusses controversy over HEW's requirement that universities increase the hiring of women and minorities on their faculty or lose Federal aid; notes there is much confusion over exact terms of federal requirements and fear among many university officials of federal interference with academic freedom. Chart compares salaries of men and women on university faculties.

674. "Faculty Backlash. " Newsweek. 80 (December 4, 1972), 127-128.

Discusses male backlash in academia, as a result of efforts by women to secure positions and promotions. Article describes organized efforts by Committee on Academic Nondiscrimination and Integrity, led by Sidney Hook, to persuade Congress to lift HEW's guidelines on affirmative action. HEW's response to this male backlash described, along with reaction of many equal rights crusaders who believe that male critics are over-reacting, upset because white males must suddenly compete with blacks and women.

675. Faia, Michael A. "Discrimination and Exchange: The Double Burden of the Female Academic. " Pacific Sociological Review. 20 (January, 1977), 3-20.

Recent survey data indicate that a large part of the "discrimination gap" has been eliminated. Article focuses on evidence that females who wish to pursue careers in academe often suffer "opportunity costs" in terms of involvement in familism. Exchange theory suggests the hypothesis that reduced salary discrimination, over the long run, may be associated with an increase in opportunity costs for females entering the academic profession.

676.   Falk, Carol H.   "The 'Benign Discrimination' Issue. "   Wall
       Street Journal. 189 (April 1, 1977), 12.

       Discusses the concept of affirmative action, arguments for
       and against it, pending cases on preferential hiring before
       the U. S. Supreme Court, including the Bakke case, and how
       the Justices have ruled in the past on compensatory hiring.
       Author believes that the central issue is the point at which
       extending the constitution's guarantees to minorities and wom-
       en infringes on the equal protection and due process rights
       of whites and males.

677.   Farber, Stephen.   "The Earnings and Promotion of Women
       Faculty. "   American Economic Review.   67 (March, 1977),
       199-206.

       Purpose of study is to test whether the results of cross-sec-
       tional studies of sex differences in academic rank, promotion
       and earnings profiles are similar to results derived from
       longitudinal data.   Male and female academic scientists were
       compared by ranks and ages.

678.   Faust, Pamela.   "Title IX: It Means More than Pink Foot-
       balls. "   Thrust for Educational Leadership.   5 (May, 1976),
       6-8.

       Discusses Title IX legislation: admissions, treatment of stu-
       dents, courses, athletics, student health, financial aid to
       students, counseling, and employment.

679.   "Federal Hearings Planned on College Hiring Policies. "
       The New York Times.   August 18, 1975, p. 26.

       HEW Department begins series of informal hearings to study
       rules governing affirmative action plans to end employment
       discrimination in higher education; issues new guidelines to
       clarify what information colleges must give Federal govern-
       ment to comply with affirmative action programs; comment
       by HEW Department official Martin H. Gerry and Clark Kerr.

680.   Feiner, John.   "Preferential Admissions from the Economic
       Perspective of Information Costs. "   UCLA Law Review.   26
       (October, 1978), 162-202.

       Presents an economic justification for racially preferential
       admissions programs and discusses programs within the con-
       text of current debates over the constitutionality of such pro-
       grams.   Explores an alternative economic justification for
       preferential admissions policies.

681.   Feldman, Saul D.   Escape from the Doll's House.   Carnegie
       Foundation for the Advancement of Teaching.   New York:
       McGraw-Hill Book Co. , 1974.

Analysis of data relating to women in higher education, male and female attitudes, and disciplines.

682.   "Female Academics Find Progress Slow. " The New York Times. November 13, 1977, XII, p. 13.

Article shows slow progress, setbacks women teachers facing in struggle for sex equality in academe. Cites statistics on faculty, by rank and sex, based on U. S. Office of Education study.

683.   Ferber, Marianne A. , and Kordick, Betty. "Sex Differentials in the Earnings of Academic Women. " Industrial and Labor Relations Review. 31 (January, 1978), 227-238.

Replicates the type of regressions used by Bayer and Astin to determine rewards of male and female members of college faculties. Addresses the impact of women's life styles on their performance in order to test the hypothesis of the critics of affirmative action whose arguments on behalf of "human capital" cause salary differentials between male and female faculty members. Considers also whether reward differentials may be the cause, as well as result, of differences in performance.

684.   _____, and Loeb, Jane W. "Performance, Rewards, and Perceptions of Sex Discrimination Among Male and Female Faculty. " American Journal of Sociology. 78 (January, 1973), 995-1002.

Study relates marital and parental status to productivity, salary, and rank for men and women. Productivity and reward of men and women are related to the percentage of the department which is female. Question is whether "women's" fields differ from "men's" in either the productivity or the reward of their specialists. Deals also with the perceptions concerning the existence of sex discrimination.

685.   _____, and Westmiller, Anne. "Sex and Race Differences in Nonacademic Wages on a University Campus. " Journal of Human Resources. 11 (Summer, 1976), 366-373.

Study tests the hypothesis that, when other variables are taken into account, race and sex are not statistically significant in explaining wages in different occupations. The results, using data for the nonacademic work force of a large university campus, do not support the hypothesis. On the contrary, they show that sex and race influence the pattern of wage rates and earnings by occupation.

686.   Ferguson, Mary Anne. "Affirmative Action: HEW, Women, and the Law. " Association of the Departments of Foreign Languages. Bulletin. 3 (March, 1972), 43-46.

Describes the affirmative action regulations as applied to
higher education. Gives evidence that improvements in the
position of women in 1971 bore a close correlation to the
presence or threat of presence of HEW. Discrimination because of sex is more apparent in promotion and tenure than
in hiring.

687.   Fields, Cheryl. "Affirmative Action: Campus Officers Or-
         ganize, Assess Their Status. " The Chronicle of Higher Edu-
         cation. 10 (May 5, 1975), 8.

Describes the conference of 400 affirmative action officers
and other interested persons held at the University of Texas
in which they formed the American Association for Affirmative Action. Presents brief summaries of speeches by various federal and university officials on the status and future
prospects of affirmative action in higher education and employment.

688.   _____ . "Affirmative Action, 4 Years Later. " The Chron-
         icle of Higher Education. 8 (August 5, 1974), 1, 8-9.

Describes the status of affirmative action on college campuses
four years after its inception, with no dramatic changes in
the composition of college faculties and staff. Cites various
problems in assuring compliance with affirmative action regulations.

689.   _____ . "Are Job 'Goals' Quotas? " The Chronicle of High-
         er Education. 9 (October 15, 1974), 7.

Cites testimony of witnesses for and against affirmative action
in higher education before the House Special Subcommittee on
Education, chaired by James G. O'Hara.

690.   _____ . "Colleges Told: Hire the Best-Qualified: U. S.
         Memo Says Race, Sex, and Ethnicity Must Play No Part in
         Selecting People. " The Chronicle of Higher Education. 9
         (December 23, 1974), 1.

Describes, and provides text of memo sent to heads of 2, 800
institutions by the Director of the Office for Civil Rights,
Peter Holmes. Outlines examples of acceptable affirmative
action. Designed to explain more clearly the hiring obligations of colleges subject to affirmative action regulations.

691.   _____ . "Fifty-Seven Rights Groups Hit HEW on Anti-Bias
         Enforcement. " The Chronicle of Higher Education. 11
         (January 22, 1976), 7-8.

Civil rights groups criticize the Office for Civil Rights for
failure to enforce laws prohibiting race and sex discrimination
in higher education.

692.   _____, and Winkler, Karen J.   "U. S. Rights Agency
Caught in Crossfire. "   The Chronicle of Higher Education.
11 (February 23, 1976), 1, 10.

Minority and civil rights groups call the U. S. Office for
Civil Rights lax and colleges say they are swamped in paperwork complying with affirmative action regulations and anti-
bias laws.

693.   "The Fight for a Fair Shake on Campus. "   The New York
Times.   October 8, 1972, IV, p. 11.

Article finds fewer women attend college than men, that only
19. 6 per cent of college administrators are women and do
not get as high salaries nor tenure as easily as their male
counterparts; graphs show percentages of men and women
holding various academic positions and their comparative
salaries.

694.   Fineberg, Solomon A.   "Must Affirmative Action Be Divi-
sive? "   Crisis.   82 (October, 1975), 287-291.

Affirmative action is seen as causing dissension and cleavage
in civil rights coalition.   Requisites suggested for winning
support for affirmative action are thorough knowledge of its
rationale and components, assuring whites that they will not
be pushed out of jobs, and continued emphasis on the urgency
for affirmative action.

695.   Fishel, Andrew.   "Review of 'Making Affirmative Action
Work in Higher Education, ' a report by the Carnegie Council
on Policy Studies in Higher Education. "   Journal of Higher
Education.   47 (July/August, 1976), 481-484.

Author, an official of HEW, concludes that the wide spectrum
of views on affirmative action in higher education were considered but not fairly represented in the report itself.

696.   _____.   "Organizational Positions on Title IX. " Journal
of Higher Education.   47 (January/February, 1976), 93-105.

Comments submitted by organizations and individuals to the
Department of HEW on the proposed regulations to implement
Title IX of the Education Amendments of 1972 reveals that
groups representing women, teachers, students, and civil
rights commissions substantially differ on sex discrimination
issues from education administrators and other education
groups.

697.   Fleming, John E. , and others.   The Case for Affirmative
Action for Blacks in Higher Education.   Washington, D. C. :
Howard University.   Institute for the Study of Educational
Policy, 1978.   436 p.

Discusses the importance of affirmative action and other
strategies for achieving equal opportunity, the status of black
education prior to the Civil War to the time prior to affirmative action, the constitutional and legal basis for affirmative
action and related Federal programs, policies and practices
of implementation by the Federal government; and four case
studies of affirmative action in institutions of higher education are analyzed.   Contains a lengthy bibliography.

698.   .   The Lengthening Shadow of Slavery: A Historical
Justification for Affirmative Action for Blacks in Higher Edu-
cation.   Howard University: Institute for the Study of Educational Policy.   Washington, D. C.:   Howard University Press,
1976.   162p.

Study chronicles selected events in the history of black people in America, from slavery t the present, and examines
certain key factors which impeded or enhanced their struggle
to acquire an education.   As noted in the Preface, the history of black education "pointedly" illustrates that a sustained commitment to affirmative action is necessary to
rectify generations of denial.

699.   Florida State University, Tallahassee.   Manual for Affirma-
tive Action Program Development and Implementation in
Higher Education Institutions.   Tallahassee: Florida State
University, 1974.   70 p.
(ED 107 193)

The purpose of the manual is to provide clearly defined information, instructions, and processes that can direct and
facilitate development and provide effective implementation
of affirmative action plans as action-oriented procedures in
higher education.   The goals are included under three broad
headings: background information, writing an affirmative action program, and affirmative action implementation.

700.   Fontham, Michael R.   "Legalization of Employment Discrimination Against White Males. "   Journal of Intergroup Relations.   6 (December, 1978), 30-39.

Argues that the intervention of government to require special
treatment of designated groups on the basis of race, color,
or sex is inconsistent with principles of equal treatment under American law.   Regardless of past discrimination, governmental action to favor minorities at the expense of white
males is unjustified.

701.   Fort, Vance.   "Affirmative Action in the 80s: Toward a
Politics of Equality. "   Cross Reference: A Journal of Public Policy and Multicultural Education.   1 (March-April,
1978), 182-209.

Suggests that institutions of higher education adopt admissions procedures which take into account indices of social and economic disadvantage, thereby recruiting disadvantaged whites.

702.   Foster, Ashley. "Some Implications of Quotas." Intellect. 102 (February, 1974), 293.

Discusses the question of quotas in higher education as related to the idea of merit, proportional representation, opportunity for social mobility, and diversity in talents. Asks whether quotas really will create an equality of opportunity.

703.   Fratkin, Susan. "Collective Bargaining and Affirmative Action." Journal of the College and University Personnel Association. 26 (July-August, 1975), 53-62.

Reviews the laws and decisions applicable to affirmative action and collective bargaining. Identifies conflict areas such as seniority rights, grievance procedures, and fair representation. Author concludes that unionization can merely institutionalize present-day discrimination unless bargaining parties give more than lip service to equality mandates.

704.   Freeman, Bonnie Cook. "Faculty Women in the American University: Up the Down Staircase." Higher Education. 6 (May, 1977), 165-188.

Discusses the status of academic women, particularly in the most prestigious institutions, compared to that of faculty men. Reveals inequalities in rank, prestige, rewards, work environment, and social expectations. Situation discussed in terms of women's movement, in general, government policy, and university personnel policies.

705.   Freeman, Richard B. "The New Job Market for Black Academicians." Industrial and Labor Relations Review. 20 (January, 1974), 161-174.

Study shows that the historic employment pattern of black academicians has been significantly altered in recent years. An analysis of data for 1969 and 1973 indicates that among other changes, black male faculty members have received more job offers than white faculty members with similar qualification; black faculty have obtained an income advantage over white colleagues; the number of blacks in primarily white institutions has increased substantially; and using the number of publications as a criterion, hiring standards appear to have been lowered for blacks. Author suggests federal affirmative action programs one reason for these changes.

706.   Fuerst, J. S. "Quotas as an Instrument of Public Policy." Society. 13 (January-February, 1976), 11, 18-21.

Suggests that the key question is not whether quotas are right,
or wrong, but at what level particular quotas should be set,
what the rate of change to achieve a particular goal should
be, when to increase or eliminate them, and the establishment of procedures and personnel used for executing them.

707.   Furniss, W. Todd and Albjerg, Patricia, eds. Women in
Higher Education. Washington, D. C.: American Council on
Education, 1974. 336 p.

Contents grouped under headings: Women in higher education; the woman student; the woman professional in higher
education; academic programs; affirmative action; contexts
for decisions. Section on Affirmative Action includes:

708.   Fleming, Robben W. , The Implementation of Affirmative Action Programs

709.   Kanowitz, Leo, Some Legal Aspects of Affirmative Action
Programs

710.   Klotzburger, Katherine M. , Advisory Committee Role in
Constructing Affirmative Action Programs

711.   Rogers, Martha P. , The Role of the Equal Employment Opportunity Commission

712.   Rumbarger, Margaret L. , The Great Quota Debate and Other
Issues in Affirmative Action

713.   Gallup Opinion Poll.   "Ability, Not Preferential Treatment,
Should Resolve Hiring, Placing Students. " Gallup Opinion
Index. Report No. 143. (June, 1977), pp. 22-23.

Poll indicates that 83 per cent of 1550 people believed that
reverse discrimination should not be used in hiring in college admissions; differences in opinions by sex, race, education, and geographical region noted.

714.   Garcia, Ricardo L. "Affirmative Action Hiring: Some Perceptions. " Journal of Higher Education. 45 (April, 1974),
268-272.

Discusses the concerns of both the minority candidates and
the institutions as related to affirmative action in higher education.

715.   Geadelmann, Patricia L. , and others. Equality in Sport for
Women. Washington, D. C.: American Alliance for Health,
Physical Education, and Recreation, 1977. 207 p.

Discusses equal rights and opportunities for women in the
field of physical education in nine articles. The major em-

phasis is on the legal aspects of sex discrimination. Appendix includes a list of organizations actively engaged in affirmative action.

716. Gemmell, Suzanne. "The Affirmative Action Officer."
      Journal of the National Association for Women Deans, Administrators, and Counselors. 9 (Winter, 1975), 87-92.

      Study of affirmative action officers in colleges and universities with enrollments of 10,000 or more students.   Discusses how affirmative action officers are appointed and salary discrimination against female officers.   Lack of support within the university community comes from misunderstanding of the need for goals of affirmative action and fear on the part of white males, with department chairmen and faculty members most likely to obstruct affirmative action efforts.   Only half of full time officers considered that they had the necessary authority to ensure proper implementation of affirmative action plans.

717. Gilbert, Neil, and Specht, Harry. "'Institutional Racism' and Educational Policy." Journal of Social Policy. 2 (January, 1973), 27-39.

      Divides institutional racism into collective racism, statistical racism, and institutional inequality. Describes the characteristics of each and what types of social policies and programs are required to solve them.   Sees a fundamental conflict between the values of equal opportunity and academic standards.

718. Gittell, Marilyn. "The Illusion of Affirmative Action."
      Change. 7 (October, 1975), 39-43.

      Traces resistance to affirmative action in universities, noting that federal agencies backed off from their tough stance, and concludes that "with the exception of an increase in lower-level class action suits, the status of women in the university has changed little."

719. Glazer, Nathan. Affirmative Discrimination: Ethnic Inequality and Public Policy. New York: Basic Books, 1975. 248 p.

      Reviews the background, including the laws, relating to governmental imposition of affirmative action upon employers, in housing, and in education.   Describes America's experience with ethnic groups, and how, in the 1960's, the principle of equal rights for all citizens gave way to affirmative discrimination--to group representation and statistical parity. Author calls for the reestablishment of the principle that rights attach to the individual, not the group, and that public policy must be exercised without distinction of race, color, or national origin.

720. _____. "Equal Opportunity Gone Wrong. " New Society.
      35 (January 22, 1976), 151-153.

      Discusses how American policy has moved strongly towards
      job quotas for minority groups. Argues that affirmative ac-
      tion tramples on individual rights and are unnecessary.

721. Goldstein, Jinny M. "Affirmative Action: Equal Employ-
      ment Rights for Women in Academia. " Teachers College
      Record. 74 (February, 1973), 395-422.

      Article seeks to analyze the genesis of the evolving relation-
      ship between the colleges and the federal government in the
      field of sex discrimination, to identify its patterns, and to
      project its implications, if any, upon both the rights of wom-
      en and the future of higher education. Also discusses the
      laws and court cases relating to affirmative action in aca-
      demia.

722. Goodman, Walter. "The Return of the Quota System. " The
      New York Times. September 10, 1972, VI, 29, 103-108+.

      Cites examples of increasing use of racial and sexual quotas
      in hiring policies at many of the nation's universities.

723. Goodwin, James C. "Playing Games with Affirmative Ac-
      tion. " The Chronicle of Higher Education. 10 (April 28,
      1975), 24.

      Claims that university structures are antithetical to affirma-
      tive action. Affirmative action offices are being demoted or
      rendered ineffective throughout the nation by means of policy,
      inaction and manipulation of data by the universities and by
      HEW. Serious open searches and objective selection of fac-
      ulty members have failed. Author gives examples of seven
      tactics to subvert affirmative action.

724. Gordon, Milton A. "An Analysis of Enrollment Data for
      Black Students in Institutions of Higher Education, from
      1940-1972. " Journal of Negro Education. 45 (Spring, 1976),
      117-121.

      Examines enrollment figures for blacks in colleges during
      the period 1940-1972; develops a statistic which author be-
      lieves is more significant than either enrollment figures or
      percentages in order to determine exactly what progress is
      being made by black college students, and predicts when
      black students will exist on college campuses in same pro-
      portion as blacks in population.

725. Gordon, Nancy M.; Morton, Thomas E.; and Braden, Ina C.
      "Faculty Salaries: Is There Discrimination by Sex, Race,
      and Discipline?" American Economic Review. 64 (June,
      1974), 419-427.

Investigates wage differentials for the faculty of a large urban university. Salary profile for the female faculty differs
from that for males primarily in the effects of race, age,
and department. Salary increments between the ranks are
similar on the average. A woman faculty member earns 11
per cent less than would be predicted for a man with her
characteristics. Blacks earn 13 per cent more than comparable whites.

726. _____, and Morton, Thomas E. "Staff Salary Structure
of a Large University." Journal of Human Resources. 11
(Summer, 1976), 374-382.

Uses data on all full-time staff (non-faculty) employees at a
large urban university and controls for age, education, sex,
marital status, years at the university, and job. Three
separate analyses were undertaken using three job-classifi-
cation schemes. Regression analyses for all three schemes
yield similar, unambiguous results. On average, after con-
trolling for variables listed above, a woman staff member
earns 7, 13, and 17 per cent less than a man.

727. Gordon, Vivian V. "An Analysis of the Legal, Moral, and
Practical Aspects of Affirmative Action." Western Journal
of Black Studies. 2 (March, 1978), 2-9.

Reviews the historical background of federal preferential
treatment to particular groups, such as affirmative action
programs. Author criticizes some arguments against affirmative action and cites necessity for such programs.

728. Gould, Ketayun H. "Goals and Timetables vs. Quotas: Non-
discrimination or Reverse Discrimination?" Journal of the
National Association for Women Deans, Administrators, and
Counselors. 40 (February, 1976), 3-6.

Explores the issues of the universities' commitments under
Executive Orders 11246 and 11375, and the current controversy revolving around the issue of goals vs. quotas. Available statistics show that the position of women and minorities
in academia has not improved significantly.

729. _____, and Kim, Bok-lim C. "Salary Inequities Between
Men and Women in Schools of Social Work: Myth or Reality?" Journal of Education for Social Work. 12 (Winter,
1976), 50-55.

Studies the effects of sex on salary differentials between men
and women faculty in schools of social work in the U.S. and
Canada. Results indicate a significant difference in mean
salaries of men and women when five variables are controlled for, and on all possible combinations of the five.

730.   Gould, Stuart H. and Van Den Berghe, Pierre L. "Particularism in Sociology Departments' Hiring Practices." Race. 15 (1973), 106-111.

Authors applied to sociology departments in 176 universities, using fictitious resumes. They mentioned whether they were black or female. Concluded that blacks have a decided edge in today's job market.

731.   "Government Accused of Laxity in Enforcing Sex Bias in the Statutes." The New York Times. November 27, 1974, p. 34.

Women's Equity Action League (WEAL) and four other organizations file class-action lawsuit accusing the federal government of failing to enforce antisex-discrimination laws. Suit, first of its kind in U. S. District Court, seeks order directing the Department of Labor and HEW to withhold millions of dollars in Federal funds from colleges and universities that allegedly discriminate against women; also seeks to force the two agencies to enforce antibias provisions of Executive Orders and Public Health Service law, and 1972 Education Amendments applying to colleges.

732.   Government Regulation of Higher Education. Edited by Walter C. Hobbs. Cambridge, Mass.: Ballinger Publishing Co., 1978. 128 p.

Collection of essays analyze government regulation of academe, including such issues as the purposes of regulation, whether legitimate or not, methods, and consequences of such regulation. Includes sections on affirmative action.

733.   Greckel, Fay E. "Affirmative Action: The Development of a Plan." The Journal of the College and University Personnel Association. 25 (October-November, 1974), 40-51.

Suggests how one might go about planning and implementing an affirmative action program. Sections include self-education, identify general areas of concern, assessing the campus situation, setting goals, writing an affirmative action plan, and implementing it.

734.   Green, Agnes A. Women on the Chemistry Faculties of Institutions Granting the Ph. D. in Chemistry. Report of survey conducted by the Women Chemists Committee of the American Chemical Society, 1976.

Report contains data for 186 chemistry departments for the 1974-75 academic years. Updates an earlier study, prepared by Green, for the years 1972-73. Two thirds of the faculties of Ph. D. granting chemistry departments in the U. S. in 1975 are still all-male institutions. A little more

than a quarter of them have just one woman.   Women make
up 2.16 per cent of 186 departments studied.

735.   Green, Edith.   "The Road Is Paved with Good Intentions:
       Title IX and What It Is Not."   Vital Speeches.   43 (March 1,
       1977), 300-303.

       Former U. S. Representative from Oregon charges that the
       Civil Rights legislation such as Title IX was designed to
       bring about equality of opportunity, not to bring about re-
       verse discrimination and the imposition of quotas, as is now
       happening.   It is not fair, wise, or just to design a social
       system based on the mistakes and injustices of our fore-
       fathers.

736.   Greenberg, Deborah M.   "Public Policy Issues in the Quota
       Controversy."   Education and Urban Society.   8 (November,
       1975), 73-85.

       Presents three cases based on actual federal court litigation
       to illustrate the problems involved in whether to set quotas
       or goals in affirmative action programs, discusses how she
       would adjudicate them if she were presiding judge, and ex-
       amines the issues involved in an attempt to clarify the areas
       of disagreement concerning quotas.

737.   Greenberg, Jack.   "Affirmative Action, Quotas and Merit."
       The New York Times.   February 7, 1976, p. 21.

       Article on legitimacy of affirmative action and quota systems;
       notes that while most schools usually rely on grades as a
       measure of student competency, some prestigious schools
       may waive grades to obtain geographically and otherwise di-
       verse student body or to permit enrollment of children from
       wealthy families in order to enhance fund-raising; contends
       that race as a basis of selection of candidates is as morally
       justified as any other criterion.

738.   Greenfield, Ester.   "From Equal to Equivalent Pay: Salary
       Discrimination in Academia."   Journal of Law and Education.
       6 (January, 1977), 41-62.

       Sketches the Education Amendments of 1972 and Title VII of
       the Civil Rights Act of 1964 which bars sex discrimination
       in employment; discusses why the work performed by male
       and female professors is comparable but not equal; presents
       the statistical technique of regression analysis as a practical
       method of proving salary discrimination by equalizing for the
       differences between professors which rightfully effect their
       salaries, and explores the legal justification for adopting re-
       gression analysis and the standards of comparable pay for
       comparable work.

739.   Greenfield, Lois B.   "Women in Engineering Education. "
       Contemporary Education.   43 (February, 1972), 224-226.

       Discusses why there are few women in engineering education,
       with only four-tenths of one per cent of Ph. D. degrees
       granted in engineering earned by women.   One reason is the
       attainment of faculty positions by informal referrals infre-
       quently given women.

740.   Gregory, Gwendolyn H.   "Making the Affirmative Action Plan
       Work. "   Journal of College and University Law.   1 (Febru-
       ary, 1973), 16-19.

       Director of Policy Communications, Office for Civil Rights,
       makes suggestions for implementing affirmative action plans:
       identify employment patterns and practices that discriminate
       against minorities and women, take necessary steps to avoid
       them, and monitor the effectiveness of the corrective action.

741.   Gross, Barry R.   "Of Affirmative Action. "   The New York
       Times.   April 12, 1975, p. 26.

       In letter, replies to Mordeca Jane Pollock, sees equal appli-
       cation of laws as proper remedy for unjust discrimination in
       faculty hiring; contends some who oppose quotas and reverse
       discrimination are now tenured professors who were originally
       responsible for discrimination.

742.   _____, ed.   Reverse Discrimination.   New York: Prome-
       theus, 1977.   401 p.

       Compilation of the pros and cons of reverse discrimination
       in education and employment.   Selections reprinted from
       various sources, and divided into three sections: facts and
       polemics, the law, and value.   Excellent bibliography in-
       cluded.   Section on "facts and polemics" includes the follow-
       ing:

743.   Barasch, F. K., HEW, the University, and Women

744.   Glazer, Nathan, The Emergence of an American Ethnic Pat-
       tern

745.   Hook, Sidney, The Bias in Anti-Bias Regulations

746.   _____, Discrimination, Color Blindness, and the Quota
       System

747.   Nisbet, Lee, Affirmative Action--A Liberal Program?

748.   O'Neil, R. M., The Case for Preferential Admissions

749.   Pottinger, J. Stanley, The Drive Toward Equality

750.   Seabury, Paul, HEW and the Universities

751.   Sowell, Thomas, "Affirmative Action" Reconsidered

752/3.   Todorovich, Miro and Glickstein, Howard A., Discrimination in Higher Education: A Debate on Faculty Employment

754.   "HEW Cracks Down on Major Universities: 'Gross Violations' of Anti-Bias Order Discovered." The Chronicle of Higher Education. 15 (January 16, 1978), 16.

Office for Civil Rights signed lengthy agreements with four major universities to comply with equal opportunity laws; agreements followed on-campus investigations at Ohio State University, Purdue University, University of Michigan, and the University of Wisconsin.

755.   "HEW Report on Schools and Sex Bias." The San Francisco Chronicle, March 16, 1977, p. 5.

Nearly two-thirds of the nation's schools and colleges have failed to meet legal requirements for banning sex discrimination in classes and activities. Schools will be given 60 days to assure the government that they are complying with laws on sex discrimination or face possible withdrawal of federal aid.

756.   Habecker, Eugene B. Affirmative Action in the Independent College: A Practical Planning Model. Washington, D. C.: Council for the Advancement of Small Colleges, 1977. 213 p.

Book is divided into three parts: 1) a broad statement about the procedures and expectations of equal employment opportunity, from the perspective of a small, independent college; 2) charts, instructions, for institutional planning; and 3) appendixes containing references and statistical sources, federal regulations, and the like on nondiscrimination and affirmative action.

757.   Hammond, Edward H. "Sex Discrimination in Student Personnel Functions." NASPA Journal. 11 (Winter, 1974), 27-32.

Discusses sex discrimination and how it relates to student personnel work. Deals specifically with co-curricular activities that are part of higher educational institutions, and examines pertinent court decisions.

758.   Harris, Ann Sutherland. "The Second Sex in Academe." AAUP Bulletin. 56 (September, 1970), 283-295.

Discusses the widespread discrimination against women in higher education, as undergraduate and graduate students, faculty, and staff. Brief bibliography included.

759.   Haycock, Richard C.   An Assessment of Affirmative Action
        Programs in Selected Rocky Mountain Institutions of Higher
        Education as Viewed from the Perspective of the Affirmative
        Action Officer.   Ph. D. Dissertation, University of Utah,
        1976. 115 p.

        Purpose of study was to assess the impact of and changes in
        selected institutions of higher education as a result of the
        federally imposed affirmative action program from the per-
        spective of institutional affirmative action officers.   It was
        found that affirmative action has had a positive impact in em-
        ployment practices in higher education; however, little statis-
        tical evidence can be produced indicating greater numbers of
        women and minorities are now in institutional work forces.

760.   Henson, James W. and Astin, Alexander W.   "The Minority
        Pipeline: Minorities at Different Educational Transition
        Points. "   New Directions for Higher Education.   6 (1978),
        41-46.

        Suggests that increasing the participation of minority groups
        at lower educational levels appears to offer substantially
        greater potential for eventually increasing the representation
        of minorities in graduate and professional schools then do
        changes in graduate and professional school admissions pro-
        cedures.   Data collected from a Cooperative Institutional Re-
        search Program (CIRP) survey.

761.   Herbstritt, Michael R.   "Development and Implementation of
        Minimum Hiring Specifications. "   Journal of the College and
        University Personnel Association.   29 (February, 1978), 1-5.

        Describes the specifications developed at a large southeastern
        university to avoid possible discrimination and confusion in
        the hiring practices.   Job analysis and systematic file
        searches were designed to find the education and prior re-
        lated work experience possessed by each incumbent.   The
        specifications were validated as nondiscriminatory.

762.   Hewitt, Barbara N. and Cortes, Carlos E.   "To Serve Soci-
        ety: An Alternative Model for the Selection of Professional
        School Students. "   Aztlan--International Journal of Chicano
        Studies Research.   8 (Spring-Summer-Fall, 1977), 201-216.

        Suggests that graduate schools should provide greater access
        to Chicanos by changing the process and criteria for graduate
        admissions.   Recommends that the traditional admissions
        qualifications be reexamined as to their ability to predict
        valid success criteria in terms of professional success and
        societal needs.

763.   Higgins, James M.   "The Complicated Process of Establish-
        ing Goals for Equal Employment Opportunity. "   Personnel
        Journal.   54 (December, 1975), 631-636.

Two requirements related to the Federal Equal Employment Opportunity (EEO) laws and Executive Orders have been especially difficult: utilization analysis and employment goal-setting for minorities and females. Associated problems and solutions are examined.

764.   "The High Cost of Compliance." The Chronicle of Higher Education. 10 (July 21, 1975), 1.

Discusses the cost of processing the paperwork associated with meeting the federal government's requirements for equal opportunities in higher education.

765.   Hill, Herbert. "Affirmative Action and the Quest for Job Equality." The Review of Black Political Economy. 6 (Spring, 1976), 263-278.

Criticizes the opponents of affirmative action for their systematic misrepresentation of affirmative action (by use of the fiction of quotas and reverse discrimination), their ignoring of major legal and case law upholding numerical goals and affirmative action programs to eliminate job discrimination, and their assumption that no qualified Blacks and women exist, hence affirmative action replaces merit. Concludes that the debate over affirmative action is not preferential treatment of women and minorities but "that a substantial body of law now requires that discriminatory system which operate to favor whites at the expense of women and Blacks must be eliminated."

766.   Hill, Norman. "For Liberty and Equality." Current. No. 129 (May, 1971), 32-35.

Debates whether racial minorities should be granted preferential treatment regarding entrance requirements and achievement at college levels. Presents a rationale that does not favor this proposal.

767.   Hilton, William J. "DeFunis Revisited." Journal of the National Association of College Admissions Counselors. 19 (March, 1975), 8-9.

In an attempt to put the DeFunis case into proper perspective, author examines some key issues involved in preferential minority admissions.

768.   Hixson, Judson, and Epps, Edgar G. "The Failure of Selection and the Problem of Prediction: Racism vs. Measurement in Higher Education." Journal of Afro-American Issues. 3 (Winter, 1975), 117-128.

Discusses the selection of black students for college admission. Suggests that the traditional criteria, such as SAT

scores and high school grade point averages, have been
shown not to be valid predicators of future college performance. Therefore, their continued use raises questions of
whether this is a measurement problem or an instance of
racism.

769.   Hoffman, Emily P. "Determinants of Faculty Rank: The
Discriminant Analysis Approach. " Quarterly Review of Eco-
nomics and Business. 17 (Summer, 1977), 79-88.

Case study of whether females are assigned to faculty rank
on the same basis as males. Previous studies are surveyed. Discusses the suitability of multiple regression analysis, multidimensional contingency table analysis, and discriminant analysis techniques for such an investigation.
Based on discriminant analysis, the results show that sex
is more important than number of publications in predicting
rank. Males and females have a different structure for
determinants of rank, which is evidence of occupational discrimination against females. Female assistant professors
publish more per year of professional experience than any
other group, including males of all ranks.

770.   _____ . "Faculty Salaries: Is There Discrimination by
Sex, Race, and Discipline? Additional Evidence. " American Economic Review. 66 (March, 1976), 196-198.

Replicates the Gordon, Morton, Braden study of faculty salaries, but uses data from another institution and results
from tests of alternative models. Concludes that sex discrimination in faculty salaries is higher than shown in the
Gordon model and that omitting rank as a variable increased
the measured amount of discrimination, almost doubling it.

771.   Holmes, Peter E. "Affirmative Action: Myth and Reality. "
Toward Affirmative Action. Lucy W. Sells, Issue Editor.
San Francisco: Jossey-Bass, 1974. Pp. 39-54.

Former Director of the Office for Civil Rights (HEW),
Holmes responds to critics of affirmative action. Denies
that it leads to lowered qualifications or the substitution of
quotas for merit and the subversion of university independence. Defines affirmative action as a process to equalize
opportunities to groups previously underrepresented and disadvantaged relative to other persons.

772.   Hook, Sidney. "The Bias in Anti-Bias Regulations [Review
of Richard Lester's Antibias Regulation of Universities,
(1974)]" Measure. #30 (Summer, 1974), 1-2, 4-6.

Favorably reviews Lester's book. Agrees with Lester that
few women and minorities qualify for academic positions and
that quotas and preferential treatment erode the principles of
merit in faculty positions.

773.   . "Discrimination Against the Qualified?" The New
York Times. November 5, 1971, p. 43.

Article criticizes recent threats by HEW to cut off Federal
funds to colleges unless they admit minority groups such as
women and blacks as students and teachers as percentages
based on employment figures; says that to insist on equality
on the basis of quotas compels institutions to hire unqualified
persons and causes them to discriminate against qualified
candidates, who he feels would scorn preferential treatment.
(See item 897.)

774.   . "Discrimination, Color Blindness, and the Quota
System." Measure. #1 (October, 1971), 2-3.

Charges that the Office for Civil Rights (HEW) compels institutions of higher education to hire unqualified women and
Negroes, thereby debasing educational standards.

775.   . "H. E. W. Regulations--A New Threat to Educational Integrity. " Freedom at Issue. No. 10 (1971), 12-14.

776.   . "The Road to a University Quota System. "
Freedom at Issue. No. 12 (March/April, 1972), 1-2, 21-22.

Criticizes HEW for imposing quotas upon faculty hiring and
student admissions, thereby subordinating academic qualifications. Also addresses the question whether preferential hiring is illegal and if present injustice compensates for past
injustice.

777.   . "Semantic Evasions. " College and University
Journal. 11 (September, 1972), 16-18.

HEW's affirmative action, which imposes quotas on colleges
and universities, is continuing and largely succeeding because
of administrative cowardice. A quota system is never morally legitimate when seeking the best qualified person for a
position. If a quota system is morally undesirable, then the
effort to achieve it is likewise undesirable.

778.   , and Todorovich, Miro. "The Tyranny of Reverse
Discrimination. " Change. 7 (December/January, 1975-76),
322-423.

Presents alternative views to some of the comments regarding opposition to affirmative action made by Marilyn Gittell
in "The Illusion of Affirmative Action. "

779. Hopkins, Elaine B. "Unemployed! An Academic Woman's
Saga. " Change. 5 (Winter, 1973), 49-53.

A study of women in academe and policies that discriminate
against them.

780.   Horn, Stephen.   "Affirmative Action and Collective Bargain-
        ing: Opportunity and Uncertainty for American Higher Edu-
        cation. " Vital Speeches.   42 (December 15, 1975), 143-147.

        President, California State University, Long Beach, asserts
        that the affirmative action mandate of the federal government
        is simply asking institutions of higher education to rationalize
        their personnel processes so that the best qualified are being
        hired rather than relying upon the "old boy" network and the
        appointment of faculty based more on where candidates were
        educated and whom they knew rather than on what they knew.
        Author believes that the precepts of affirmative action and
        the process of collective bargaining are possibly on a col-
        lision course.

781.   Hornby, D. Brock.   "Implications of the De Funis Case for
        Undergraduate Admissions. " Liberal Education.   71 (May,
        1975), 216-226.

        Examines two legal problems in higher education brought
        about by the De Funis case: proper role of race in under-
        graduate admissions and procedures of undergraduate admis-
        sions.   Focuses upon state institutions of higher education.

782.   Horvitz, Jerome S.   "Tax Subsidies to Promote Affirmative
        Action in Admission Procedures for Institutions of Higher
        Learning--Their Inherent Danger. " Taxes.   52 (August,
        1974), 452-465.

        Discusses the substantive issues that run parallel in the Bob
        Jones University and the De Funis decisions, which the au-
        thor believes have created a social experiment that may result
        in severing the life support system of both public and private
        higher education.

783.   Howard, Bill.   "Blacks and Professional Schools. " Change.
        4 (February, 1972), 13-16.

        Black students encounter difficulty in gaining admissions to
        graduate schools, and once in, attrition rate is great for
        financial and scholastic reasons.

784.   Howard, John A.   "Principles in Default; the Government
        Seizure of Education. " Vital Speeches.   41 (February 1,
        1975), 241-245.

        President of Rockford College criticizes governmental usurpa-
        tion of the control of education, as evidenced in affirmative
        action programs and Title IX regulations of the Education
        Amendments of 1972.

785.   Howard, Suzanne. Campus '70: Revisited 1976. Washing-
        ton, D. C.: American Association of University Women, 1978.

Update of the Ruth Oltman study of 1970.   Survey of 600
four-year institutions of higher education, covering the years
1973 through 1975, to determine whether progress was made
by women on campus since the advent of federal equal opportunity and affirmative action regulations.   Some results of
the survey were that no gains have been made since 1973 in
the percentage of women holding top-level positions in administration and tenured faculty in either public or private
higher education institutions; women are clustered in the
lower professorial ranks, holding only 8 per cent of the full
professorships and 16 per cent of the associate professorships, but 49 per cent of the instructor positions and 37 per
cent of the lecturer slots.   The report concluded that legislation is seen as the most effective force in reducing sex
discrimination.

786.   Howard University.   Institute for the Study of Educational
        Policy.   Affirmative Action for Blacks in Higher Education:
        A Report.   Washington, D. C. :   Howard University Press,
        1978.   106 p.

        Report is divided into three parts: 1) presents the results
        of an historical analysis of the efforts of blacks to obtain an
        education, examines the extent to which equal opportunity has
        existed in higher education, discusses the findings concerning
        the legal and constitutional foundations of affirmative action,
        and examines the criticisms of affirmative action; 2) presents
        the results of the analysis of the government's role in af-
        firmative action and examines the current practices of af-
        firmative action within selected institutions of higher educa-
        tion; 3) discusses the current position of blacks in faculty
        employment in higher education.

787.   _____ .   Equal Educational Opportunity for Blacks in U. S.
        Higher Education: An Assessment.   Report No. 1, 1973-74
        Academic Year.   Washington, D. C. :   Howard University
        Press, 1975.   695 p.

        Provides an exhaustive review of the recent status of blacks
        in higher education, the economic return of education for
        blacks, the continuing barriers to equal educational oppor-
        tunity, and the problems in the racial data which are used
        to determine federal policy.

788.   _____ .   Equal Educational Opportunity for Blacks in U. S.
        Higher Education; an Assessment.   Washington, D. C. :
        Howard University Press, 1976.   330 p.

        Chapters include problems of the data on blacks in college;
        access, distribution, and persistence of blacks in college;
        barriers to equal educational opportunity for blacks; impact
        of higher education on black income; federal policies related
        to equal educational opportunity; and appendices on federal

legislation, enrollment, graduate and professional school enrollment, and other data.

789. Hughes, Helen M. The Status of Women in Sociology, 1968-1972. Washington, D. C.: American Sociological Association, 1973.

Reviews the status of women in sociology, particularly in institutions of higher education. Findings reveal discrimination against women.

790. Humphreys, Lloyd G. "Race and Sex Differences and Their Implications for Educational and Occupational Equality." Educational Theory. 26 (Spring, 1976), 135-146.

Views with trepidation certain procedures and criteria used to implement basic policies on equal employment opportunity, particularly the concept of proportional representation and that initial deficiencies in qualifications can easily, quickly, and cheaply be overcome after selection. Also considers the erroneous number of generalizations made concerning race, sex differences, and individual differences within groups.

791. Hutchins, Trova K. "Affirmative Action for the Physically Disabled in Social Work Education." Journal of Education for Social Work. 14 (Fall, 1978), 64-70.

Describes the issues and needs that should be considered in developing affirmative action programs for the disabled and suggestions are made for identifying and recruiting qualified disabled students for the field of social work.

792. "Is Reverse Discrimination Justified? Interviews. Frank Askin; Eugene Rostow." U. S. News & World Report. 83 (October 3, 1977), 39-40.

Askin, Professor of Law at Rutgers University and General Counsel of the ACLU, defends affirmative action as an effective means for bringing racial minorities into full participation in American life. Rostow, Professor of Law, Yale University, criticizes the use of quotas because they threaten the basic standard of equality as a principle of constitutional law, and for having a dangerous impact on university practices and on the people themselves who may be admitted to a university who are underqualified.

793. Jackson, Reid E., II. "The Effectiveness of a Special Program for Minority Group Students." Journal of Medical Education. 47 (August, 1972), 620-624.

Discusses the need for physicians in minority group communities which should be met by medical schools actively recruiting and educating minority group students.

794.   "Job Action Plans on Campus Urged. " <u>The New York Times.</u>
        October 1, 1975, p. 56.

        Secretary of HEW, David Mathews, testifying before the
        House of Representatives Equal Opportunities Subcommittee
        hearings to explore growing concern that colleges are trying
        to gain exemption from affirmative action laws, says he is
        opposed to such exemptions; backs "refining" rules under
        which colleges have to set up goals and timetables to end
        racial and sexual bias.

795.   "Job Drive Backed by HEW's Chief. " <u>The New York Times.</u>
        November 17, 1973, p. 18.

        Secretary of HEW, Caspar Weinberger, in speech before
        B'Nai B'rith Anti-Defamation League, says that his depart-
        ment's drive for equal employment in higher education does
        not compel universities to institute quota systems and that
        HEW does not recommend hiring unqualified candidates.

796.   "Job Rights Role of U. S. Disputed. " <u>The New York Times.</u>
        November 18, 1972, p. 27.

        B'nai B'rith Anti-Defamation League criticizes the Govern-
        ment's supervision of the way universities hire minorities
        and women, charges that Federal "goals" inevitably become
        quotas, contending that this is a distortion of antidiscrimina-
        tion policies; J. Stanley Pottinger, Director, Office for Civil
        Rights, defends Government's policy of numerical goals as
        proper and useful for measuring colleges' progress in rem-
        edying past discrimination.

797.   Johnson, George E. , and Stafford, Frank P.   "The Earnings
        and Promotion of Women Faculty. " <u>American Economic Re-
        view.</u>   64 (December, 1974), 888-903.

        Examines data from the National Science Foundation to deter-
        mine the extent of male-female salary and promotion differ-
        ential of Ph. D. 's in academic employment and the extent by
        which lifetime choice of training vs. nonmarket work in the
        home influences the differential.   Concludes that the aca-
        demic salaries of females start out at not much less than
        those of males (4 to 11 per cent less in six disciplines
        studied) and then decline to result in a fairly substantial
        differential after a number of years of potential experience
        (13 to 23 per cent at 15 years completion of the doctorate).
        Attributes these differentials between men and women by the
        fact that roughly two-fifths of the wage disadvantage is at-
        tributable to discrimination, three-fifths to human capital
        differences, such as child-care and other home choices made
        by females.

798.   _____ .   "Earnings and Promotion of Women Faculty: Re-
        ply. " <u>American Economic Review.</u>   67 (March, 1977), 214-217.

Responds to Farber and Strober's comments on original 1974
article in American Economic Review, and Quester's analysis.   Repeats conclusion that salary differentials between
men and women faculty is largely the result of historical
differences in patterns of work attachment between home and
work.

799.   Johnson, Roosevelt.   "Blacks and Higher Education--A Decade in Review. " Journal of Afro-American Issues.   5 (Winter, 1977), 88-97.

Concludes that the social growth and development which
blacks gained over the last ten years now are being seriously threatened by changes in the social policy which may
become sanctioned by law.

800.   Jordan, Vernon E. , Jr.   "Blacks and Higher Education--
Some Reflections. " Daedalus.   104 (Winter, 1975), 160-165.

Criticizes higher educational institutions for discriminating
against blacks, stalling on meeting affirmative action requirements, and elevating the concepts of "merit" and "excellence" to the heights of mythology in its efforts to preserve the prerogatives of white males.   Author perceives
universities as "instruments of economic and social mobility
whose claim on the public and private purpose implies social usefulness and engagement. " Author is Executive Director, National Urban League.

801.   _____.   "Blacks and Jewish Communities: The Quota System. " Vital Speeches.   40 (August 1, 1974), 629-632.

Describes affirmative action as the issue which most visibly
separates the black and Jewish communities.   Speaks of the
quota system as historically operating in America to freeze
blacks out of universities, professions, and social and economic mainstream.   Special affirmative action programs are
necessary to include blacks in the spheres of jobs, education, and the professions.

802.   Josey, E. J.   "Affirmative Action for Blacks and Other Minority Librarians. " Negro History Bulletin.   38 (June-July,
1975), 423-427.

Argues that, by and large, minority Americans are short-
changed when it comes to higher education and that the library profession is a case in point.   Maintains that although
an Equal Employment Opportunity Policy Statement was
passed by the American Library Association in 1974, no
mechanism was established for libraries to file affirmative
action plans with the Association.

803.   _____.   "Can Library Affirmative Action Succeed? " Library Journal.   100 (January 1, 1975), 28-31.

Discusses the results of a 1974 survey of minority librarians
in 22 leading libraries, 12 of them academic. Survey was
conducted by the Black Caucus of the American Library Association. The number of minority librarians, and how many
have middle management or higher administrative positions
were surveyed, with poor representation described. Author
concludes that libraries and the ALA must commit themselves to a real affirmative action program and not content
themselves with a mere policy statement. Author cites evidence of a great reservoir of potential black and other minority librarians.

804.   Kane, Roslyn D. Sex Discrimination in Education: A Study
       of Employment Practices Affecting Professional Personnel.
       Volume I: Study Report. 321 p. Volume II: Annotated
       Bibliography. 258 p. Washington, D.C.: National Center
       for Education Statistics, 1976.
       (ED 132 743)

       The current status of women employed in professional posi-
       tions in educational institutions from preschool through the
       universities is reviewed to determine their relative employ-
       ment status in comparison to men, and to identify discrim-
       inatory employment practices that have limited women's op-
       portunities. Chapters discuss the methodological approach;
       employment and salary; minority women; policymakers; hir-
       ing and promotion; discriminatory practices relating to fringe
       benefits; women's patterns of life and work; legislation,
       regulations, and executive orders; court cases; and recom-
       mendations.

805.   Katz, David A. "Faculty Salaries, Promotions, and Pro-
       ductivity at a Large University." American Economic Re-
       view. 63 (June, 1973), 469-477.

       Data analyzed from a large highly ranked public university
       in order to study the determinants of faculty salaries and
       promotions. The primary purpose was to develop a more
       rational means of evaluating and rewarding university pro-
       fessors. Study demonstrates that even after taking into con-
       sideration their lower productivity, women are still paid less
       than men.

806.   Keller, Suzanne. "Reply to Borgatta's 'The Concept of Re-
       verse Discrimination and Equality of Opportunity.'" The
       American Sociologist. 11 (May, 1976), 79-81.

       Discusses preferential treatment of minorities and women as
       necessary to improve their chances of access to opportunity
       and as compensation for their historic exclusion and neglect.

807.   Kerr, Clark. "Solving the Selective Admissions Dilemma:
       A Two-Stage Model for Higher Education." Phi Kappa Phi
       Journal. 58 (Winter, 1978), 4-6.

Chairman of the Carnegie Council on Policy Studies in Higher Education reviews the findings of the Council's publication, Selective Admissions in Higher Education. Author believes that race and other minority status can be considered in admissions decisions without lowering academic standards or causing unfair disadvantage to other students. Race should be considered in admissions selection where individual's racial identity reflects prior adverse circumstances, a promise to contribute to the educational experience of other students, or to the diversity of services to be provided to society.

808.   Kilberg, William J. "Application of Equal Employment Laws to Higher Education." The Journal of the College & University Personnel Association. 27 (April-May, 1976), 28-32.

Kilberg, Solicitor, U. S. Department of Labor, responds to critics in the higher education community who deny the applicability of equal employment laws to academia. Points out the reality of salary differentials between men and women faculty, the exaggerated debate over goals and timetables, and that the goal is equality of opportunity and not equality of result.

809.   Kilson, Martin. "The Black Experience at Harvard." The New York Times. September 2, 1973, VI, p. 13.

Professor Kilson discusses how self-imposed black separatism at Harvard University, as at many colleges across the U. S., has had "nearly disastrous impact on academic achievement and intellectual growth" of black students; sees hopeful sign of end of separatism in attitude of some blacks now in school; advocates quota system for admission of blacks to colleges; scores prejudices shown against middle-class blacks by admissions officials.

810.   [Kilson's critics respond.] The New York Times. September 23, VI, p. 10, 74; September 30, VI, p. 24, 28; October 14, VII, p. 16; November 4, VII, p. 121, 1973.

Replies focus on whether black students are succeeding academically, and his defense of racial quotas.

811.   Kimball, Bruce A. "An Historical Perspective on the Constitutional Debate Over Affirmative Action Admissions." Journal of Law and Education. 7 (January, 1978), 31-49.

Examines the history of admissions policies in postsecondary institutions and reveals that the constitutional debate over affirmative action admissions involves a dispute about the purposes of American postsecondary education. Opponents of affirmative action consistently uphold intellectual meritocracy as the purpose of a university. Supporters of affirmative action recognize a plurality of purposes for the univer-

sity including not only intellectual merit but also service to
society. Examines the DeFunis and Bakke court cases within these conflicting assumptions and suggests that affirmative
action admissions policies are historically consistent with
the purposes of American postsecondary education insofar as
desegregation is a judicially mandated form of service to
society.

812.   King, Joseph A. "Affirmative Action Gone Wild. " America.
        134 (April 17, 1976), 334-336.

        Critical look at affirmative action in its continuation of ra-
        cism and sexism and its pitting of ethnics against ethnics.
        Cites affirmative action for violating the equal protection
        clause of the Fourteenth Amendment.

813.   Koch, James V., and Chizmar, John F. "The Unfairness
        of 'How to Analyze the Fairness of Women's Salaries on
        Your Own Campus' [by Bergmann and Maxfield]. " AAUP
        Bulletin. 62 (April, 1976), 123-236.

        Criticizes the Bergmann-Maxfield method of analyzing fair-
        ness because it excludes from consideration explicit meas-
        ures of "on the job" productivity and performance.

814.   _____. "Sex Discrimination and Affirmative Action in
        Faculty Salaries. " Economic Inquiry. 14 (March, 1976),
        16-24.

        A counterfactual model is used to determine if sex discrim-
        ination in salaries existed at Illinois State University. The
        analysis makes use of detailed peer evaluations of each fac-
        ulty member's productivity in scholarly productivity, teach-
        ing, and service. Model examines the effects of Affirmative
        Action salary increments given female faculty members.
        Evidence of sex discrimination in salaries against female
        faculty is found. The Affirmative Action salary program
        erased this discrimination and introduced statistically signi-
        ficant discrimination against male faculty.

815.   Kommers, Donald P. "Affirmative Action: An Academi-
        cian's Viewpoint. " Social Research Administrators Journal.
        9 (Fall, 1977), 45-48.

816.   Konheim, Beatrice G. "Report of the AAUP Council Com-
        mittee on Discrimination. " AAUP Bulletin. 58 (Summer,
        1972), 160-163.

        Report recommends that appointments are to be made on the
        basis of fitness of faculty members in professional capacities
        without prejudice with respect to race, sex, religion, or na-
        tional origin. Affirmative action calls for rejection of stand-
        ards and practices which do not allow equal opportunity for

all.   Affirmative action calls for genuine efforts to bring into faculties members of groups previously denied full equality of opportunity.   Report denies that affirmative action requires the employment of unqualified persons or the imposition of quotas.

817.   Kristol, Irving.   "How Hiring Quotas Came to the Campuses. "
       Fortune.   90 (September, 1974), 203+

       Claims that the federal bureaucracy has imposed a discrim-
       inatory quota system upon college faculties, which has re-
       sulted in the subversion of the American democratic ideal--
       the reconciliation of equality and excellence.

818.   Kuk, Linda.   "Beyond Affirmative Action. "   Journal of the
       College and University Personnel Association.   29 (Fall,
       1978),   17-20.

       Describes affirmative action compliance as insufficient; indi-
       vidual institutions must work to create a climate in which
       women faculty are able to contribute to their full potentials.

819.   Kuttner, Bob.   "'Quota' Hiring/White Males and Jews Need
       Not Apply. "   Village Voice.   17 (August 31, 1972), 5+

       Claims that the immediate future is bleak for white male ap-
       plicants in fields where jobs are tight, such as university
       teaching.   Many employers are hiring only blacks and wom-
       en, with Jews standing to lose the most if ethnic quotas are
       established.   Unfortunately, the history of fair employment
       enforcement leaves little doubt that it requires "affirmative
       action" bordering on quotas to break traditional white-male
       employment patterns.   What is required is a civil rights en-
       forcement effort machinery with sensitivity to the competing
       equities.

820.   Ladd, Everett C. and Lipset, Seymour Martin.   "How Fac-
       ulty Members Feel About Equality. "   The Chronicle of Higher
       Education.   12 (March 1, 1976), 12.

       Ladd-Lipset survey points up sharp divisions over the ques-
       tions of merit and equality and much ambivalence.   Faculty
       members equally divided on the question of whether univer-
       sities have behaved meritocratically.   Only a fourth to a
       third endorse the use of "benign" quotas or preferential
       treatment in the recruitment process.

821.   _____.   "Professors' Religion and Ethnic Background. "
       The Chronicle of Higher Education.   11 (September 22, 1975),
       2.

       Survey of U. S. faculty members demonstrates that blacks
       represent about 2 per cent of faculty of major research uni-

versities and "that proportion has remained basically the same over the last decade."

822.   LaNoue, George R.   "Athletics and Equality: How to Comply with Title IX Without Tearing Down the Stadium."
Change.   8 (November, 1976), 27-30, 63-64.

Suggests that Title IX needs to be implemented within the concept of athletic equality which improves opportunities for women, is legally defensible, and reflects the multiple purposes of collegiate sports.

823.   _____, and Miller, Nancy Lloyd.   "Professional Societies and Equal Employment."   Society.   13 (January-February, 1976), 53-58.

Study of a number of professional organizations was done by a questionnaire in 1973; it describes affirmative action efforts by these associations.   The groups find universities under pressure, the traditional old-boy network for jobs under attack, and affirmative action regulations taking effect. All of these factors put pressure on the associations to define professional competence and roles before nonprofessional agencies and pressure groups do so for them.

824.   LaSorte, Michael A.   "Academic Women's Salaries: Equal Pay for Equal Work?"   Journal of Higher Education.   42 (April, 1971), 265-278.

Compares salary differentials of academic men and women from 1959 to 1968.   Analyzes academic degrees, geographical region, professional experience, and age to ascertain effect upon salary differentials.   Concludes that men are rewarded above women regardless of whether they do research in addition to teaching or teaching only and that women teachers entering academia initially encounter a small salary inequity which then increases in size with the acquisition of high rank tenure, and professional experience.

825.   Leepson, Marc.   "Medical Education."   Editorial Research.
Reports.   11 (November 25, 1977), 891-908.

Discusses the Bakke case as a challenge to affirmative action, heavy demand for entering medical school, minority group representation in medicine, increases in the number of women students, evolution of U. S. medical study, and foreign training of doctors.   Brief bibliography included.

826.   Leonard, Walter J.   "Affirmative Action at Harvard."   The Chronicle of Higher Education.   10 (March 31, 1975), 13.

Third annual report by the person in charge of Harvard's affirmative action plan indicates that there has been a moving backward since 1971 in affirmative action, both in staff and student population. Those who do not want to understand affirmative action use two myths: the take-over by minorities/women in employment, and the red herring of reverse discrimination and preferential treatment. Refutes these myths by showing statistics on the number of women and minority faculty members, and their rank within Harvard.

827.   Lester, Richard A. "The AAUP Salary Survey: Comments and Suggestions." AAUP Bulletin. 62 (August, 1976), 156-159.

Suggests that the AAUP, in publishing salary and compensation averages each year for individual institutions and for categories of institutions, should alert readers to the shortcomings of the data for various purposes, and especially for comparisons between institutions and between categories of institutions and sexes on a nationwide basis.

828.   _____. Antibias Regulation of Universities: Faculty Problems and Their Solutions. A Report Prepared for the Carnegie Commission on Higher Education. New York: McGraw-Hill, 1974. 168 p.

Critical review of the federal government's affirmative action programs as applied to higher education. Charges that the programs compel colleges to hire unqualified women and minorities, thereby lowering the standards and undermining faculty quality. Colleges, lacking an adequate pool of qualified women and blacks, are pirating from each other; some new minority and female appointees are paid more than white male faculty members at the same level; and numerical quotas should not be applied to professional jobs. (See item 925.)

829.   _____. "The Equal Pay Boondoggle." Change. 7 (September, 1975), 38-43.

Studies the problems of bringing the Equal Pay Act to university faculty. Presents solutions to the problems.

830.   _____. "The Fallacies of Numerical Goals." Educational Record. 57 (Winter, 1976), 58-64.

Discusses the problems inherent in the federal government's statistical methods of determining and enforcing goals for hiring and composition of the faculty. The government's use of recipients of Ph.D. degrees as a pool of persons qualified and available for all levels of academic appointment tends to disregard important individual differences in quality. There is a need to correct the serious flaws in government regulation, eliminate the wasteful red tape of federal mechanisms, and work out a sensible, effective program against discrimination in employment.

831.   Levinson, Richard M. "An Encounter with Sex Discrimina-
        tion. " Teaching Sociology. 3 (January, 1975), 191-193.

        Phoned job inquiries by students for positions not tradition-
        ally held by persons of their sex were followed by calls from
        those for whom the jobs would have been traditionally ap-
        propriate. Results indicate that there is still much sex dis-
        crimination.

832.   Lewis, Lionel Stanley. Scaling the Ivory Tower: Merit and
        Its Limits in Academic Careers. Baltimore: Johns Hopkins
        University Press, 1975. 238 p.

        Contends that it is untrue that the evaluation and advancement
        of academics turns on merit. Presents evidence that ascrip-
        tion and sponsored mobility are at least as potent in affect-
        ing the careers of university professors as are achievement
        and contest mobility. Includes evidence of sex discrimination
        in graduate school admissions, recruitment and promotion of
        women faculty, and salary discrimination. Contains a sec-
        tion on common fictions and half-truths regarding academic
        women.

833.   Linnell, Robert H. and Gray, Paul. "Faculty Planning and
        Affirmative Action. " The Journal of College and University
        Personnel Association. 28 (Spring, 1977), 6-9.

        Reports the use of a model to examine the impact of affirm-
        ative action policies on the female/male ratio of a faculty
        of natural sciences. Concludes that increased analysis and
        detailed study of suggested alternatives can lead to better
        resolution of the problems and potentials of affirmative ac-
        tion programs.

834.   Liss, Lora. "Affirmative Action Officers: Are They Change
        Agents?" Educational Record. 58 (Fall, 1977). 418-428.

        Describes affirmative action officers as internal change
        agents in higher education. Their chief obstacle in bringing
        change are the conflicting perceptions of their role among
        different constituencies within academe. Describes models
        for action available to the affirmative action officer.

835.   _____. "Why Academic Women Do Not Revolt: Implica-
        tions for Affirmative Action. " Sex Roles, A Journal of Re-
        search. 1 (September, 1975), 209-223.

        Low perceptions of sex discrimination among full-time female
        faculty explained and compared with statistical data, docu-
        ments on inequities in salary, promotion, rank, and tenure.
        Structural reasons for misperceptions offered, including con-
        centration in the lowest ranks, pluralistic ignorance, merit
        myths, and cooptation. Includes recommendations for solving
        status inequalities.

836.   Loeb, Jane W. , Ferber, Marianne A. , and Lowrey, Helen
        M.   "The Effectiveness of Affirmative Action for Women. "
        Journal of Higher Education. 49 (May-June, 1978), 218-230.

        Examines data from the University of Illinois at Urbana-
        Champaign and concludes that government regulation is costly
        and has not been well enforced.   It is also largely ineffec-
        tual in decreasing salary differentials between men and
        women.   Rather than depending on regulation to achieve
        equality in hiring, pay and salary, these programs should
        be redesigned in order to build on incentives.

837.   _____ and Ferber, Marianne.   "Sex as Predictive of Sal-
        ary and Status on a University Faculty. " Journal of Educa-
        tional Measurement.   8 (Winter, 1971), 235-244.

        Results indicate the existence of discrimination against wom-
        en in pay as well as in rank but do not allow a clear esti-
        mation of the magnitude of the discrepancy.

838.   Loftus, Elizabeth.   "Follies of Affirmative Action. " Society.
        14 (January / February, 1977), 21-24.

        Explains how one possible reason why affirmative action pro-
        grams have not been more successful is that the punishment
        --removal of federal funds--is so severe that it almost is
        never invoked.   Universities know that it is unlikely this
        "atom bomb" will be dropped.   Suggests alternatives to the
        practices used in the present system.

839.   Loggins, Philip R.   "Calculating Staff Affirmative Action
        Goals and Timetables. " The Journal of the College and
        University Personnel Association.   24 (September, 1973),
        64-77.

        Describes the contents of a report developed by the Office
        for Equal Employment Opportunity in the Office of the Pre-
        sident of the University of California.

840.   Lopiano, Donna A.   "A Fact-Finding Model for Conducting a
        Title IX Self-Evaluation Study in Athletic Programs.   Title
        IX--Prospects and Problems. " Journal of Physical Educa-
        tion and Recreation.   47 (May, 1976), 25-30.

        Guidelines are given to conduct a self-evaluation study as
        required by Title IX.

841.   Lorch, Barbara R.   "Reverse Discrimination in Sociology
        Departments: A Preliminary Report. " American Sociolo-
        gist.   8 (August, 1973), 116-120.

        Questionnaire was sent to sociology department chairmen, 32
        per cent of which indicated they had positions to fill in the

past two years. Replied that they felt coerced to practice
reverse discrimination; 16 per cent reported that they actually did so. Concludes that this reaction is cause for great
concern.

842.   Lyons, Paul J. The College and University Affirmative Ac-
        tion Manual. New York: Executive Enterprises Publica-
        tions, Co., 1976.

843.   McCarthy, Joseph L. and Wolfle, D. "Doctorates Granted
        to Women and Minority Group Members." Science. 189
        (September 12, 1975), 856-859.

        Data presented from the Association of American Univer-
        sities. Fields dominant for women and blacks included.

844.   Maccia, Elizabeth S. "Affirmative Action Plans: A Policy
        Analysis." Viewpoints. 51 (May, 1975), 33-44.

        Discusses affirmative action policy and plans, and its rela-
        tion to the kinds of society in which we want to live and the
        kind of men and women we wish to see nurtured in such a
        society.

845.   McCune, Shirley. "Title IX--Sexism in Education." Hu-
        manist Educator. 14 (June, 1975), 195-207.

        Article discusses the historic trends leading to the develop-
        ment and implementation of Title IX. Major provisions of
        regulations listed under admissions, treatment of students,
        employment, and a general section. Implications of Title
        IX and an institutional compliance checklist are presented.

846.   McGill, William J. "The University and the State." Educa-
        tional Record. 58 (Spring, 1977), 132-145.

        Reflects on academic freedom, federal regulations (including
        affirmative action) and government interference in higher
        education. Suggests ways to improve the regulations and
        how to rewrite and enforce them.

847.   Magarrell, Jack. "Faculty Salary Gap Widens Between Men
        and Women." The Chronicle of Higher Education. 13 (Sep-
        tember 27, 1976), 1.

        Figures from the National Center for Educational Statistics
        show that salary inequalities between men and women faculty
        have increased in the year 1975-76. Differences were great-
        est at the instructor level. On the average, women faculty
        earned $3,096 less than men in 1975-76. The percentage of
        faculty positions held by women increased one half of one
        per cent--from 23.8 per cent in 1974-75 to 24.3 per cent in
        1975-76.

848.   Marcus, Laurence C.   "Affirmative Action in Higher Educa-
        tion. " Journal of Intergroup Relations. 6 (April, 1977), 24-53.

        Notes that the affirmative action effort has taken longer than
        five years to reduce empirically sex and racial discrimina-
        tory practices in higher education, the enforcement effort
        has been slow, and higher education has stopped growing.

849.   Marshall, Eliot.   "Race Certification. " The New Republic.
        177 (October 15, 1977), 18-20.

        Explains how the enforcement of affirmative action plans
        means preference to people because of race and sex.   Af-
        firmative action also means unholy deference to statistics.
        We have come full circle--from removal of racial and ethnic
        identification to back again.

850.   Martin, Michael.   "Pedogogical Arguments for Preferential
        Hiring and Tenuring of University Teachers. "   Philosophical
        Forum.   5 (Fall/Winter, 1973/74), 325-333.

        Argues that women university teachers provide role models
        and empathy with female students, and ability to teach non-
        sexist courses.   Pedogogical arguments against preferential
        hiring are discussed, then refuted.

851.   Mathews, John.   "Female and Faculty Rights. " Change.   3
        (Summer, 1971), 13-15.

        Describes the efforts of the Women's Equity Action League
        (WEAL) to end sex discrimination in higher education.   Also
        presents evidence of nation-wide sex discrimination in hiring
        and promoting women faculty.

852.   Meckley, Shirley M. , and Anthony, William P.   "Experience
        with Affirmative Action. " The Journal of the College & Uni-
        versity Personnel Association. 28 (Winter, 1977), 11-17.

        Outlines the affirmative action program and the role of the
        Personnel Officer in implementing affirmative action policies
        and regulations.   Presents highlights of the most successful
        aspects of the program at Florida State University and those
        needing more effort.

853.   "Meritocracy and Its Discontents; Symposium. " The New
        Republic.   177 (October 15, 1977), 5-9+.

        Briefly discusses arguments for and against quotas.   Be-
        lieves that the "fateful flaw" is any system that confers ad-
        vantage on the basis of group membership.   Writes that the
        purpose of affirmative action is to make sure that talented
        individuals, from every social group, have an opportunity to
        shine

854.   Meyers, Michael. "Faculty Desegregation: The Rational-
        izers. " The New York Times. April 24, 1976, p. 26.

        NAACP official questions assertions by Professor Jaroslav
        Pelikan about efforts by Yale and other universities to de-
        segregate faculty and administration and become equal oppor-
        tunity employers.

855.   Michigan University, Ann Arbor. Center for the Study of
        Higher Education. Affirmative Action: Its Legal Mandate
        and Organizational Implications, No. 2. By Jamie B. Cat-
        lin and others. Michigan University: Center for the Study
        of Higher Education, 1974. 81 p.
        (ED 092 050)

        Discusses affirmative action legislation and regulations as
        applied to institutions of higher education. Includes section
        on legal aspects with emphasis on historical and legal per-
        spectives of affirmative action, summary of the guidelines
        and compliance procedures for administrations and their
        legal implications. Organizational section reviews a con-
        ceptual framework and history of HEW/university interac-
        tion, institutional response; and some organizational implica-
        tions for affirmative action.

856.   "Minority Enrollments: Some Second Thoughts. " The New
        York Times. May 20, 1973, IV, p. 11.

        Conference of U. S. college admissions officials at Oberlin
        College reveals that some schools are having second thoughts
        about nature of commitment to increase minority enrollments;
        much of criticism aimed at double standards and quota sys-
        tems under which minority students are admitted despite
        lower test scores and lower high school averages than whites;
        chart of black enrollment in U. S. colleges, 1964-1972 also
        included.

857.   "A Model [Affirmative Action Plan] AAP. " College Manage-
        ment. 8 (February, 1973), 34-35.

        Presents the plan at Rutgers University, one of the first af-
        firmative action plans, and one of the best.

858.   Modern Language Association. Women in Modern Language
        Departments, 1972-1973: A Report by the Commission on
        the Status of Women in the Profession. New York: Modern
        Language Association, 1976. 13 p.

        Report based on data gathered by the American Council on
        Education, includes an analysis of rank, tenure, and salary
        in the modern language departments.

859.   Mollenhauer, Rosalie. "Quantifying Minority Student Enroll-
         ment Goals." Journal of Education for Social Work. 14
         (Fall, 1978), 100-106.

         Address the need for quantitatively defined minority enroll-
         ment goals for graduate social work education. Provides
         brief overview of minority enrollment efforts, a summary of
         federal regulations, an exploration of the legitimacy of quan-
         titative goals, and concludes with a formula that yields
         quantified minority enrollment goals.

860.   Mommsen, Kent G. "Black Doctorates in American Higher
         Education: A Cohort Analysis." Journal of Social and Be-
         havioral Science. 20 (Spring, 1974), 101-117.

         Examines the educational and career experiences of black
         doctorates in higher education. Data on 785 black doctorates
         collected in 1970 through the use of a mailed questionnaire.
         Weak support is found for the major hypothesis that institu-
         tional racism is decreasing in American higher education.

861.   _____. "Black Ph. D. 's in the Academic Marketplace:
         Supply, Demand, and Price." Journal of Higher Education.
         45 (April, 1974), 253-262.

         Presents the results of a questionnaire based upon national
         nonprobability sample of all living black American Ph. D. 's.
         Data on the educational origins, career patterns, demand,
         salaries, and mobility. Suggests that greater institutional
         efforts be directed to recruit, support, and increase the
         supply of black students rather than aggravating the situation
         by continuing to drive demand and price levels even higher.

862.   Moore, Dwight. "Preferential Minority Admission in Higher
         Education." Journal of the National Association of College
         Admissions Counselors. 19 (March, 1975), 5-7.

         Article reviews some key historical cases, addresses com-
         ponents of the issue, and concludes with a look at some
         solutions and unanswered questions.

863.   Moore, William J. and Newman, Robert J. "An Analysis
         of the Quality Differentials in Male-Female Academic Place-
         ments." Economic Inquiry. 15 (July, 1977), 413-434.

         Analyzes whether a significant differential exists in the qual-
         ity of the academic placements of male and female econo-
         mists for the period 1960 to 1974. Concludes that males
         had a 22.2 per cent advantage in placement quality over
         women and that most of this can be attributed to some form
         of discrimination.

864.   "More on 'Affirmative Action and the AAUP. '" AAUP Bul-
         letin. 62 (October, 1976), 326-332.

Several authors reply, pro and con, to Malcolm Sherman's article "Affirmative Action and the AAUP, " (AAUP Bulletin, December, 1975). Sherman replies to his critics.

865.   "More Women Seeking Redress. " The New York Times. March 26, 1975, p. 36.

Article points up the increasing number of women college educators who are resorting to legal action to counter alleged discrimination in areas of hiring, promotion, tenure, fringe benefits and forced retirement; underlying causes of trend are evident in figures released recently by the National Center for Educational Statistics which show that percentage of males holding tenured positions is more than twice that of women and average salary of women academics is only 83 per cent of what men receive; options open to women who feel that they are victims of discrimination detailed.

866.   Muffo, John and others. Equal Pay for Equal Qualifications? A Model for Determining Race or Sex Discrimination in Salaries. AIR Forum Paper 1978. Paper presented at the annual Association for Institutional Research Forum, Houston, Texas, May 21-25, 1978. May 1978. 16 p.

Describes a four step process to determine the existence and extent of discrimination: policy, data collection and analysis, salary adjustment determination, and follow-up and monitoring.

867.   National Board on Graduate Education. Minority Group Participation in Graduate Education: A Report with Recommendations. Washington, D. C.: National Academy of Sciences, 1976. 273 p.

Chapters include patterns of minority participation, barriers to participation, present context of graduate education and impact on minority participation, activities and concerns of graduate schools, and current efforts to promote minority participation. Of particular importance are the sections on labor market for advanced-degree holders, implications of affirmative action in higher education, and legal issues. Excellent bibliography provided.

868.   National Education Association. Salaries Paid and Salary-Related Practices in Higher Education, 1971-72. Washington, D. C.: National Education Association, 1972.

Compares salaries between men and women faculty, although statistics are not broken down by rank.

869.   Nelson, Bernard W. and others. "Expanding Educational Opportunities in Medicine for Black and Other Minority Students. " Journal of Medical Education. 45 (October, 1970), 731-736.

Condensation of "Report of the Association of American Medical Colleges Task Force to the Inter-Association Committee on Expanding Education Opportunity in Medicine for Black and Other Minority Students. "

870.   Nevill, Dorothy. "Achieving Salary Equity. " Educational Record. 56 (Fall, 1975), 266-270.

Outlines three techniques for use by higher education institutions to achieve salary equity: salary prediction, counterparting, and grievance procedures.

871.   "New Group Backs Hiring Guidelines. " The New York Times. February 27, 1975, p. 12.

New national organization, Committee for Affirmative Action in Universities, is being formed to support the Federal government's guidelines for hiring women and minorities; committee rejects arguments of program's critics that affirmative action has led to the establishment of quotas discriminatory to white males and that standards have sometimes been lowered to give preference to less-qualified groups; hundreds of professors said to have signed petition on behalf of affirmative action.

872.   "New Guidelines Set for Affirmative-Action Negotiations. " The Chronicle of Higher Education. 16 (April 17, 1978), 15.

Discusses the Department of Labor's new guidelines for the Office for Civil Rights (HEW) to use in negotiating "conciliation agreements" with colleges and universities found to have inadequate affirmative action plans. Guidelines focus on "in-place" plans such as utilization analyses and goals and timetables rather than prospective plans. The OCR is not to rely upon the universities to conduct programs to discover possible discrimination, but rather, the OCR itself would conduct "on-site" reviews of affirmative action plans.

873.   Newcomb, Betty. "The Affirmative Action Critics: A New Mythology. " Social Research Administrators Journal. 9 (Fall, 1977), 49-53.

Describes employment practices in higher education; based upon a round table presentation.

874.   Nies, Judith. Women and Fellowships. Washington, D. C.: Women's Equity Action League, 1974. 27 p.

Explains why the vast majority of major fellowship awards go to men, including the image of the fellowship as male and that information about many programs is informal, passing through word-of-mouth networks. Describes how recent developments are helping to change the situation.

875.   Nisbet, Lee.   "Affirmative Action--A Liberal Program?"
        Reverse Discrimination.   Edited by Barry R. Gross.   New
        York: Prometheus, 1977.   Pp. 50-53.

        Author criticizes liberals for shifting from traditional liberal
        concern with individual rights to a concern with abstract
        groups.   Government-administered program is trying to ac-
        complish impossible feat of securing just ends (equal job op-
        portunity) through unjust means (reverse discrimination).

876.   "No Progress This Year: Report on the Economic Status of
        the Profession, 1976-1977. "   AAUP Bulletin.   63 (August,
        1977), 146-228.

        Includes the average salaries given by rank and by sex, and
        by name of institution.

877.   Nordvall, Robert C.   "Affirmative Action Implementation:
        Rightness and Self-Righteousness. "   Journal of the College
        & University Personnel Association.   25 (July, 1974), 21-24.

        Author suggests that anti-discrimination legislation can create
        reverse discrimination and enforcing agencies that exceed the
        intent of the law.

878.   Oaks, Dallin H.   "Title IX: Administrative, Legal and Con-
        stitutional Aspects. "   Vital Speeches.   43 (April 1, 1977),
        372-375.

        President of Brigham Young University concludes that Title
        IX legislation is an acceptable moral and legal principle, but
        the regulations have driven it beyond law and reason.   Regu-
        lations exceed statutory authority granted by Congress.

879.   Oats, William R.   "Affirmative Action: A Question of Edu-
        cational Deprivation. "   Crisis.   85 (May, 1978), 172-174.

        Points out how debate over affirmative action has failed to
        realize that if race as a concept was used in the past to de-
        cide who would not benefit from the American Dream, it
        must now be used to remedy the effects of what has hap-
        pened.

880.   Odegaard, Charles.   Minorities in Medicine: From Recep-
        tive Passivity to Positive Action.   New York: Josiah Macy
        Foundation, 1976.

        Assesses medical schools' efforts to increase minority stu-
        dent enrollment the past decade.

881.   Oltman, Ruth M.   Campus 1970:   Where Do Women Stand?
        Washington, D. C.:   American Association of University
        Women, 1970.   46 p.

Presents the results of a questionnaire sent to presidents of
750 colleges and universities which hold institutional membership in the AAUW.   Its purpose is to evaluate the activities of women and the extent of their participation at all
levels of involvement--as students, administrators, faculty,
and trustees.   The results indicate that at every level, wom-
en are underrepresented or placed in a position with little
power in decision-making.

882.   O'Neil, Robert M.   "Federal Forays and Academic Autono-
        my. " Viewpoints.   52 (September, 1976), 73-79.

        Discusses federal regulation of higher education and academic
        reaction to such regulations.   Poses three questions: what
        troubles the university administrators, what are the consti-
        tutional limits on federal regulations, and what are the lim-
        its of public policy?   Particular emphasis is placed upon ad-
        ministrators reaction to Title IX and affirmative action regu-
        lations.   Concludes that there must be a rapprochement be-
        tween regulators and those subject to regulation.

883.   On Campus with Women.   Number 20, June 1978.   Washing-
        ton, D. C. :   Association of American Colleges.   Project on
        the Status and Education of Women, 1978.   11 p.
        (ED 162 571)

        Occasional newsletter publishes information on affirmative ac-
        tion and employment, education of women, Title IX, women's
        studies, medicine, sports, and institutional news.   HEW in-
        vestigations of educational institutions, court decisions on
        discrimination, and the status of women in academe are par-
        ticularly newsworthy.

884.   Ornstein, Allan C.   "Affirmative Action and the Education
        Industry. " Policy Issues in Education.   Edited by Allan C.
        Ornstein and Steven I. Miller.   Lexington, Mass. :   Lexington
        Books, 1976.

        Criticizes federal bureaucrats for substituting proportional
        representation for individual merit in higher education.
        Claims that the concept of equal opportunity has been trans-
        formed into the ideology of equal results.

885.   _____ .   "Quality, Not Quotas. " Society.   13 (January-
        February, 1976), 10, 14-17.

        Criticizes the federal bureaucrats for undermining the integ-
        rity and scholarly functions of the university by forcing in-
        stitutions to hire not the most qualified candidates but from
        a limited and sometimes qualifiable pool in order to fill a
        government-imposed quota.

886.   _____ .   "What Does Affirmative Action Affirm?   A View-
        point. " Phi Delta Kappan.   57 (December, 1975), 242-245.

Contends that the federal government is undermining the
scholarly functions of the university by its reliance on statistical guides for detecting discrimination and ignoring the
criterion of qualification.

887.   Ortiz de Montellano, Bernard.   "Affirmative Action. "   Sci-
        ence.   190 (November, 1975), 508, 510.

        Replies to HEW Secretary Caspar Weinberger's statements
        on affirmative action in an earlier article.   Criticizes HEW
        for failure to force universities to comply with affirmative
        action regulations, for perpetuating the old-boy network, to
        the exclusion of women and minorities, and for reporting the
        number of minorities as a percentage of the total faculty of
        the entire institution in order to disguise the "abominable
        record" of individual departments, such as colleges of sci-
        ence.   Gives statistics to show that women and minority fac-
        ulty have not appreciably changed in the last three years.

888.   "Pact Gives U. S. Contracts to 13 Colleges Despite Lack of
        Approved Hiring Plans. "   The New York Times.   June 25,
        1975, p. 48.

        HEW and Labor Departments negotiated proposed agreement
        to let 13 colleges and universities with unapproved affirma-
        tive action hiring plans get over $20 million in Federal pacts
        despite rule requiring that such plans be approved before
        pacts are awarded.

889.   Pati, Gopal C. , and Mezey, Michael J.   "Designing an Af-
        firmative Action Program for the Handicapped. "   Training
        and Development Journal.   32 (June, 1978), 14-22.

        Presents guidelines from the U. S. Department of Labor for
        developing an affirmative action employment program for the
        handicapped.   Includes checklists of affirmative action items
        and a sample program policy plan.

890.   Patterson, Michelle.   "Alice in Wonderland: A Study of
        Women Faculty in Graduate Departments of Sociology. "   The
        American Sociologist.   6 (August, 1971), 226-234.

        Study investigates the interaction between the personal char-
        acteristics of male and female sociologists and the organiza-
        tional rewards and treatment accorded both sexes.   Concludes
        that evidence exists of a systematic pattern of excluding
        women from the two organizational rewards that most influ-
        ence an individual's prestige within the discipline.   Women
        are excluded from high-ranking departments and from high-
        ranking positions in almost all departments.

891.   Pelikan, Jaroslav.   "Quality and Equality. "   The New York
        Times.   March 29, 1976, p. 29.

Discusses the need to increase the quantity and improve the quality of available pool of minority group candidates in order to assure equal employment opportunity at the college level; notes that Yale University is among the institutions with moderately successful programs of minority recruitment in various graduate schools.

892.   Persson, Leonard N.   "Impact of Collective Bargaining and Programs of Equal Employment Opportunity and Affirmative Action on the Role of the Personnel Officer. " Journal of the College & University Personnel Association.   27 (July-August, 1976), 21-67.

Results of a mail survey of 300 full-time personnel officers concerning the impact of collective bargaining and Equal Employment Opportunity programs on the personnel officer.   Also examined are the possible consequences that impact may have for other groups within the institutions.   Excellent bibliography included.

893.   Pettigrew, L. Eudora.   "Reverse Discrimination--Fact or Fancy?" Integrated Education.   14 (November-December, 1976), 3-4.

Concludes that even though federal legislation designed to equalize employment opportunity for all U. S. citizens has been enacted, the only group to enhance its employment status over the past ten years has been white males.

894.   Pollock, Mordeca Jane.   "On Academic Quotas. " The New York Times.   March 4, 1975, p. 33.

Article discusses the Executive Order 11246 as it applies to higher education; charges that HEW is responsible for the failure of affirmative action to increase the employment of women despite their qualifications and availability on the job market; cites log-rolling system from which women rarely benefit, but which is the norm for faculty hiring; notes that colleges and universities face about 500 complaints of discrimination against academic hiring bias and no such complaint has been proven unjustified upon HEW inquiry.

895.   Pondrom, Cyrena N.   "Setting Priorities in Developing an Affirmative Action Program. " Journal of Medical Education.   50 (May, 1975), 427-434.

Discusses how affirmative action programs should include special activities to ensure that women and minorities participate in employment and educational opportunities in the numbers in which qualified members of these groups are represented in the nation or community.   Describes six kinds of activities which should receive priority in establishing a medical school affirmative action program, including a review of salaries for equity; establishing goals for hiring; review of admissions criteria; survey of physical facilities for women.

896.   Pottinger, J. Stanley. "Administering a Solution: Goals Versus Quotas. " Journal of the College & University Personnel Association. 26 (January, 1975), 21-25.

Former Director of the Office for Civil Rights (HEW), responsible for implementing affirmative action regulations in higher education, notes the federal regulation guidelines and critical responses to them from the academic community. Sketches the difference between numerical quotas and realistic goals in equal employment opportunity.
(ED 100 246)

897.   _____.   "Come Now, Professor Hook. " The New York Times. December 18, 1971, p. 29.

Office for Civil Rights Director, Pottinger, replies to Sidney Hook's November 5, 1971 article. Director claims that concrete evidence of discrimination in jobs cannot be dismissed with claims of reverse discrimination.

898.   _____.   "The Drive for Employment Equality. " Protean. 2 (Summer, 1972), 6-11.

Discusses the Executive Order 11246 on equal employment opportunity requirements on college campuses. Order embodies two concepts: nondiscrimination and affirmative action, the latter defined as requiring a contractor to go beyond a passive stance of nondiscrimination and to employ members of groups which have traditionally been excluded, thereby mitigating the effect of discrimination in society at large. Defines quotas as numerical level of employment that must be met while goals signify projected levels of achievement resulting from analysis by the contractor of his deficiencies and what he believes he can do about them.

899.   _____.   "Race, Sex and Jobs: The Drive Toward Equality. " Change. 4 (October, 1972), 26-29.

Discusses the two concepts of nondiscrimination and affirmative action. Latter requires universities to determine whether it has failed to recruit, employ, and promote women and minorities commensurate with their availability. Where women and minorities are not represented on a university's rolls, despite their availability (when they are "under-utilized"), the university has an obligation to initiate affirmative efforts to recruit and hire them, and to arrange a schedule for how such recruitment is to take place. Explains why the attack on "quotas" is a phony and rhetorical issue. Explains why goals are required and suggests that many uni-

versity spokesmen have as their real target affirmative action itself, rather than "quotas." Too many institutions fail
to deal voluntarily with such issues as salary reviews, fair
grievance procedures, and safeguards against clustering of
segregation of women and minorities.

900.   Pottker, Janice.   "Overt and Covert Forms of Discrimination
        Against Academic Women." Sex Bias in the Schools.   Ruth-
        erford, N.J.:   Fairleigh Dickinson University, 1977.   Pp.
        380-410.

        The study deals primarily with the overt forms of bias
        against women such as hiring and promotions, and the covert
        forms such as maternity leave regulations.   Author places
        such discrimination within the larger concept of institutional
        discrimination.

901.   Prestage, Jewel L.   "Quelling the Mythical Revolution in
        Higher Education: Retreat from the Affirmative Action Con-
        cept." Journal of Politics.   41 (August, 1979), 763-783.

        Describes the general status of blacks in American graduate
        education and in political science and the South, in particu-
        lar, in terms of black faculty, political science doctorates
        conferred on blacks, current enrollment of blacks in Ph.D.
        programs and impediments to their access in this field of
        study.

902.   "Program to Spur College Hiring of Women and Minority
        Teachers Lags Amid Continuing Controversy." The New
        York Times.   December 28, 1975, p. 23.

        Article on the Times survey of the effectiveness of the 5-
        year old affirmative action program to promote the hiring of
        more women and minorities as faculty members; finds that
        opponents and supporters of affirmative action agree that it
        is not being well carried out and has not been a success;
        notes that Office for Civil Rights has approved affirmative
        action plans for 31 of nation's 1, 300 eligible institutions;
        claims that there is no monitoring of such plans to assure
        compliance, and that no college has lost its Federal funding,
        as law provides, for failing to comply.   Additional comments
        by supporters and opponents of affirmative action noted.

903.   Pruitt, Anne S.   "Stop the Revolving Door." AGB Reports.
        21 (March-April, 1979), 17-19.

        Suggests a comprehensive developmental program for disad-
        vantaged students in college, especially in graduate and pro-
        fessional schools.   Recommends kinds of institutional and
        state support, and on campus, a decision-making structure
        and an advisory structure.

904.   Pyles, Jackson.   "Rights in Conflict."   Journal of Inter-
        Group Relations.   6 (April, 1977), 18-23.

        Discusses the DeFunis case of alleged reverse discrimination
        to admissions in professional school within the context of
        whether one group's gains have to be another group's loss.

905.   "'Quotas' Assailed in Faculty Hiring."   The New York Times.
        December 8, 1974, p. 47.

        In letter to President Ford, several dozen prominent univer-
        sity professors, including three Nobel laureates, signify op-
        position to the Federal government's affirmative action plan
        for increasing the proportion of women and minorities on fac-
        ulties in higher education; signers listed; brief discussion of
        the pros and cons of affirmative action; Director of the Of-
        fice for Civil Rights, Peter Holmes, responds to criticism
        by denying that quotas are being imposed by HEW and that
        they are in violation of the law; repeats assertion that insti-
        tutions who do not comply with affirmative action approach
        run the risk of having their Federal funds withheld.

906.   Rabinove, Samuel.   "Law School Minorities: What Price Ad-
        mission?"   America.   128 (April 28, 1973), 387-389.

        Discusses why the professional school is caught between a
        social need to grant preferential admission to disadvantaged
        minority applicants and the risks that go with reverse dis-
        crimination.

907.   Rafky, David M.   "The Black Scholar in the Academic Mar-
        ketplace."   Teachers College Record.   74 (December, 1972),
        225-260.

        Study of barriers to employment of blacks in predominantly
        white, non-Southern institutions.   Data based upon results of
        questionnaire.   Results are mixed, although author does not
        believe that the system of hiring generates discrimination.

908.   Reagan, Barbara R.   "Report of the Committee on the Status
        of Women in the Economics Profession."   American Eco-
        nomic Review.   65 (May, 1975), 490-501.

        Presents data on women in academic departments and in non-
        academic positions, for the year 1974-75.   Data and analysis
        on number of degrees, by sex; number of graduate students,
        employment by level of degree; number of faculty by rank;
        distribution of department of economics by number of women
        faculty; net change in faculty positions from 1973 to 1975;
        relative salaries for rank and time; promotion and tenure de-
        cisions; and affirmative action in economics departments on
        campus.

909.   _____, and Maynard, Betty. "Sex Discrimination in Universities: An Approach Through Internal Labor Market Analyses. " AAUP Bulletin. 60 (March, 1974), 11-21.

Analyzes the internal labor market concept and its application to faculty. Such a concept in determining sex discrimination focuses on two aspects: differences among departments in entrance rate; and policies on promotion and salary increases. Salaries of individual women were found to be 5 to 50 per cent less than average for comparable men. Reasons for such discrepancies discussed.

910.   "The Rebellion of the Chancellors. " The Washington Post. (Editorial.) June 27, 1975, p. A-14.

Editorial concerns the hesitation and misgivings among administrators in higher education regarding federal intervention to implement and monitor affirmative action policies on campus.

911.   Record, Jane Cassels, and Record, Wilson. "Ethnic Studies and Affirmative Action: Ideological Roots and Implications for the Quality of American Life. " Social Science Quarterly. 55 (September, 1974), 502-519.

Reviews the background and interaction of minority studies and affirmative action program as they developed in the 1960's. Also discusses some middle and long-range developments for black colleges, graduate, and professional schools, and society as a whole.

912.   "Report of Committee W on the Status of Women in the Academic Profession, 1978-79. " Academe. 65 (October, 1979), 413-15.

Annual report of Committee W on the status of women in the academic professions. Efforts center on achieving economic parity and equal benefits compared to male academicians. Reports also deal with affirmative action, efforts to end sex discrimination, pension benefits, and Title IX.

913.   Rigby, Sandra. "The Work May Be Equal, but Is the Pay?" Journal of the College & University Personnel Association. 25 (January, 1974), 14-21.

Discusses some implications of the Equal Pay Act as it applies to faculty, and suggests that educational institutions within the states should group together to develop uniform criteria for adjustment of salary inequities.

914.   Ringer, Benjamin B. "Affirmative Action, Quotas, and Meritocracy. " Society. 13 (January-February, 1976), 12, 22-25.

Defends affirmative action policy not only on the grounds of
social justice but also on the serious inadequacies of the
merit system as it actually operates, including in universities. Regards the goal of affirmative action programs as a
"merit system rid of inherent biases, subjectivities, and en-
crustations, a system that recognizes its responsibilities" to
incorporate "affected classes" as a functioning part of the
system.

915. "Rise in Black Students Brings Disputes on Law School Re-
      cruiting. " The New York Times. April 7, 1974, p. 48.

      A Times survey of quota systems and minority recruitment
      policies at U. S. graduate schools reports white students are
      now charging reverse discrimination is being practiced against
      them and professionals are worried about decline in profes-
      sional standards.

916. Roark, Anne C. "Federal Sex Bias Forms Seen Inviting
      Dishonesty. " The Chronicle of Higher Education. 13 (De-
      cember 6, 1976), 8.

      Assurance forms which must be signed by administrators in
      higher education to assert their compliance with anti-dis-
      crimination legislation actually encourage college officials to
      lie. Officials encouraged to say that discrimination does not
      exist on their campuses or that they are eliminating it when
      no progress is actually being made.

917. Roberts, Sylvia. "Equality of Opportunity in Higher Educa-
      tion: Impact of Contract Compliance and the Equal Rights
      Amendment. " Liberal Education. 59 (May, 1973), 202-216.

      Focuses on women employed as faculty members and staff at
      colleges and universities. Discusses affirmative action legis-
      lation and regulations, including Revised Order #4. Dis-
      cusses court cases related to race and sex discrimination in
      higher education.

918. Robustelli, Joseph A. and Ericsson, Carl W. "Affirmative
      Action in the Academic Community. " Journal of the College
      & University Personnel Association. 26 (October-November,
      1975), 7-14.

      Describes the progress made and the problems encountered
      in implementating affirmative action plans from the vantage
      point of the personnel office.

919. Roche, George C., III. "On Campus: 'An Iceberg of Gov-
      ernment Intervention'? " U. S. News & World Report. 74
      (January 1, 1973), 48-52.

      Excerpts of a report entitled "Government Intervention in
      Private Education" to the American Association of Presidents

of Independent Colleges and Universities, by the President of
Hillsdale College in Michigan.   Author criticizes federal regulations for forcing colleges to admit unqualified students and
to hire second-best applicants for faculty jobs.   Regulations
force the substitution of quotas for quality and assaults institutional self-determination and integrity of many schools.

920.   Rossi, Alice S. and Calderwood, Ann, eds.   Academic Wom-
       en on the Move.   New York: Russell Sage Foundation, 1973.
       560 p.

       Contents are grouped under the headings: recruitment, train-
       ing, and employment; women on the contemporary academic
       scene; and action toward change.   This collection of essays,
       research findings, and field manuals provide documentation
       that women have not achieved full equality and participation
       in higher education.   Examined also is the pattern of govern-
       ment enforcement (or non-enforcement) of equal opportunity
       mandates.   Bibliography included.

921.   Roybal, Edward R.   "Minorities in Medicine: The Next Dec-
       ade. "   Journal of Medical Education.   54 (August, 1979),
       652-655.

       Discusses the participation of minority groups in medical
       education, focusing upon the health status and needs of mi-
       norities, student recruitment and affirmative action programs,
       and rising educational costs.   Discusses also the future of
       minority group participation and the support needed from
       schools, foundations, and government.

922.   Rumbarger, Margaret L.   "The Great Quota Debate and Oth-
       er Issues in Affirmative Action: Some Observations. "
       Marquette University Education Review.   4 (Spring, 1973),
       2-6.

       Associate Secretary for the AAUP briefly describes affirma-
       tive action regulations applied to higher education and the
       critical response to them by the academic community.   Be-
       lieves that the charges and rebuttals of debased standards
       and lost institutional autonomy have obscured the real objec-
       tives of the law against discrimination of women and minor-
       ities.   The objective, in part, "is to discover, preserve and
       transmit knowledge and experience, not selectively for one
       group, but for all people. "

923.   Russell, Joseph J.   "Institutionalizing Affirmative Action. "
       Journal of Afro-American Issues.   5 (Winter, 1977), 33-42.

       Explains how patterns of racial and sexual exclusion can be
       broken only by sweeping legal measures and institutionally
       determined modification of employment practices.   University
       decision-makers must focus on the problems of institutional-
       izing affirmative action programs.

924.   Sammons, Jeffrey.   "I Am a White Male. "   Crisis.   82 (October, 1975),   292-296.

Suggests that competence and merit are elements in need of examination, and gives four reasons why being a black, woman, or Spanish-American is a qualification for academic appointment.   Stresses that energy ought to be directed to increasing support of colleges and universities and not to fighting affirmative action.

925.   Sandler, Bernice.   "Backlash in Academe: A Critique of the Lester Report. "   Teachers College Record.   76 (February, 1975), 401-419.

Director of the Association of American Colleges' Project on the Status and Education of Women, Sandler criticizes Richard Lester's Antibias Regulation of Universities (1974) for its lack of supporting data and its innumerable inaccuracies. Gives statistics to refute Lester's charge that universities are being forced to hire less-qualified women and minorities or that affirmative action lowers academic qualifications. Author describes affirmative action as meaning to prohibit hiring based upon the "old boy" system which often excludes women and minorities.   Refutes Lester's claim that only a small supply of women and minorities are available and qualified for faculty employment.

926.   _____ .   "Discrimination Is Immoral, Illegal and, Offenders Find, Costly. "   College and University Business.   56 (February, 1974), 27-30.

Briefly describes the regulations and laws prohibiting sex discrimination in higher education.   Refutes charges that affirmative action results in lower academic standards, "reverse discrimination, " and the imposition of quotas.   Includes information on the more than 400 institutions which have been charged with sex discrimination, none of which have been refuted by HEW investigations.

927.   _____ .   "Equity for Women in Higher Education. "   Current Issues in Higher Education.   27 (1972), 78-90.

Discusses what women want from higher education: equality of opportunity, freedom from myths, such as a "shortage of qualified women, " equal pay, and full integration of women, as faculty and students, on campus.   Women also want comprehensive plans of affirmative action to remedy effects of past discrimination.

928.   _____ .   "The Hand That Rocked the Cradle Has Learned to Rock the Boat. "   Toward Affirmative Action.   Lucy W. Sells, issue editor.   San Francisco: Jossey-Bass, 1974. Pp.   1-22.

Leading advocate of affirmative action programs reviews legislation banning discrimination in higher education, summarizes issues faced by colleges and universities, and analyzes some of the myths of affirmative action as seen by its advocates.

929. _____. "Sex Discrimination, Admissions in Higher Education and the Law. " College and University. 50 (Spring, 1975), 197-212.

Defines sex discrimination in higher education in these areas: admissions and Title IX provisions, types of discrimination in admissions, additional factors that affect admissions policies (such as myths and arguments used to limit the admission of women), affirmative recruiting and preferential admissions, and how to end discrimination in admissions.

930. _____. "Women in Higher Education: What Constitutes Equity?" Vital Speeches. 38 (June 15, 1972), 532-537.

Explains what women want from institutions of higher education: equality of opportunity, equal pay, end of the nepotism rule, comprehensive plans of affirmative action to remedy the effects of past discrimination, and full integration of women on campus.

931. _____, and Steinbach, Sheldon Elliot. HEW Contract Compliance--Major Concerns of Institutions. Washington, D. C.: Association of American Colleges, 1973?

Explains how HEW conducts its contract compliance procedures, as directed under Executive Order 11246, as amended by Executive Order 11375. At first, priority went to individual complaints, but now it has shifted to pattern complaints and to preaward compliance reviews. Article identifies nine issues in the compliance review process: lack of uniform action by regional HEW offices; the need for federal guidelines; access to personnel files; due process of law in compliance reviews; time requirement for response; status of retroactive pay under Order 11246, as amended; publication of affirmative action programs; criteria for measuring discrimination; and graduate admissions. On each of these subjects the institutions and women's groups present their points of view.

932. Schiller, A. R. "Aware: Report on Women in Librarianship. " American Libraries. 2 (December, 1971), 1215-1216.

Review of women's representation in top positions shows rapid decline; also reports on affirmative action plans in academe.

933. Scientific Manpower Commission. Professional Women and Minorities: A Manpower Resource Service /prepared by

Betty M. Vetter and Eleanor L. Babco. Washington, D. C.:
Scientific Manpower Commission, 1975-   . (Loose-leaf for
updating.)

Book is designed to assist persons or groups seeking data on
the participation of women and/or minorities in those professional areas generally requiring formal education such as
the Baccalaureate level or above. Data based on years 1970
through 1975, with semi-annual updates provided. Over 100
data sources are used. Data covers women and minorities
in terms of their enrollment, participation, and degrees
earned in the science professions, social sciences, engineering, arts, humanities, and in professional occupations overall. Also contains sections on recruitment sources, bibliography, and data sources, with subject index included.

934.   Scott, Ann. "It's Time for Equal Education. " Ms. 1 (Oc-
       tober, 1972), 122-125.

Legislative Vice President for NOW describes sex discrimination in higher education in the areas of admissions policies, financial aid, and health services. Outlines a model
affirmative action plan to implement the Higher Education
Act of 1972 which prohibits sex discrimination against students and employees in federally assisted education programs.

935.   Scott, Madison H.   "Affirmative Action/Personnel as a Vi-
       able Institutional Process. " Journal of the College & Univer-
       sity Personnel Association. 26 (October-November, 1975),
       3-6.

Contends that affirmative action is an expression of, and an
ingredient of, thoughtful and progressive personnel administration. Suggests that by establishing clear identification for
a personnel function and meshing affirmative action with it,
the institution would secure a number of advantages.

936.   Scott, Robert A.   "The Opening of Admissions: Implications
       for Policies and Procedures. " College and University. 52
       (Spring, 1977), 247-275.

Issues of equality and excellence examined along with barriers to postsecondary schooling, the organization of college
admissions, and widening of access to further schooling.
These factors are used in an intensive study of a single institution (Roosevelt University) and its policies and procedures.

937.   Seabury, Paul.   "HEW and the Universities. " Commentary.
       53 (February, 1972), 38-42.

Outlines the history of HEW's regulations relating to discriminatory hiring. Charges that the universities must now
prove their innocence and that HEW fails to understand the

complexities of hiring practices and inequities that might result from hiring goals based upon race and sex. Concludes that historically all experience with quotas and preferences interferes with individual rights. Employment goals and access to recruitment files, if necessary, have pernicious effects on faculty, administration, students, and white males highly qualified for jobs.

938. Sedlacek, William E. "Should Higher Education Students Be Admitted Differentially by Race and Sex: The Evidence." Journal of the National Association of College Admissions Counselors. 22 (September, 1977), 22-23.

Abstract of a study by the Cultural Study Center at the University of Maryland, in 1975. Cites studies that show no negative relationships between traditional predictors and college grades for black students and that if traditional predictors are employed, optimum validity is achieved by separate equations of cut-off scores for each race-sex subgroup.

939. Seligman, Daniel. "How 'Equal Opportunity' Turned Into Employment Quotas." Fortune. 8 (March, 1973), 160-168.

Explains how non-discrimination legislation turned into the imposition of quotas in business and higher education.

940. Sells, Lucy W. "Critical Points for Affirmative Action." Toward Affirmative Action. Edited by Lucy W. Sells. San Francisco: Jossey-Bass, 1974. Pp. 71-80.

Data on sex and ethnic differences in academic achievement document a pervasive climate of different expectations about behavior on the basis of sex and ethnicity and indicate the need for affirmative action at five critical points in the academic system.

941. "Sex Discrimination and Contract Compliance Beyond the Legal Requirement." Educational Record. 53 (Summer, 1972), 265-266.

Statement by Roger Heyns, President of the American Council on Education. Discusses the steps colleges and universities can take to reduce barriers to women in higher education.

942. Shapley, Deborah. "University Women's Rights: Whose Feet Are Dragging?" Science. 175 (January, 1972), 151-154.

Surveys progress made by HEW in enforcing equal opportunity for employment of women in university research projects sponsored by federal funds. Concludes that "contract compliance is proving a clumsy mechanism" for women's groups anxious to make rapid changes in their universities.

943.   Sherman, Malcolm J.   "Affirmative Action and the AAUP. "
        AAUP Bulletin.   61 (December, 1975), 293-303.

        Discusses why the implementation of affirmative action pro-
        grams on college campuses is inconsistent with equal em-
        ployment opportunity.   Criticizes HEW's imposition of quotas
        on colleges which result in reverse discrimination.   Dis-
        cusses, then refutes arguments made on behalf of affirmative
        action.   Reviews the report of the AAUP Council Committee
        on Discrimination and explains what the AAUP must do to
        promote equal opportunity and high professional standards in
        institutions of higher education.

944.   Shiffrin, Mark A.   "What's Ahead: OCR Enforcement of
        Anti-Discrimination Regulations. "   Change.   10 (February,
        1978),   44-45.

        Describes the problem areas the Office for Civil Rights
        (HEW) will focus upon in the following months: stricter en-
        forcement of civil rights legislation and Executive Orders;
        particularly Title IX regulations, age and handicapped dis-
        crimination.

945.   Shoemaker, Elwood A. and McKeen, Ronald L.   "Affirmative
        Action and Hiring Practices in Higher Education. "   Research
        in Higher Education.   3 (December, 1975),   359-364.

        Analyzes data from 191 institutions which placed notices in
        "The Chronicle of Higher Education. "   Reveals that there
        are qualified minority and female candidates available and
        members of minority groups are making progress toward
        employment (females even greater progress) while white
        males are not being closed out of the hiring process.

946.   Silberman, Laurence H.   "The Road to Racial Quotas. "
        Wall Street Journal.   190 (August 11, 1977),   14.

        Author served in the Labor Department and helped devise
        goals for government minority employment contractors.
        Concludes that the Labor Department's use of numerical
        standards led inequitably to the very quotas that the depart-
        ment initially wished to avoid.

947.   Silverman, B. I. and others.   "Minority Group Status and
        Bias in College Admissions Criteria. "   Educational and Psy-
        chological Measurement.   36 (Summer, 1976),   401-407.

        Cleary's & Thorndike's definition of bias in college admis-
        sions criteria (ACT scores and high school percentile rank)
        were examined for black, white, and Jewish students.   Use
        of the admissions criteria tended to overpredict blacks' per-
        formance, accurately predict white's performance, and un-
        derpredict that of Jews.

948. Silverman, Bernie I. "Reverse Discrimination. " Peabody
      Journal of Education. 52 (January, 1975), 116-121.

      Discusses the arguments in favor of affirmative action and
      shows why reverse discrimination is unfair, illegal, and
      stigmatizing.

949. Silvestri, Marco J. and Kane, Paul L. "How Affirmative
      Is the Action for Administrative Positions in Higher Educa-
      tion?" Journal of Higher Education. 46 (July, 1975), 445-
      450.

      Discusses the study that analyzed responses to fictitious posi-
      tion-wanted ads of females and minority candidates for ad-
      ministrative positions in higher education. Date suggests
      reluctant institutional commitment to locate and recruit fe-
      male and minority candidates for administrative positions.

950. Simon, H. J. and Covell, J. W. "Performance of Medical
      Students Admitted via Regular and Admission-Variance
      Routes. " Journal of Medical Education. 50 (March, 1975),
      237-241.

      Results of a survey of students granted admission variances
      at the University of California at San Diego School of Medi-
      cine in 1970-71 indicate that they achieved much success,
      attributed to the flexible curriculum at the school.

951. "Six Jewish Groups Charge Colleges with Reverse Bias. "
      The New York Times. January 14, 1973, p. 56.

      Six national Jewish organizations have sent 19 new examples
      of reverse discrimination against white males in college ad-
      missions and hiring practices to HEW Department; call on
      agency to carry out legal responsibility to prevent or elimi-
      nate preferential treatment; 19 examples are cases of white
      male applicants who were told that they could not be hired
      or admitted to schools of higher education because of their
      race or sex.

952. Slawson, John. "Affirmative Action and Quotas. " Com-
      mentary. 54 (December, 1972), 26, 28.

      Favors affirmative action in effort to advance the condition
      of minority groups to expedite their entry into the main-
      stream of American society. Describes the criteria to ful-
      fill the goals of affirmative action: search for applicants,
      compensatory services in education for disadvantaged indi-
      viduals, the utilization of the "pattern" approach as a crite-
      rion for ascertaining the presence or absence of discrimina-
      tory practices.

953. Sleeth, Boyd C. and Mishell, Robert I. "Black Under-
      Representation in United States Medical Schools. " The New

England Journal of Medicine. 297 (November 24, 1977), 1146-1148.

Analyzes statistics on medical-school applicants, medical-school students and college undergraduates. Concludes that the pool of qualified black applicants to medical schools has not been large enough to achieve appropriate black representation. Affirmative action programs for blacks who are already in college are unlikely to be sufficient by themselves to increase the pool of black applicants substantially. Such programs, therefore, should be developed for high-school students.

954. Smith, Cynthia J., ed. Advancing Equality of Opportunity: A Matter of Justice. New York: Ford Foundation, 1978. 213 p.

Papers presented from the proceedings of a national invitational conference held in Washington, D.C. in May, 1977 dealing with affirmative action in higher education. Topics include the ramifications of Bakke, public responsibility for assuring justice, reverse discrimination arguments and other legislative and administrative attacks on affirmative action, faculty and nonacademic problems in implementing affirmative action, affirmative action in a declining economy, increasing the supply of women and minorities, and higher education's responsibility for advancing equality of opportunity and justice, among other topics.

955. Smith, James F. "Reflections of a Respondent Attorney." Journal of Intergroup Relations. 6 (December, 1978), 40-48.

Suggests that while the book is far from closed on the issue of reverse discrimination, in light of Bakke, there is justification for rethinking and rewriting Equal Employment Opportunity Commission guidelines to focus upon opportunities rather than on numbers and goals.

956. Solomon, Lewis C. Male and Female Graduate Students: The Question of Equal Opportunity. New York: Praeger, 1976. 146 p.

Study of differential opportunities for men and women graduate students. Analysis provides some evidence that differential treatment exists, but also some data indicating that conditions have improved from the past.

957. _____. "Women in Doctoral Education: Clues and Puzzles Regarding Institutional Discrimination." Research in Higher Education. 1 (1973), 299-332.

Abstract of larger study mentioned above.

958.   Solomon, Henry, ed. "The Growing Influence of Federal
        Regulations. " Educational Record. 58 (Summer, 1977),
        270-289.

        Staff of George Washington University assessed the effects of
        federal legislation on university affairs, including academic,
        administrative, and research concerns.   The study analyzed
        civil rights legislation and compliance; non-civil rights legis-
        lation requiring compliance; government funding priorities;
        and funds administration.   Negative and positive effects are
        discussed.

959.   Sowell, Thomas.   "Affirmative Action Reconsidered. "   Public
        Interest.   No. 42 (Winter, 1976), 47-65.

        Discusses basic concepts and legal rationale of affirmative
        action; measures in some general terms the magnitude and
        severity of the problem that was intended to be solved or
        ameliorated by affirmative action programs; considers actual
        results achieved and general trends set in motion by such
        programs, and weighs implications of affirmative action poli-
        cies.   Statistics demonstrate that minorities have made con-
        siderable progress in appointment to institutions of higher
        education before current affirmative action programs were
        begun.   Minority and female academics are relatively well
        off, contrary to popular accounts.

960.   _____ .   "Affirmative Action Reconsidered. "   Urban
        League Review.   2 (Summer, 1977), 9-24.

        The academic profession is used to study the necessity and
        effectiveness of affirmative action programs.   Demonstrates
        that this is an area in which crucial career characteristics
        can be quantified and have been researched extensively over
        the years.

961.   _____ .   Affirmative Action Reconsidered: Was It Neces-
        sary in Academia?   Washington, D. C.:   American Enterprise
        Institute for Public Policy Research, 1975.   45 p.

        Draws on a large general literature on race and sex differ-
        entials in employment, pay, and promotion prospects, with
        emphasis on academic careers.   Criticizes government regu-
        latory agencies for their burdensome requirements, unsup-
        ported presumptions, ignorance of academic norms and prac-
        tices, and presumption of university guilt on discrimination
        unless they can prove otherwise.   Suggests that so-called
        discrimination is actually the result of individual career
        choices.

962.   _____ .   "Are Quotas Good for Blacks?"   Commentary.
        65 (June, 1978), 39-43.

Discusses the fallacy that statistical representation of a group in jobs, etc., measures discrimination, the fallacy that preferential treatment compensates people for past wrongs, the mismatching of minority students and the institutions they attend, even though the minorities meet standards in a wide range of colleges and universities, and the stigma attached to minorities who are given preferential treatment.

963.   . "Compensatory Education: Two Views." The New York Times. November 14, 1976, XII, p. 19.

Describes the compensatory mismatching of students with institutions. Believes that the existing range of American colleges and universities can easily accommodate the range of academic preparation of minority students. Believes it wrong to emphasize that academic institutions have a "need" for certain minority body count, for legal, moral, or public relations purposes.

964.   . Dissenting from Liberal Orthodoxy: A Black Scholar Speaks for the "Angry Moderates." Reprint No. 29. Washington, D. C.: American Enterprise Institute for Public Policy Research, 1976. 16 p.

Describes the situations whereby the grand delusion of contemporary liberals is that they have both the right and ability to move fellow creatures around like blocks of wood, in effect denying other people's humanity. In affirmative action programs, there is very little hard evidence that quotas meet the purpose of such programs to compensate minorities and women for past injustices.

965.   . "The Plight of Black Students in the United States." Daedalus. 103 (Spring, 1974), 179-196.

Discusses the arguments for special admissions of black students, the question of whether academic standards are lowered for minority students, the hiring of minority faculty members to meet affirmative action quotas, the fact that black students at all levels of ability are systematically mismatched upward. Describes how the government has imposed race and sex quotas without accepting responsibility for them, while carefully preserving its "deniability." Maintains that some of the gains under affirmative action are illusory because black bodies count not only for hiring but also sending recruiting letters and conducting interviews, whether or not officials have any intention of proceeding beyond these first stages.

966. Speck, David G. "Title IX: The Death of Athletics and Other Myths." NASPA Journal. 13 (Winter, 1976), 73-75.

Author tries to refute all the misinterpretations of the law enacted by Congress which prohibits sex discrimination in education. Concludes that this law has achieved long due improvements in the status of women in colleges.

967.   Spivak, Jonathan. "Red Tape in Academe: Universities See Their Autonomy Slipping Away Due to U. S. Rules on Bias, Pensions, and Privacy. " Wall Street Journal. 188 (December 8, 1976), 46.

Discusses the belief that the government is engulfing the university in bureaucratic rules and regulations which are costly to implement and which challenge the university's autonomy.

968.   Squires, Gregory D. Affirmative Action: A Guide for the Perplexed. East Lansing: Michigan State University, Center for Continuing Education, 1977. 204 p.

Gives views on some of the controversies which emerged with the advent of affirmative action; leverage provided by civil rights law to successfully overcome discrimination and to improve the life chances of women and minorities.

969.   _____. "Affirmative Action, Quotas and Inequality. " The Journal of Intergroup Relations. 3 (Fall, 1974), 26-37.

Argues that equalizing opportunity alone will not bring about equality with respect to the way our society distributes its resources; changing individuals in some fashion without altering social structural relationships will effect a relatively small change in the present unequal distribution of goods and services.

970.   _____, ed. Inequality and Public Policy: The Ethics of Affirmative Action. East Lansing: Michigan State University. Institute for Community Development, Continuing Education Service, 1977. 50 p.

Proceedings of a conference held at Michigan State University, December 6, 1976.

971.   Steele, Claude M. and Green, Stephen G. "Affirmative Action and Academic Hiring: A Case Study of a Value Conflict. " Journal of Higher Education. 47 (July, 1976), 413-435.

A study of responses to affirmative action at a large university revealed that using estimates of the minorities available at prestige schools, as opposed to more comprehensive availability estimates, led to smaller departmental hiring goals, and that once such goals were met, and no minorities already hired were lost, the subsequent pursuit of minorities was abandoned, even to the point of reduced advertising.

Other data suggested that the relative importance of academic selection criteria may have shifted in response to the race, sex, and quality of the candidates. Several affirmative policies are derived from these findings.

972. Steinbach, Sheldon E. "Equal Employment Opportunity on Campus: Issues in 1974." Journal of the College & University Personnel Association. 25 (July-August, 1974), 1-9.

Discusses the ramifications of recent cases and federal regulations on equal employment opportunity efforts on campus, citing real and potential problem areas.

973. _____. "Washington: Fighting Campus Job Discrimination." Change. 5 (November, 1973), 51-52.

Discusses the myriad federal regulations prohibiting race and sex discrimination in higher education, and the problems colleges and universities face in complying with such regulations, such as equal pay and retirement benefits.

974. Steiner, Elizabeth. "Affirmative Action Plans." Educational Researcher. 4 (October, 1975), 29-30.

Notes that affirmative action plan for women in educational research should be a policy document and not simply a passive statement of principles or a statement for commitment to goals and timetables.

975. Stiles, Lindley J. and Nystrand, P. Martin. "The Politics of Sex in Education." Educational Forum. 38 (May, 1974), 431-440.

Notes that women are poorly represented at the administrative level and in higher academic positions, even in those fields where the majority of Ph. D. recipients are women. Describes the legal steps necessary to guarantee equity for women, effects of legal protections, and politics and public opinion.

976. Strober, Myra and Quester, Aline O. "The Earnings and Promotion of Women Faculty: Comment." American Economic Review. 67 (March, 1977), 207-213.

Responds to George Johnson and Frank Stafford article. Found latter's evidence on salary differentials unconvincing and misleading.

977. "Study Finds Women Academicians' Salaries Lag." The New York Times. September 18, 1973, p. 70.

Quotes from the Carnegie Commission Study on Opportunities for Women in Higher Education. Women faculty members earn $1500-$2000 less per year than do men in comparable jobs, finds that percentage of women in academic world declines at successfully higher levels.

978. Sugent, Charles J. "The Uncertain Progress of Affirmative Action. " Change. 6 (May, 1974), 37-42.

Professor at the University of Minnesota analyzes the affirmative action program at that university, including the waning enforcement efforts by HEW. Notes the omission of data on the long-range effects of affirmative action and figures on the distribution of women and minorities by rank, department, tenure, status, and salary.

979. Sullivan, Louis W. "The Education of Black Health Professionals. " Phylon. 38 (June, 1977), 181-193.

While American minority groups comprise close to one fifth of the nation's total population, only one in every 15 first-year medical school seats is held by a black, a Mexican American, a mainland Puerto Rican or a Native American.

980. Tanur, Judith M. and Coser, Rose L. "Pockets of 'Poverty' in the Salaries of Academic Women. " AAUP Bulletin. 64 (March, 1978), 26-30.

Explores some factors that may account for the existence of pockets of poverty in academic women's salaries, particularly emphasizing length of service, rank, and proportion of females in the field.

981. Tarr, S. A. "The Status of Women in Academic Libraries. " North Carolina Libraries. 31 (Fall, 1973), 22-32.

Surveys factual information in library literature as well as general studies of academic members and myths regarding women workers.

982. Tenzer, Morton J. "A Debate on Affirmative Action: Tenzer Replies to Rose Coser. " Dissent. 23 (Spring, 1976), 207-210.

Argues that race and sex are irrelevant criteria for college admissions and appointment, that affirmative action appointments contaminate the achievement of blacks and women who arrived at their present positions through their own merit, and that affirmative action imposes bureaucratic control over the autonomy of higher education.

983. Thornton, Sandra and others. "Affirmative Action: Success or Failure?" Change. 7 (May, 1975), 48-50, 64.

Presents a variety of opinions on affirmative action in higher education including whether programs really help minorities, and whether the federal government is actively enforcing regulations.

984.   Tidball, M. Elizabeth. "Perspective on Academic Women
       and Affirmative Action." Educational Record. 54 (Spring,
       1973), 130-135.

       Takes a close look at the educational environment which reveals some alarming trends in both higher education and society. Warns that unless the number of women academic professionals is increased, the benefit to society from women's greater access to higher education will be minimized.

985.   Todorovich, Miro M. "On Discrimination: Part Two."
       Toward Affirmative Action. Edited by Lucy W. Sells. San
       Francisco: Jossey-Bass, 1974. Pp. 31-38.

       Coordinator of the Committee on Academic Nondiscrimination presents an alternative to present policies of preferential treatment and a return to the policy of merit.

986.   Toward Affirmative Action. Lucy W. Sells, issue editor.
       San Francisco: Jossey-Bass, 1974. (New Directions in Institutional Research: no. 3.) 99 p.

       Wide-ranging synthesis of views on affirmative action and its implications for colleges and universities. Content includes:

987.   Fleming, Robben W., Implications for Government

987A. Holmes, Peter E., Affirmative Action: Myth and Reality

988.   Hook, Sidney, On Discrimination: Part One

989.   Johnson, Robert I., Implications for Institutions

990.   Sandler, Bernice, The Hand That Rocked the Cradle Has
       Learned to Rock the Boat

991.   Sells, Lucy W., Critical Points for Affirmative Action

992.   Todorovich, Miro M., On Discrimination: Part Two

992A. Tryman, Donald L. "Colonialism and 'Reverse Discrimination': A Political Systems Approach." Western Journal of
       Black Studies. 2 (March, 1978), 10-17.

       Explains that in politics, economics, education, and religion, Blacks will largely depend upon White institutions. White resistance to affirmative action means that the subordinate position of Blacks in American society is likely to continue. The only feasible alternative is Black mobilization and organization on a scale parallel to that of the 1960's.

993.   "UC Chief Defends Minority Policy. " San Francisco Chroni-
        cle. November 17, 1976, p. 16.

        David Saxon, president of the University of California, says
        that the school's program to encourage minority enrollment
        is the only way to correct social inequities caused by past
        racial discrimination. The University has a responsibility
        to attract more minority students.

994.   "UC Deadline Passes on Affirmative Action. " San Francisco
        Chronicle. May 2, 1978, p. 18.

        Describes the University of California at Berkeley dispute
        with HEW officials over faculty hiring practices. At issue
        is the opening of personnel files. The History Department
        refuses to show investigators letters of recommendation writ-
        ten in behalf of job candidates. The Art History Department
        refuses to allow HEW investigators copy a file which they
        consider to be evidence of discrimination against one appli-
        cant. The University stands to lose $55 million a year in
        federal contracts and grants unless the dispute is resolved.

995.   Van Alstyne, Carol and others. "Affirmative Inaction: The
        Bottom Line Tells the Tale. " Change. 9 (August, 1977),
        39-41, 60.

        National study of top-level college administrators destroys
        the illusion that these jobs and salaries are now fairly ap-
        portioned by race and sex. Women are generally concen-
        trated in lower paying jobs, and in these jobs, the women
        are paid less than the men.

996.   Van Den Haag, Ernest. "Reverse Discrimination: A Brief
        Against It. " National Review. 29 (April 29, 1977), 492-
        495.

        Describes the arguments for and against preferential admis-
        sions and affirmative action, including arguments from com-
        pensatory justice. Rejects preferential treatment because it
        elevates numerical goals over the distinctive individual quali-
        fications of candidates, reinforces prejudice against minor-
        ities, and affirmative action, being a creature of the federal
        bureaucracy, perverts democracy and common sense.

997.   Walsh, John. "Higher Education and Regulations: Counting
        the Costs of Compliance. " Science. 190 (October 31, 1975),
        444-447.

        Describes the financial crisis in colleges and universities
        caused by enactment of federal social legislation, such as
        affirmative action programs.

998.   Warren, Mary A. "Secondary Sexism and Quota Hiring. "
        Philosophy and Public Affairs. 6 (Spring, 1977), 240-261.

Discusses the defacto discriminatory hiring in universities, in the form of secondary sexism. To counteract this ongoing form of discrimination and make competition for jobs more nearly fair, minimum numerical quotas for the hiring and promotion of women are necessary.

999.   Washington, K. R.   "Special Minority Programs: 'Dupe or New Deal'?"   Journal of Afro-American Issues.   5 (Winter, 1977), 60-65.

Explains how the attrition rate suggests that special programs for minority students serve revolving door function. Responsibility for moving disadvantaged students toward actualization of their true potential equally rests with the institution, the program administrations, and the students.

1000.   Webb, Lillian O., and McCarthy, Martha M.   "Debunking the Myths of Affirmative Action."   Journal of the National Association of Women Deans, Administrators, and Counselors.   41 (Spring, 1978), 105-108.

Explains how affirmative action programs should provide opportunities for all individuals to realize their potential. However, many are thwarted by the existence of many myths about the nature of programs required. Although there are no legal grounds for these myths, they are widely held and impair the effectiveness of affirmative action efforts.

1001.   "Weinberger Sees Flaws in Quotas."   The New York Times.   July 31, 1973, p. 16.

Secretary of HEW, Caspar Weinberger, says that he opposes a quota system approach to ending college and university hiring practices that discriminate against women; says that once numerical goal is reached in such cases, efforts to end discrimination stop.

1002.   Weitzman, Lenore J.   "Affirmative Action Plans for Eliminating Sex Discrimination in Academe."   Academic Women on the Move, edited by Alice Rossi and Ann Calderwood. New York: Russell Sage Foundation, 1973.   Pp. 463-504.

Summarizes legal requirements for affirmative action, suggests effective means of meeting these requirements, and notes some of the programs that have been developed. Suggests affirmative action strategies for eliminating sex discrimination in faculty recruitment and hiring programs, promotions, equity in conditions of employment and employment benefits, and salary equity.

1003.   Wellington, John S. and Montero, Pilar.   "Equal Educational Opportunity Programs in American Medical Schools."

Journal of Medical Education. 53 (August, 1978), 633-639.

Data collected from questionnaire responses of 90 medical schools indicate that from 1968 to 1972 enrollment of minority group students increased sixfold in white-dominated institutions. Student recruitment, admission criteria, and academic support of these groups are discussed.

1004.   "White Males Challenge Affirmative Action Programs. " The New York Times. November 24, 1977, p. 1.

Professor James A. Cramer of the Virginia Commonwealth University files a reverse sex discrimination suit. Suit indicative of the growing number of white males who are fighting affirmative action programs that favor women and minorities in employment and college admissions.

1005.   Wicker, Tom. "A 'Wise Sensitivity' to Race. " The New York Times. January 17, 1975, p. 33.

Contrasts the attitudes of Dean Murray Schwartz of the U. C. L. A. Law School and Derek Bok, President of Harvard University, toward the meaning of affirmative action. Wicker finds goals to be reasonable ways to open up hiring and admissions to minorities and women formerly excluded from consideration, citing such opportunities to disadvantaged people as a matter of simple equity, benefiting higher education and society at large.

1006.   Wilcox, Lee. "Financial Aid and Admissions Quotas. " College Board Review. No. 90 (Winter, 1973/74), 10-12.

Discusses whether financial aid policy influences who is admitted and whether the probability of being admitted is a function of one's financial situation.

1007.   Williams, Roger M. "Law Schools: The Big Women Boom. " Saturday Review. 2 (September 21, 1974), 51-52, 54.

Article focuses on women's rush to law school currently underway and the difference between past and present admissions attitudes as well as the influence of feminism on women beginning a law career and later securing a position.

1008.   Winkler, Karen J. "Proliferating Federal Regulations: Is Government Now 'the Enemy'? " The Chronicle of Higher Education. 13 (December 13 and 20, 1976), 3 and 5 respectively.

Two-part article on federal regulation of colleges and universities. Discusses the complaints of colleges about con-

flicting rules, burgeoning paper work and rising compliance
costs; a survey finds institutions spend 1 to 4 per cent of
their budgets simply to meet the requirements of federal
regulations.

1009.   Winter, Ralph K. and others.   Affirmative Action: The
         Answer to Discrimination?   An AEI Round Table Held on
         May 28, 1975.   Washington, D. C.:   American Enterprise
         Institute for Public Policy Research, 1976.   45 p.

         Contributors are Owen Fiss and Richard Posner, professors
         of law; Vera Glaser and William Rasberry, newspaper col-
         umnists; and Paul Seaberry, political scientist.   Address
         various legal, ethical and practical issues related to the
         elimination of racial and sex discrimination in employment
         and admissions through affirmative action programs.

1010/11 "Women Administrators Found Unequal in Pay, Status. "
         The Chronicle of Higher Education.   14 (June 27, 1977), 8.

         The College and University Personnel Association and Alex-
         ander Astin completed studies which show that discrimina-
         tion against faculty women still continues.   Women's sal-
         aries are about four-fifths of males with the same job ti-
         tles at the same kind of school.   White women hold only
         14 per cent and minority women hold only 2 per cent of
         key administrative positions in the institutions studied.
         The overall situation for women "remains virtually un-
         changed. "

1012.   Women in Academia: Evolving Policies Toward Equal Op-
         portunity.   Edited by Elga Wasserman and others.   New
         York: Praeger, 1975.   169 p.

         Volume is based upon the symposium "Women in Academia:
         Evolving Policies Toward Equal Opportunities, " which was
         held at the 138th annual meeting of the American Associa-
         tion for the Advancement of Science in Philadelphia on De-
         cember 30, 1971.   Contents include:

1013.   Beach, Ruth, A Case History of Affirmative Action

1014.   Bunting, Mary I., Creating Opportunities for Women

1015.   Cook, Alice H., Sex Discrimination at Universities: An
         Ombudsman's View

1016.   Hornig, Lili S., Affirmative Action Through Affirmative
         Attitudes

1017.   Miner, Anne S., Affirmative Action at Stanford University

1018.   Pottinger, J. Stanley, Race, Sex, and Jobs: The Drive
         Toward Equality

1019.   Sandler, Bernice, Sex Discrimination, Educational Institu-
           tions, and the Law: A New Issue on Campus

1020.   Scott, Elizabeth L., Developing Criteria and Measures of
           Equal Opportunities for Women

1021.   Weitzman, Lenore J., Legal Requirements, Structures,
           and Strategies for Eliminating Sex Discrimination in Aca-
           deme

1022.   "Women on Campus Look to Courts for Equality." The
           New York Times. January 16, 1974, p. 72.

           Article points out how women's movement on college cam-
           puses is shifting from reliance on the Federal government
           toward use of local courts as a weapon in fights against
           alleged sex discrimination; chart compares increase in
           positions held by women in U.S. colleges between 1969 and
           1973.

1023.   "Women on College Faculties Are Pressing for Equal Pay
           and Better Positions in Academic Hierarchy." The New
           York Times. November 21, 1971, p. 41.

           Article finds women faculty members are bringing pressure
           to bear on American campuses and pushing themselves
           quietly into more substantial positions in the university
           hierarchy. Chief complaints of women professors include
           claim that they are paid less for the same work and are
           in lower echelons of faculty hierarchy; women are asking
           the Government to insist that more women be enrolled in
           doctoral programs which are apprenticeships for higher fac-
           ulty positions.

1024.   "Women on the Campus Find a 'Weapon.'" The New York
           Times. January 10, 1972, XX, p. 22.

           In Annual Education Review, article notes growing militancy
           among women about sex discrimination in college hiring
           practices and the activities of the Women's Equity Action
           League (WEAL) to prohibit such discrimination.

1025.   "Women Professors Said to Lose Ground on Wages and
           Rank." The New York Times. February 9, 1976, p. 29.

           U.S. Office of Education reports that women accounted for
           24 per cent of all faculty members on academic year con-
           tracts in 1975, same as in 1974, but that there were fewer
           women professors, lecturers, and undesignated positions
           than in 1974; salaries of women faculty members in 1975
           averaged $14,710 while male faculty averaged $17,558 at
           public colleges. 42 per cent of women and 60 per cent of
           men were tenured.

1026.   "Women, Too, Shall Overcome. " College Management.   7
        (April, 1972), 4-6.

        Article shows that 350 institutions of higher education have
        been charged with violating the federal prohibition against
        sex discrimination.   Under the fear of losing federal funds
        and the impetus of affirmative action regulations, a number
        of large institutions have appointed more women to admin-
        istrative positions, converted male colleges to co-educa-
        tion, and awarded prestigious scholarships to women for the
        first time.

1027.   Women's Equity Action League Educational and Legal De-
        fense Fund, Washington, D. C.   Facts About Women in
        Higher Education.   Washington, D. C. :   WEAL Educational
        and Legal Defense Fund, 1977.   14 p.
        (ED 163 885)

        Information is presented on women as students, women
        graduates in the job market, women as faculty members
        and administrators, and the status of affirmative action.

1028.   "Women's Toehold on Chemistry Faculties Still Just That. "
        Chemical and Engineering News.   54 (November 22, 1976),
        47-48.

        Discusses the status of women on chemistry faculties in
        higher education.   Article is based upon a study conducted
        by Agnes Green.   Data was collected from the years 1974-
        1975.   Overall, women make up 2. 16 per cent of Ph. D.
        granting chemistry departments in the U. S.

1029.   Wright, James R.   "Affirmative Action: A Plan for Amer-
        ica. "   Freedomways.   17, no. 1 (1977), 30-34.

        Argues that affirmative action plan is the best designed
        measure to guard against bigotry and institutionalized ra-
        cism in employment.   Many of author's remarks directed
        to the necessity of affirmative action plans in libraries.

1030.   Wright, Stephen J.   "Redressing the Imbalance of Minority
        Groups in the Professions. "   Journal of Higher Education.
        48 (March, 1972), 239-248.

        Argues that the representation of major minority groups
        must be raised in various major vocations and professions
        to levels equal to their percentage of the population.

1031.   Zitron, Celia.   "Reverse Racism: The Great White Hoax. "
        Freedomways.   15 (Summer, 1975), 188-195.

        Article focuses on controversy around quotas, school inte-
        gration, open admissions, reverse discrimination, all of

which indicates serious problems for equal educational opportunity and employment for minorities. Calls for united action of all people for effective integrated education.

ERIC RESOURCES

Bibliographies

1032/33. Lockheed, Mariane E. and others, comps. Sex Discrimination in Education: A Literature Review and Bibliography. Princeton, N.J.: Educational Testing Service, 1977. 90 p.
(ED 144 976)

1000 item bibliography of published and unpublished materials focuses on studies which relate discrimination in education to sex differences in the attainment of roles and rewards both in the educational system and in the larger society.

1034. Oltman, Ruth M. Status of Graduate and Professional Education of Women--1974: A Review of the Literature and Bibliography. 1974. 15 p.
(ED 092 022)

Contains two sections: a review of the literature and a 68-item bibliography on graduate and professional education of women.

1035. Pemberton, S. Macpherson. Research Reports on Affirmative Action Programs in Colleges and Universities: An Annotated Bibliography. Washington, D.C., U.S. Office of Education, 1977. 16 p.
(ED 147 247)

Provides narrative summaries of 31 articles and books dealing with affirmative action in higher education that appeared between 1972 and 1977.

1036. Schrader, Jerry G. and Kent, Marion. Education of Minorities and the Disadvantaged: A Partial Annotated Bibliography. Madison: University of Wisconsin. Center for the Study of Minorities and the Disadvantaged, 1978. 328 p.
(ED 152 945)

Citations drawn from ERIC data base and covers a period from approximately 1963 to 1978.

1037. Silver, Donna and Magee, Jane. Women Administrators in Higher Education: A Selected Bibliography. 1978. 27 p.
(ED 151 024)

Material includes the history of women in academia, future trends affecting equal opportunity for women administrators, and on the issue of women and power.

1038. Wheeler, Helen Rippier. Alice in Wonderland, or, Through the Looking Glass; Resources for Implementing Principles of Affirmative Action Employment of Women. July, 1975. 14 p.
(ED 110 776)

Annotated bibliography of resources consisting of 64 references of periodicals, organizations, films, books, pamphlets, tapes, slides, and microfilms.

Studies and Monographs

1039. Alford, Howard Lee. The Impact of Special Admissions Programs on General Admissions Policies in Five San Francisco Bay Area Public Institutions of Higher Education 1966-1971. Stanford: Stanford University, 1972. 367 p.
(ED 066 146)

The study was conducted to determine such questions as the quality of services provided to special admissions students, what general admissions polices were waived for special admissions students, how did these students perform as compared to other students, how did the ethnic population of the student body change as a result of special admissions programs, what were the differences in admissions policies among the institutions studied, what procedures and policies were incorporated into the general admissions policies.

1040. American Council on Education, Washington, D. C. Framework for Evaluating Institutional Commitment to Minorities: A Guide to Institutional Self Study. Washington, D. C.: American Council on Education, 1976. 18 p.
(ED 123 981)

Guide focuses on such areas as admissions, financial aid, counseling, curriculum, graduate and professional programs, faculty and staff hiring, evaluation, and retention, and administrative policies.

1041. American Library Association. Survey of Graduates and Faculty of U. S. Library Education Programs Awarding Degrees and Certificates, 1973-1974. Chicago: American Library Association, 1975. 17 p.
(ED 116 646)

Study was made to provide information for affirmative action programs. Data collected on the ethnic and sexual com-

position of graduates and faculty of U. S. library education
programs. Blacks were being recruited into the library
profession in numbers comparable to their representation,
as were Asian Americans. Mexican Americans were underrepresented.

1042.   Association of American Colleges, Washington, D. C.   Pro-
        ject on the Status and Education of Women. Women in
        Higher Education Administration. Washington, D. C.: As-
        sociation of American Colleges, 1978. 8 p.
        (ED 162 572)

        Two papers are presented which examine the barriers to
        women in academic decision making and identify a variety
        of effective strategies for improving the status of women
        in higher education administration. Affirmative hiring goals
        and search procedures are also discussed.

1043.   Astin, Alexander W.   Data Pertaining to the Education of
        Women: A Challenge to the Federal Government.   1978.
        24 p.
        (ED 158 626)

        Evaluates data requirements for a comprehensive assess-
        ment of the educational status of women. Postsecondary
        and elementary/secondary education are considered separ-
        ately.

1044.   Astin, Helen S. and others. Sex Discrimination in Educa-
        tion: Access to Postsecondary Education. Los Angeles:
        Higher Education Research Institute, 1976. 2 vols. 394 p.
        (ED 132 966)

1045.   _____ . Executive Summary. 1976. 50 p.
        (ED 132 967)

        Both documents were undertaken to identify the kinds and
        extent of sex discrimination in access to postsecondary edu-
        cation. Recommendations are included to increase women's
        access to postsecondary education.

1046.   Bailey, Merrill-Jean. The Status and Future of Minority
        Group Representation in the Graduate and Professional Pro-
        grams. 1977. 13 p.
        (ED 161 977)

        Discusses the underrepresentation of minorities in graduate
        and professional schools based upon philosophical, socio-
        logical, and economic reasons. Minorities are relegated
        to a predetermined status in society. Those favoring af-
        firmative action should make their support known.

1047.   Barksdale, Milton K. Graduate and Professional School
         Admissions: Social and Legal Considerations. 1977. 43p.
         (ED 138 181)

         Discusses the difficulty in maintaining a balance between the
         rights guaranteed to both minority and nonminority Ameri-
         cans. Analyzes the court cases of Bakke and DeFunis
         within this dilemma.

1048.   Blackwell, James E. Access of Black Students to Graduate
         and Professional Schools. Atlanta: Southern Education
         Foundation, 1975. 81 p.
         (ED 119 555)

         Study focuses upon admissions policies, enrollment trends
         and patterns, barriers to professional practices, and efforts
         to increase the number and proportion of blacks in graduate
         and professional schools.

1049.   California. University. Berkeley. Office of the President.
         Task Force on Undergraduate Admissions. Final Report.
         Berkeley: Office of the President. University of Califor-
         nia. Berkeley, 1977. 94 p.
         (ED 136 648)

         Discusses the criteria for admission to the University of
         California system, including the question of affirmative ac-
         tion policies in admissions.

1050.   Chait, Richard and Ford, Andrew T. Affirmative Action.
         Tenure, and Unionization: Can There Be Peaceful Coexis-
         tence? 1973. 13 p.
         (ED 090 808)

         Explains why affirmative action and unionization are likely
         to force an end to current tenure practices.

1051.   Education Commission of the States, Denver, Colo. Re-
         trenchment in Education: The Outlook for Women and Mi-
         norities. Report No. F76-9. Denver: Education Commis-
         sion of the States, 1977. 39 p.
         (ED 141 954)

         Presents evidence that, in view of the retrenchment prac-
         tices now being undertaken by educational institutions, more
         successful remedies to eliminate inequalities affecting wom-
         en and minorities must be found.

1052.   Florida State University. Tallahassee. Manual for Affirm-
         ative Action Program Development and Implementation in
         Higher Education Institutions. Tallahassee: Florida State

University.   Office of University Minority Affairs, 1974.
70 p.
(ED 107 193)

Manual provides instructions and processes to facilitate implementation of affirmative action plans as action-oriented
procedures within higher education institutions.

1053.   Gilford, Dorothy M. and Snyder, Joan.   Women and Minor-
ity Ph. D. 's in the 1970's: A Data Book.   Washington,
D. C.:   National Academy of Sciences.   National Research
Council.   Commission on Human Resources, 1977.   247 p.
(ED 148 197)

Selected data from the Commission on Human Resources
are reported for two major groups that have been underrepresented in doctoral education: minorities and women.

1054.   McLean, Marquita and others.   Affirmative Action Data
Collection and Reporting System.   1976.   20 p.
(ED 131 369)

Describes a computerized Affirmative Action Data Collection
and Reporting System used at the University of Cincinnati.

1055.   Mickey, Melissa.   Developing a Plan for Affirmative-Ac-
tion--Human Rights Bibliography.   Working Paper No. 3.
Chicago: Medical Library Association, 1973.   58 p.
(ED 136 763)

Presents a literature search to locate materials useful in
designing, producing, and evaluating a human relations
training program for the Medical Library Association.

1056.   Ohio University, Athens.   Affirmative Action Plan: Ohio
University.   Athens: Ohio University, 1973.   29 p.
(ED 078 766)

Describes the Affirmative Action Plan of Ohio University.
Explains its policy, purpose, responsibility for implementation, dissemination of policy and communication of related
measures, university policy procedures, affirmative employment practices, and other topics included.

1057.   Pemberton, S. MacPherson.   Affirmative Action in Higher
Education.   1977.   18 p.
(ED 142 148)

Describes barriers to affirmative action, including a pervasive institutional attitude ranging from neutral to negative.

1058.   Rivas, Richard G.   Implementation of a System for Gathering Data for the Purpose of Conducting an Affirmative Ac-

tion Utilization Availability Analysis and Setting of Goals
and Time Tables at a Large University.   1976.   29 p.
(ED 129 185)

Provides a systems approach for gathering data for affirmative action analysis and for setting goals and timetables.

1059.   Roberts, Sylvia.   Equality of Opportunity in Higher Educa-
        tion: The Impact of Contract Compliance and the Equal
        Rights Amendment.   Washington, D. C.:   National Organi-
        zation for Women, 1973.   30 p.
        (ED 074 920)

        Focuses upon women employed as faculty members and staff
        at universities and colleges.   Concludes that women are
        not hired and promoted at the same rate nor have they been
        paid as well as their male counterparts.

1060.   Rose, Clare and others.   Responsiveness vs. Resources:
        The Implementation and Impact of Affirmative Action Pro-
        grams for Women Scientists in Postsecondary Education.
        AIR Forum Paper, 1978.   1978.   30 p.
        (ED 161 389)

        Includes a series of statistical analyses of institutional and
        departmental trends in women's graduate enrollment and
        employment in science and engineering in the 50 leading
        doctorate-granting institutions.

1061.   Roye, W. J.   The Myth of Affirmative Action.   1976.
        38 p.
        (ED 143 724)

        Discusses the principles of affirmative action policies and
        their implementation in American businesses and universi-
        ties.   Reasons for resistance to affirmative action are
        noted, particularly the accusatory fashion in which affirma-
        tive action regulations are often initiated.

1062.   Sedlacek, William E.   Should Higher Education Students Be
        Admitted Differentially by Race and Sex: The Evidence.
        Research Report No. 5-75.   College Park: Maryland Uni-
        versity.   Cultural Study Center, 1976.   11 p.
        (ED 119 558)

        Concludes that students should be selected by race-sex sub-
        group.   Support for this position centers on the dearth of
        valid predictors of academic success in higher education.

1063.   Segalman, Ralph.   Affirmative Action, Delivered Equality
        and the Concept of Community.   1976.   16 p.
        (ED 142 622)

Describes three models of society: the gemeinschaft, the
gesellschaft, and the pseudo-gemeinschaft, and examines
the affirmative action process and its relationship to the
utopian ideals of equality of opportunity and delivered
equality.

1064.   Sells, Lucy W.   Availability Pools as the Basis for Affirmative Action.   1973.   10 p.
(ED 077 461)

Argues that affirmative action requires both greater use of
persons in the existing pool of qualified persons in the context of hiring for university faculty positions, and long
range action to increase the number of women and minorities in the pool.

1065.   Shulman, Carol Herrnstadt.   Affirmative Action: Women's
Rights on Campus.   Washington, D. C.: American Associ-
ation for Higher Education, 1972.   48 p.
(ED 066 143)

Report examines the current law governing affirmative action programs and sex discrimination on campus, and describes the approaches universities and colleges have taken
to comply with the law.

1066.   _____ .   University Admissions: Dilemmas and Potential.
ERIC/Higher Education Research Report No. 5.   Washing-
ton, D. C.: George Washington University, 1977.   60 p.
(ED 146 826)

Discusses the period of the sixties and the seventies as the
admissions debate turned on the issues of merit versus
equal opportunity but changed during the later period in
light of the demand to attract students to higher education.
Also discusses the legal issues concerning quotas and reverse discrimination.

1067.   Taylor, Dalmas A. and Henry, J. Marilyn.   Ethnicity and
Bicultural Considerations in Psychology: Meeting the Needs
of Ethnic Minorities.   Washington, D. C.: American Psychological Association, 1977.   129 p.
(ED 151 251)

Summarizes the history, philosophy, and recruitment meth-
odology of the American Psychological Association Minority
Fellowship Program, particularly in recruiting minorities
leading to a Ph. D. in psychology.

1068.   Thornberry, Mary.   Unexpected Benefits, Expected Defeats:
Affirmative Action for Women.   1978.   48 p.
(ED 162 584)

Study of the effects of affirmative action on faculty hiring practices, based upon 90 questionnaires and interviews at two large state universities to determine what was happening at the departmental level.

1069.   Welch, Finis.   Employment Quotas for Minorities.   Santa Monica, Calif.:   Rand Corporation, 1976.   64 p. (ED 147 394)

The purpose of the study is the use of employment quotas as an analytical device for devising a priori notions of what the effects of government attempts to reduce employment discrimination might be.

1070.   White, Gloria W.   Affirmative Action Programs in Small Institutions.   1974.   32 p. (ED 089 564)

Speech discusses the development and implementation of an affirmative action program at Washington University at St. Louis, along with problem areas and prognosis for the future.   Copy of the program is included.

1071/72.   Willis, Virginia and others.   Affirmative Action: The Unrealized Goal.   A Debate of Equal Employment Opportunity.   Washington, D.C.:   The Potomac Institute, 1973. 148 p. (ED 089 649)

Concludes that more than a decade of affirmative action policies on the part of the federal government has yielded inadequate results.   Assumption blacks are being given unfair and undeserved advantage over whites is found to be unjustified.

PART THREE:

THE PHILOSOPHICAL DEBATE

An Analysis of the Philosophical Debate on Affirmative Action and

Preferential Admissions in Higher Education

The philosophical debate pertaining to affirmative action and preferential treatment revolve around conflicting interpretations of the meaning and nature of justice and equality.

Political theorists, taking their cue from Aristotle, write of two kinds of justice: distributive and corrective. Distributive justice involves the fair distribution of goods, offices, honors, and burdens among citizens of the state. Corrective justice concerns a rectifying or compensatory transaction between individuals. Under corrective justice, the person who commits a wrongful injury to another is obligated to compensate the injured party, with the objective of restoring the equality which existed prior to the wrongful injury. A corollary is that the penalty to the person who committed the wrongful injury and the benefit bestowed on the injured person should be proportional to the difference created by the injury. [1]

In applying the principles of corrective justice to the debate over affirmative action and preferential treatment (which to critics is "reverse discrimination"), the literature reveals little disagreement that justice requires compensation or reparations to individuals injured by past or ongoing discrimination. The conflict arises over the issue of what form that compensation should take and who deserves such compensation.

The remaining part of this introduction will focus upon the philosophical bases which underlie the debate over affirmative action and preferential treatment.

It should be emphasized, however, that the literature cited in Part Three of this bibliography--The Philosophical Debate Over Affirmative Action and Preferential Admissions in Higher Education --concentrates on whether racial minorities are deserving of preferential treatment based upon principles of compensatory justice. Throughout the preceding sections of this bibliography relating to affirmative action and preferential admissions in the law and the courts and the academic community response, philosophical judgments abound as to whether affirmative action and preferential treatment advances or inhibits justice and equality in America. This introduction, therefore, provides a summary of the philosophical underpinnings relating to affirmative action and preferential treatment.

Philosophical Arguments Against Preferential Treatment

To critics of affirmative action and preferential treatment, reward-
ing individuals with status, honors, power and the like based upon
their inherent characteristics such as race and sex subverts the
foundations of a just society: benefits should be distributed according to individual merit.   Affirmative action programs, moreover,
which substitute proportional group representation (based upon race,
ethnicity, and sex) undermine the democratic concept of equality of
opportunity: individuals ought to be allowed the opportunity to compete fairly for society's benefits based upon their abilities rather
than benefits allocated on the basis of such genetically determined
characteristics as race, ethnicity, and sex.

    To critics of preferential treatment such as Daniel Bell,
what is at stake is the redefinition of equality:

> As a principle, equality of opportunity denies the prece-
> dence of birth, of nepotism, of patronage or any other
> criterion which allocates place, other than fair competition
> open equally to talent and ambition.   It asserts ... uni-
> versalism over particularism, achievement over ascrip-
> tion. [2]

In the past, Bell continues, men were to be judged and rewarded
on the bases of individual merit, but that principle today "is held
to be the new source of inequality and of social, if not psychological, injustice. "   The new equality means "equality not at the start
of a race, but at the finish, equality not of opportunity but of result. "   Under the new equality, ascription (the gaining of place by
assignment or inheritance) replaces achievement (the principle that
persons ought to be judged and rewarded on the basis not of birth
or primordial ties, but of individual merit). [3]

    The merit principle, thus being subordinated to group as-
criptive rights, is further subverted, according to critics of affirmative action, by deliberate governmental practices and policies, accompanied by punitive sanctions in the threat of federal funding being cut off, if educational institutions and corporations do not engage
in proportional group representation in jobs and educational opportunities.   Thus, a further democratic principle is violated, namely,
that a prime function of government is to remove artificial barriers
to equal opportunity (e. g. , by passing and enforcing laws prohibiting
discrimination based upon race, sex, and nationality).   Instead, the
government, through its imposition of affirmative action programs,
forces educational institutions to set up those very barriers the government had once sought to eliminate; now, proportional group representation based upon race, nationality, and sex is thus enshrined as
the criteria for employment and admission to higher education, individual merit thus relegated to the outer reaches.

    Critics of affirmative action and preferential treatment further
point out that the allocation of the benefits of society based upon

race, sex and the like not only undermine principles of equality but also principles of distributive and compensatory justice. Justice requires that the benefits of society in the form of wealth, status, power, honors, and the like ought to be distributed according to the individual's talents and abilities, not on the basis of inherited characteristics as race and sex. Justice further requires that compensation be made to individuals wrongfully injured; it does not require (indeed it would be unjust) that compensation be made to entire groups or classes of persons by another group or class or by society at large.

Preferential treatment, critics argue, penalizes qualified white males, who, through no fault of their own (being personally innocent of discrimination against racial and ethnic minorities and women) nevertheless are expected to sacrifice their opportunities in education and employment on behalf of a greater social good (e. g., to eliminate racial and sexual injustice in America). Preferential treatment thus subordinates the individual's right to equal treatment to broader social aims and particularly places an unfair burden upon white males to assist the preferred groups of women and minorities while they themselves are excluded from educational and employment opportunities.

The principle of compensatory justice is further undermined by forcing present generations to compensate or make reparations for injuries inflicted by past generations in the form of discrimination. Justice ought not require those presently living to atone for the sins of their fathers.

An additional problem is: Who is to be compensated for wrongful injuries? Critics of preferential treatment note that individuals deserve compensation only if they have been personally injured and have been unable to overcome the debilitating effects of that injury (e. g., unjust discrimination). Preferential treatment is not deserved simply by membership in a group or class which has been traditionally discriminated against; personal injury must be demonstrated. A corollary argument against compensatory treatment is that not all members of minority groups or women have been discriminated against and also that some members of minority groups or women through their own efforts have been able to overcome discrimination aimed at them. Government imposition of statistical or proportional representation of preferred groups is wrong because it overrides considerations as to whether individuals deserve special treatment.

An additional argument relating to justice is that utilitarian values, that is, the public welfare or the common good requires special treatment to groups traditionally discriminated against. Utilitarian considerations will be discussed in greater detail below; for the moment let us consider the critics' response to claims that preferences are necessary to achieve social cohesion, to reduce racial stereotypes, and to provide minority services. Social cohesion and integration of the races, critics contend, will not be achieved by preferential treatment; rather such preference will increase hostility between the races, particularly causing resentment of white males and ethnic groups who perceive themselves deprived of educational and employment opportunities, not because they are unqualified but because they do not belong to the "right" sex or race to obtain preferential treatment. Preferential treatment will also cause social chaos as competing group interests fight for a greater share of the distribution of goods and services.

Far from reducing stereotyping of women and minorities, critics continue, preferential treatment reinforces the image that these preferred groups cannot "make it" on their own; they need governmental sanctions to succeed. Preferential treatment thus contributes to the very stigma and loss of respect that it was supposed to eliminate. Minorities and women who receive preferential treatment will suffer lowered self-esteem, the argument goes, because they will not know whether they advanced economically or educationally because of their abilities or because they received special treatment.

As to the question of whether minority doctors and lawyers will serve minority communities, the evidence is still out; there are no definitive studies to prove that this is happening.

Philosophical Arguments for Preferential Treatment

Proponents of preferential treatment contend that groups which have been traditionally discriminated against deserve compensation for wrongful injuries that they have suffered. Increased benefits to these wronged groups--women and minorities--are justified in order to bring them up to the level of wealth, status, honors, and power which they would now have, were it not for the discrimination they have endured.

As to the critics' contention that race and sex are morally irrelevant characteristics, proponents of preferential treatment answer that these characteristics have been made morally relevant because discrimination is directed against them because they are black or female, not because as individuals they are victims of discrimination. Since institutionalized injustice is directed at them as members of these victimized groups, then society as a whole owes them some form of compensation or reparations. Affirmative action programs are perceived as appropriate means for society to discharge its obligations to these wronged groups.

In terms of distributive justice, proponents of preferential treatment contend that discrimination aimed at women and minorities generates a pervasive and deep-seated maldistribution of wealth, status, and power. In the past, white males were the preferred group, receiving the greater benefits of society by virtue of their being white and male. Under affirmative action and preferential policies, women and minorities, previously underrepresented in education and employment, are now given increased opportunities, based upon their abilities, needs, and contributions they can make to society. These increased opportunities have taken the form of special apprenticeship and training programs for those groups previously excluded from promotional opportunities.

Those favoring special programs and affirmative action reject the oft-repeated argument that women and minorities are hired and promoted over more qualified white males. There is indeed some suspicion about the resurgence of the "meritocratic" concept at the same time affirmative action programs have been instituted. As Howard Glickstein of the Center for Civil Rights at Notre Dame writes: "if there were some foolproof litmus test for determining merit, perhaps I would be fearful of tampering with the system. But the rules have been so rubbery in the past that I become a bit suspicious when a new rigidity is demanded as women and minorities appear at the gates. "[4]

What is different under affirmative action programs from past preferences for white males, is that the pool of qualified applicants in education and employment is now enlarged to include groups previously excluded.

A third philosophical underpinning of preferential treatment, in addition to compensatory and distributive justice considerations, are appeals to social utility. A major reason advanced for preferential treatment is the chronic underrepresentation of minority professionals, particularly in law and medicine. Without preferential admissions programs to professional schools, proponents point out, lawyers and doctors needed to serve minority groups would be practically non-existent. For example, lawyers from minority groups represent under 2 per cent of the entire bar. [5] As for black physicians, in 1950 they constituted 2.2 per cent of the total number of physicians; by 1970, blacks in medicine remained at 2.2 per cent while the Negro population increased to 11.1 per cent of the total American population, compared to 10 per cent in 1950. These figures prompted four Justices (Brennan, White, Marshall, and Blackmun) in the Bakke case before the U.S. Supreme Court to write that "until at least 1973, the practice of medicine in this country was, in fact, if not in law, largely the prerogative of whites. "[6]

Social utility justifications for preferential treatment also are based upon the need to promote the public welfare or the common good. For example, by increasing educational and employment opportunities for disadvantaged minorities, poverty and inequality can thus be reduced, thereby lessening the potential for racial conflict. Increased minority opportunities, moreover, will enhance cohesion by eliminating racial stereotypes, providing role models for disadvantaged youth, and enhancing the self-esteem of chronically depressed racial groups.

Utilitarian considerations which assumed major significance in the debate over preferential admissions to professional schools

involved the necessity for a racially diverse student body. It will
be recalled that in the Bakke case before the U. S. Supreme Court,
Justice Lewis Powell, in delivering the swing vote upholding the
consideration of race in admissions programs, relied largely upon
the attainment of a racially diverse student body as a constitutionally permissible goal for institutions of higher education. Such
diversity, Powell wrote, contributes to the "robust exchange of
ideas" and an "atmosphere of speculation, experiment and creation ... essential to the quality of higher education. "[7]

But if Justice Powell accepted diversity as a compelling
utilitarian goal justifying the consideration of race in admissions to
higher education, he rejected additional philosophical justifications
for preferential treatment.

In the clash of opinions between Justices Powell and the
Brennan group (Justices Brennan, White, Marshall, and Blackmun), [8]
the U. S. Supreme Court addressed the same kind of philosophical
issues that are debated in the vast literature on affirmative action
and preferential admissions--the same appeals (or rejections) of
compensatory or distributive justice, social utility considerations,
and the dilemma of choosing between the right of the individual to
equal treatment versus the necessity to remedy the effects of past
discrimination against historically disadvantaged groups by granting
them (at least temporarily) preferred treatment to overcome that
discrimination.

In his Bakke decision, Justice Powell repeatedly emphasized
the right of the individual to equal treatment, regardless of one's
race, ethnicity, or sex. The keynote to his thinking is that preferring members of any one group for no reason other than race or
ethnic origin is discrimination for its own sake. The rights guaranteed by the equal protection clause of the Fourteenth Amendment,
Powell wrote, are "guaranteed to the individual. The rights established are personal rights.... The guarantee of equal protection
cannot mean one thing when applied to one individual and something
else when applied to a person of another color. If both are not
accorded the same protection, then it is not equal. "[9] Again, "it
is the individual who is entitled to judicial protection against classifications based on his racial or ethnic background because such
distinctions impinge upon personal rights, rather than the individual
only because of his membership in a particular race. "[10]

According to Powell, the idea of preference raises serious
problems of justice for the following reasons: 1) It is unclear
whether a so-called preference is benign; courts may be called upon
to impose burdens on individuals of particular groups in order to
advance the group's general interest; 2) Preferential programs may
reinforce common stereotypes that members of particular groups
cannot succeed on their own; and 3) There is inequity in forcing innocent persons of nonminority groups to bear the burdens of redressing past injustices. [11]

The unfairness of assigning benefits and burdens on a racial basis, moreover, "are likely to be viewed with deep resentment by the individuals burdened. "

> The denial to innocent persons of equal rights and oppor-
> tunities may outrage those so deprived and therefore may
> be perceived as invidious.   These individuals are likely
> to find little comfort in the notion that the deprivation
> they are asked to indure is merely the price of member-
> ship in the dominant majority and that its imposition is
> inspired by the supposedly benign purpose of aiding oth-
> ers.   One should not lightly dismiss the inherent unfair-
> ness of, and the perception of mistreatment that accom-
> panies a system of allocating benefits and privileges on
> the basis of skin color and ethnic origin. [12]

In answering proponents of affirmative action who believe that such programs enhance racial cohesion, Powell pointed out that "disparate constitutional tolerance of such [racial and ethnic] classifications well may serve to exacerbate racial and ethnic antagonisms rather than alleviate them. "[13]

The trouble with granting preferential treatment, Powell argued, is that today's preferred group may be replaced by a different preferred group tomorrow; such changing sociological and political analysis necessary to produce such rankings of preferred groups "simply does not lie within the judicial competence. "[14]

Justice Powell saved his sharpest criticism in attacking the Brennan group's central thesis that Davis' preferential admissions program was constitutionally permissible because it sought to remedy the disparate effects of societal discrimination.   Such discrimination was "an amorphous concept of injury that may be ageless in its reach into the past. "   Moreover, to grant preferential treatment based upon "societal discrimination" flew in the face of past decisions of the Court in which it had "never approved a classification that aids persons perceived as members of relatively victimized groups at the expense of the innocent individuals in the absence of judicial, legislative, or administrative findings of constitutional or statutory violations. "[15]   Without findings of identified discrimination, Powell emphasized, the government has no greater interest "in helping one individual than in refraining from harming another. " There is no compelling justification for government to inflict such harm. [16]   Once such violations have been found, however, there is a "substantial" governmental interest in preferring members of the injured groups at the expense of others in order to vindicate the legal rights of the victims.   But continuing oversight of such remedial action is necessary, according to Powell, to assure that the least possible harm is incurred to other innocent persons competing for the same benefit. [17]   To help certain groups perceived as victims of "societal discrimination, " moreover, imposes unjust disadvantages upon members of the white majority who bear no responsibility for causing harm to minority beneficiaries of preferential admissions programs. [18]

> To hold otherwise would be to convert a remedy hereto-
> fore reserved for violations of legal rights into a privi-
> lege that all institutions throughout the Nation could grant
> at their pleasure to whatever groups are perceived as vic-
> tims of societal discrimination.   That is a step we have
> never approved. [19]

In summarizing Justice Powell's opinion in the Bakke case,
we can see his repeated emphasis upon the rights of individuals to
equal treatment, with compensation in the form of preferential
treatment justified only upon findings of specific identified discrimination; such preferential treatment, moreover, to be continuously
reviewed so as to cause the least possible harm to persons innocent of causing discrimination.

But if Justice Powell expressed deep reservations for the
"inequity in forcing innocent persons ... to bear the burdens of redressing grievances not of their making" the Brennan group (Justices Brennan, White, Marshall, and Blackmun) displayed an equally
grave concern for redressing the consequences of a pervasive racism in American society.   At the heart of their opinion is the de-
sire to remedy the damaging effects of past societal discrimination
and to provide equal opportunities for minorities to participate in
all aspects of American society.   As the Justices explained,

> Davis' articulated purpose of remedying the effects of
> past societal discrimination is ... sufficiently important
> to justify the use of race-conscious admissions programs
> where there is a sound basis for concluding that minority
> underrepresentation is substantial and chronic, and that
> the handicap of past discrimination is impeding access of
> minorities to medical school or to any other opportunities
> to participate in American Society. [20]

Race-conscious programs were needed, according to the
Brennan group, to remove the "disparate racial impact" which is
the product of past discrimination by "society at large."[21]   The
regulations issued by the Department of Health, Education, and Welfare, moreover, imply that the lingering effects of past discrimination continue to make race-conscious remedial programs appropriate
means for ensuring equal educational opportunities in universities.

In rejecting Justice Powell's contention that preferential treatment could only be accorded by judicial, legislative, or administrative findings of constitutional or statutory violations, the Brennan
group cited a number of cases and laws upholding "race-conscious
remedial programs" to put members of racial minorities in the
position they otherwise might have enjoyed were it not for discrimination aimed at them in the past.   Race-conscious action, the
Brennan group noted, does not require proof that beneficiaries of
preferential treatment have been individually discriminated against;
"it is enough that each recipient is within a general class of persons
likely to have been the victims of discrimination."[22]

In analyzing the philosophical underpinning of the Brennan group's defense of preferential treatment of minorities, there is evidence of a combination of compensatory justice and present disadvantage. Race-conscious remedial programs are necessary to overcome the chronic and substantial underrepresentation of minorities caused by past and present discrimination. Equal education opportunities thus cannot be achieved as long as the effects of past and present societal discrimination remain.

Justice Thurgood Marshall wrote eloquently of the need to remedy the cumulative effects of society's discrimination. The position of blacks in America today resulting from "the tragic but inevitable consequences of centuries of unequal treatment" makes "meaningful equality" a distant dream for the Negro. For several hundred years, Marshall explained, "Negroes have been discriminated against, not as individuals, but rather solely because of the color of their skins.... A whole people were marked as inferior by the law." Not only has the dream of America not been realized for the Negro; "because of his skin color he never even made it into the pot."[23]

In addition to appeals to compensatory and remedial justice, Marshall considered social utility and distributive justice arguments: the need to bring the Negro into the mainstream of American life in order to end racial divisions in America and the need to permit institutions in America to consider race "in making decisions about who will hold the positions of influence, affluence and prestige in America."[24]

In summarizing the philosophical debate over affirmative action and preferential admissions in higher education, we can see how differing notions about equality and justice generate a broad spectrum of opinions on the question of preferential treatment. To critics of preferential treatment, the concept of equality means the right to equal treatment and the right to compete for society's benefits on the basis of one's ability without regard to race, sex, or ethnicity. To proponents of preferential treatment, equality is a myth because of the pervasive pattern of discrimination against minority groups and women which perpetuates a massive maldistribution of power, status, wealth, and authority in America. To eliminate such maldistribution it is necessary to consider one's race, sex, and ethnicity because these characteristics are the reasons for the discrimination which brought about such maldistribution in the first place. Perhaps the most important question with regard to preferential treatment is: To what degree should individual aspirations and needs be subordinated to the broader social aims of a more just society, that just society perceived as redressing the injuries suffered by historically disadvantaged groups, women and racial minorities?

References

1. Aristotle's discourse on the various kinds of justice are found in book 5 of his Nicomachean Ethics.
2. Daniel Bell, "On Meritocracy and Equality, " Public Interest, No. 29 (Fall, 1972), 41.
3. Ibid.
4. Quoted in Daniel C. Maguire, "Unequal but Fair, " Commonweal, 104 (October 14, 1977), 651-652.
5. Brief Amicus Curiae for the Association of American Law Schools, quoted in Landmark Briefs and Arguments of the Supreme Court of the United States: Constitutional Law. 1977 Term Supplement, Vol. 99-100. (Regents of the University of California v. Bakke). Edited by Philip B. Kurland and Gerhard Casper. (Washington, D.C.: University Publications of America, Inc., 1977), v. 99, 600.
6. Regents of the University of California v. Bakke, 98 S. Ct. at 2789 (1978).
7. Ibid. at 2760-2761 (opinion Powell, J.).
8. The foregoing discussion focuses upon the sharp philosophical differences underlying the opinions of Justice Powell and the Brennan group. For an opposing viewpoint which points out the "remarkable degree of doctrinal convergence" between Powell and the Brennan four, see Kenneth L. Karst and Harold W. Horowitz, "The Bakke Opinions and Equal Protection Doctrine, " Harvard Civil Rights-Civil Liberties Law Review, 14 (Spring, 1979), 7-29.
9. 98 S. Ct. at 2748 (opinion of Powell, J.).
10. Ibid. at 2753 (opinion of Powell, J.).
11. Ibid. at 2753 (opinion of Powell, J.).
12. Ibid. at 2751 n. 34 (opinion of Powell, J.).
13. Ibid. at 2753 (opinion of Powell, J.).
14. Ibid. at 2751-2752 (opinion of Powell, J.).
15. Ibid. at 2757-2758 (opinion of Powell, J.).
16. Ibid. (opinion of Powell, J.).
17. Ibid. at 2757-2758 (opinion of Powell, J.).
18. Ibid. at 2759 (opinion of Powell, J.).
19. Ibid. (opinion of Powell, J.).
20. Ibid. at 2785 (opinion of Brennan, White, Marshall, and Blackmun, JJ.).
21. Ibid. at 2789 (opinion of Brennan, White, Marshall, and Blackmun, JJ.).
22. Ibid. at 2786 (opinion of Brennan, White, Marshall, and Blackmun, JJ.).
23. Ibid. at 2802, 2805 (opinion of Marshall, J.).
24. Ibid. at 2805 (opinion of Marshall, J.).

BOOKS AND PERIODICAL ARTICLES

1073.   Ackley, Timothy E. "Reverse Discrimination. " In Philos-
ophy of Education, 1974: Proceedings of the 30th Annual
Meeting. Edited by Michael J. Parsons. Edwardsville,
Ill.: Southern Illinois University, 1974. Pp. 351-361.

Claims that there is no inherent contradiction between the
theory of egalitarian justice and the practice of reverse
discrimination. Argues that reverse discrimination is a
procedural tool necessary to ensure that past and ongoing
discrimination which excludes women and minorities from
academia is not continued. Analyzes the most commonly
voiced objections to reverse discrimination.

1074.   Axelsen, Diana. "With All Deliberate Delay: On Justifying
Preferential Policies in Education and Employment. " Philosophical Forum. (Boston) 9 (Winter-Spring, 1977/78),
264-288.

Summarizes some of the main values relevant to the issue
of preferential policies; examines some criticisms raised
against such policies; considers some arguments which support them; and argues that an important justification for
preferential policies can be based upon the rights of individuals and groups to reparations for past and present injustices. Article focuses on Blacks in America.

1075.   Banner, William A. "Compensatory Justice and the Meaning of Equity. " (In item 1166; pp. 199-216.)

Discusses the importance of equity in compensatory justice.
Calls for a new allotment of society's resources which has
tolerated an unequal extension of opportunity and an unequal
distribution of the rewards of labor. Recent efforts at ex-
tending additional opportunity to the disadvantaged may serve
as a paradigm for this allotment.

1076.   _____. "Reverse Discrimination: Misconceptions and
Confusion. " Journal of Social Philosophy. 10 (January,
1979), 15-18.

Denies that efforts at compensatory justice are unilateral
denials of constitutional rights. Because moral responsibility is individual rather than collective, one must answer
for what one does either in direct offense or in accepting
an advantage originating from offenses committed by others.
Those who accept undeserved advantages from discrimination against others are involved in injustice just as if they
had initiated discrimination. It cannot be held that affirmative action creates victims of unilateral invasions of their
rights.

1077. Bayles, Michael D. "Compensatory Reverse Discrimination
in Hiring." Social Theory and Practice. 2 (Spring, 1973),
301-312.

Argues that it may be justifiable to prefer minority group
applicants for jobs. Develops a modified principle of compensatory justice for groups, namely, that an organization
which has wronged a minority group has an imperfect obligation to compensate that group. Author then explains the
application of this principle of compensatory discrimination.

1078. _____. "Reparations to Wronged Groups." Analysis.
33 (June, 1973), 182-184.

Argues, contrary to James Nickel and J. L. Cowan, that a
characteristic which is normally morally irrelevant, e.g.,
being black, can be derivatively morally relevant for discriminating in favor of persons as reparations. (Reprinted
in item 1124; pp. 303-305.)

1079. Beauchamp, Tom L. "The Justification of Reverse Discrimination." (In item 1166; pp. 84-110.)

Argues that policies producing reverse discrimination and
quotas are justified and morally required. Cites evidence
from sociological, historical, and legal sources to document
discriminatory social attitudes and selection procedures
which are deeply entrenched in contemporary society so that
good faith efforts alone are inadequate.

1080. Bedau, Hugo Adam. "Compensatory Justice and the Black
Manifesto." Monist. 56 (January, 1972), 20-42.

The "Black Manifesto," published in 1969, demanded "reparations" from the white religious community in the United
States to be paid to black Americans as compensation for
three centuries of "exploitation" and "degradation." Essay
formulates the argument of the manifesto and rebuts objections to it. Concludes that there is more to be said for
the demands of the manifesto on familiar moral and quasi-
legal grounds than first seems the case.

1081.   Bell, Daniel. "On Meritocracy and Equality. " Public In-
         terest. No. 29 (Fall, 1972), 29-68.

         Contains a section on affirmative action in higher education
         in which the author contends that a new principle of rights
         has been introduced into the polity. The principle has
         changed from discrimination to "representation. " The new
         ascriptive principle of corporate identity has replaced the
         principle of professional qualifications or individual achieve-
         ment.

1082.   Bittker, Boris I. The Case for Black Reparations. New
         York: Random House, 1973. 191p.

         Yale law professor presents a lawyer's perspective on the
         case for black reparations and on the practical and consti-
         tutional questions that may be involved. Believes that the
         case for reparations should be based on mistreatment and
         discrimination occurring in the last century. Reparations
         is based upon Section 1983 of the U. S. Code.

1083.   _____. "Identifying the Beneficiaries. " (In item 1124;
         pp. 279-287.)

         Excerpt of author's The Case for Black Reparations, item
         1082.

1084.   Black, Virginia. "The Erosion of Legal Principles in the
         Creation of Legal Policy. " Ethics. 84 (January, 1974),
         93-115.

         Argues that reverse discrimination legislation creates new
         inequities and hurts those they are meant to help by tend-
         ing to conceal and rigidify class structures. Concludes that
         legalized group reparations are totalitarian but voluntary
         group reparations may be morally obligatory and consonant
         with legal equity.

1085.   Blackstone, William T. "Compensatory Justice and Affirm-
         ative Action. " Catholic Philosophical Association. Pro-
         ceedings. 1975. 49 (1975), 218-227.

         Distinguishes seven questions which are often not differ-
         entiated in discussions of compensatory justice and affirma-
         tive action. Discusses whether affirmative action programs
         involve reverse discrimination and assesses the arguments
         for and against reverse discrimination.

1086.   _____. "Reverse Discrimination and Compensatory Jus-
         tice. " Social Theory and Practice. 3 (Spring, 1975), 253-
         288.

         Author discusses the appropriateness of reverse discrimina-
         tion policies, using the Marco DeFunis case (1974) as a

point of reference. Argues that compensation and remedy
to those who have suffered from past institutionalized injustice is required by moral and constitutional value commitments, but that compensation must be racially and sexu-
ally neutral, even if sex and race are used as criteria for
identifying those who suffer from past injustice. The process of eliminating racial and sexual discrimination to effect distributive justice cannot itself justifiably violate the
principle of non-discrimination which it seeks to establish.
(Reprinted in item 1166; pp. 52-83.)

1087.   Boxhill, Bernard R.   "The Morality of Preferential Hiring."
          Philosophy and Public Affairs.   7 (Spring, 1978), 246-286.

          Rebuts two of the principal arguments raised against prefer-
          ential hiring, namely, that hiring preferentially benefits
          only those from among the groups that have suffered dis-
          crimination who do not deserve compensation, and that
          preferential hiring is unfair to young white men.

1088.   _____.   "The Morality of Reparation."   Social Theory
          and Practice.   2 (1972), 113-123.

          Distinguishes between compensation and reparation, the lat-
          ter is aimed at rectifying past injustices and the former
          attempts to procure some future good.   Justice requires
          compensatory programs to ensure fair competition and pro-
          tection of losers.   (Reprinted in item 1124; pp. 270-278.)

1089.   Bunzel, John H.   Rescuing Equality; a bicentennial lecture
          delivered at San Jose State University on February 10,
          1976.   14p.   (Unpublished)

          President of San Jose State University (1970-1978) dis-
          cusses the various definitions of equality throughout the
          ages, including the Declaration of Independence, the differ-
          ence between freedom and equality, and how the liberal
          tradition of equality in America is undergoing a major
          transformation: individual rights are surrendering to group
          rights in the demand for equal rights.

1090.   Burke, Armand.   "Another View of Reverse Discrimina-
          tion."   Philosophical Exchange.   1 (Summer, 1974), 17-19.

          Suggests that reverse discrimination can best be understood
          by the blacks' emerging sense of brotherhood and that his-
          tory has proven that only through group action can the
          rights of individuals be assured.

1091.   Coleman, Jules.   "Justice and Preferential Hiring."   Jour-
          nal of Critical Analysis.   5 (July-October, 1973), 27-30.

          Author responds to Judith Jarvis Thomson's arguments on
          preferential hiring, particularly in private universities.

Such hiring, Coleman contends, would justify precisely the
same discriminatory policies preferential hiring is supposed
to correct. Coleman shows that Thomson's arguments rest
on the view that justice is entirely a matter of entitlement.
Coleman argues that it is sometimes unjust to give some-
one what he deserves, though he is not otherwise entitled
to it.

1092.   Conrad, Thomas R. "The Debate About Quota Systems:
         An Analysis." American Journal of Political Science. 20
         (February, 1976), 135-150.

         Article analyzes the relationships among quota systems,
         egalitarianism, and meritocracy. Shows that adoption of
         a quota system requires trade-offs among social groups.
         Debate focuses upon the proponents of meritocracy and
         those of quota systems. Both sides agree upon the pri-
         mary importance of distributive justice but they disagree
         about what it is that distributive justice demands. The two
         sides further disagree about the nature of political society
         and hence draw opposing conclusions about the morality of
         quotas.

1093.   Cowan, J. L. "Inverse Discrimination." Analysis. 33
         (October, 1972), 10-12.

         Claims that it is not proper to base reparations on such
         morally irrelevant characteristics such as race, creed or
         sex when discrimination has occurred. Individuals who
         have been discriminated against deserve reparation, but be-
         cause they have suffered injustice, and no more than oth-
         ers who have suffered equal injustice on other grounds.
         Individuals, not groups, deserve compensation when injured.
         (Reprinted in item 1124; pp. 291-293.)

1094.   Crandall, John C. "Affirmative Action: Goals and Conse-
         quences." Philosophical Exchange. 1 (Summer, 1974), 21-
         22.

         Raises several questions as to whether the application of
         the group morality principle in the form of reverse dis-
         crimination as a social instrument will produce consequences
         congruent with the desired goals.

1095.   Crocker, Lawrence. "Preferential Treatment." (In item
         1104; pp. 190-209.)

         Considers possible justifications for the policy of awarding
         employment and higher education admissions to women,
         blacks, and other racial minorities over marginally more
         qualified white or male competitors. Concludes that while
         either group or individual compensation may justify prefer-
         ring blacks or women in particular cases, neither will jus-
         tify such a policy unless for practical reasons, no more

suitable compensatory policy is possible. Argues that a
similar preferential policy is justified in terms of its non-
compensatory consequences.

1096.   Daniels, Norman.   "Merit and Meritocracy. "   Philosophy
         and Public Affairs.   7 (Spring, 1978), 206-223.

         Analyzes the notion of merit in relation to a theory of dis-
         tributive justice. Suggests that claims of merit, particular-
         ly the underlying principles that job placement awards jobs
         to individuals on the basis of merit and that there are re-
         ward schedules for jobs, are derived from considerations
         of efficiency or productivity and will not support stronger
         notions of dessert. Concludes that many proponents of
         meritocracy often ignore the distinction between principles
         governing placement and those governing reward and the
         fact that quite different rationales are involved in justifying
         two such different types of principles.

1097.   DeMarco, Joseph.   "Compensatory Justice and Equal Op-
         portunity. "   Journal of Social Philosophy.   6 (September,
         1975), 3-7.

         Surveys difficulties in the notion of compensatory justice in
         cases of preferential hiring and admissions. Argues that
         the standard of equal opportunity solves some of the prob-
         lems in correcting past injustices. Examines Justice Wil-
         liam O. Douglas' dissent in the DeFunis case.

1098.   Deane, Herbert A.   "Justice--Compensatory and Distribu-
         tive. "   (In item 1165; pp. 13-25.)

         Asserts that present theories of compensatory justice are
         based upon new and possibly revolutionary principles of
         justice, unlike Aristotle's principles of corrective justice.
         Discusses numerous theoretical and practical difficulties
         of present-day arguments for compensation. Suggests that
         social justice can best be achieved by levying taxes on the
         basis of ability to pay and of distributing benefits on the
         basis of need.

1098A.   Dworkin, Ronald.   "DeFunis v. Sweatt. "   In Equality and
         Preferential Treatment.   (In item 1100; pp. 63-83.)

         Analyzes the moral and legal justifications underlying the
         DeFunis and Sweatt cases whereby a white male and a black
         male, respectively, were denied admission to law schools
         in Washington and Texas. Distinguishes between equality
         as a policy and equality as a right; defends a preferential
         policy for minorities on the grounds that such preference
         can reasonably be supposed to benefit the community as a
         whole; examines utilitarian and ideal arguments to distin-
         guish between DeFunis and Sweatt and concludes that the

Equal Protection Clause gives constitutional standing to the
right of individuals to be treated as equals but the clause
does not make racial classifications illegal.
Article originally appeared under the title "The DeFunis
Case: The Right to Go to Law School. "   See item 303.

1099.   Edel, A.   "Preferential Consideration and Justice. "   (In
        item 1166; pp. 111-134.)

        Discusses two models of justice to determine the justness
        of preferential treatment: the collective welfare model
        (utilitarian) and the individual rights model (non-utilitarian).

1100.   Equality and Preferential Treatment.   Edited by Marshall
        Cohen, Thomas Nagel, and Thomas Scanlon.   Princeton,
        N. J.:   Princeton University Press, 1977.   209 p.

        The essays, with one exception (R. Dworkin, item 1098A),
        appeared originally in the quarterly journal Philosophy and
        Public Affairs (Vols. 2-5, 1973-76).   For other essays in
        this collection, see items 1105, 1106, 1112, 1142, 1159,
        1162, and 1172.

1101.   Ezorsky, Gertrude.   "It's Mine. "   Philosophy and Public
        Affairs.   3 (Spring, 1974), 321-330.

        Refutes as legalist fallacy Judith Jarvis Thomson's argu-
        ment in "Preferential Hiring" that wholly private employers
        have a moral right to hire whomever they please.

1102.   _____.   "On 'Groups and Justice'. "   Ethics.   87 (Janu-
        ary, 1977),   182-185.

        Replies to George Sher's "Groups and Justice. "   Concludes
        that preferential treatment based on race and sex is morally
        defensible.

1103.   Fein, Leonard J.   "Thinking About Quotas. "   Midstream.
        19 (March, 1973), 3-17.

        Suggests that the merit system is not an absolute good or
        universal truth but rather one way of organizing society for
        certain purposes.   One purpose may be to redress historic
        injustice against groups of people.   Author rejects as in-
        sulting the concept of representative equality in which soci-
        etal rewards are distributed to groups rather than to indi-
        viduals.

1104.   Feminism and Philosophy.   Edited by Mary Vetterling-Brag-
        gin, Frederick A. Elliston, Jane English.   Totowa, N. J.:
        Rowman and Littlefield, 1977.   (See items 1095, 1109,
        1115, 1149.)

1105.   Fiss, Owen M.   "Groups and the Equal Protection Clause. "
        Philosophy and Public Affairs.   5 (Winter, 1976), 107-177.

        Purpose of article is to construct a new general theory for
        the Equal Protection Clause, and thus for the constitutional
        theory of equality.   The theory tries to shift from instru-
        mental to substantive rationality, and from individuals to
        groups.   Article focuses on two different modes of inter-
        preting the Equal Protection Clause: the actual language
        of the Constitution and the "mediating principle, " the latter
        being a set of principles which give meaning and content to
        an ideal embodied in the text.   Discusses the antidiscrim-
        ination and group-disadvantaging mediating principle, par-
        ticularly as they relate to preferential treatment of groups.
        (Reprinted in item 1100; pp. 84-154.)

1106.   _____.   "School Desegregation: The Uncertain Path of
        the Law. "   Philosophy and Public Affairs.   4 (Fall, 1974),
        3-39.

        Traces the development of school desegregation law over
        the last two decades by distinguishing between two phenom-
        ena: racial assignment (the activity) and segregation (the
        demographic pattern), with the latter the more important
        consideration in court decisions.   Points out the pitfalls
        and inconsistencies of the Supreme Court's use of the con-
        cept of past discrimination in its approach to school de-
        segregation.   Explains briefly why the Court found the
        DeFunis case of racial preference much more difficult to
        decide than the racial assignment case of Swann, such dif-
        ficulty explained by the distinguishing element of scarcity--
        the limitation on the total number of educational opportuni-
        ties--and its subsequent introduction of individual unfairness.
        (Reprinted in item 1100; pp. 155-191.)

1107.   Freund, Paul A.   "Equality, Race, and Preferential Treat-
        ment. "   (In item 1165; pp. 26-33.)

        Discusses the concept of "equality" in American history;
        how the criteria of relevance, representativeness, general-
        ity, and mutuality may be applied to the question of prefer-
        ential treatment; and how such treatment may be justified
        by the application of equitable restitution and positive con-
        siderations of social welfare and public need.

1108.   Fried, Marlene G.   "In Defense of Preferential Hiring. "
        Philosophical Forum.   5 (Fall-Winter, 1973-74), 309-319.

        Argues that preferential hiring is a justified means to real-
        ize the goal of equal opportunity.   Discussion confined to
        faculty hiring in colleges and universities.   Defends prefer-
        ential hiring against three basic objections: 1) the criteria
        of merit is subordinate to such criteria as race and sex;

2) preferential hiring is inconsistent with institutional commitment to nondiscrimination in employment; 3) preferential hiring punishes those who did not commit injustices (i. e. white males) who bear the burden of rectifying these injustices. (Reprinted in item 1178; pp. 309-319.)

1109.   Fullinwider, Robert K. "Preferential Hiring and Compensation. " Social Theory and Practice. 3 (Spring, 1975), 307-320.

Analyzes Judith Jarvis Thomson's article, "Preferential Hiring. " Argues that she has failed to show that the principle of compensation justified preferential hiring in the cases she constructs. (Reprinted in item 1104; pp. 210-224.)

1110.   _____. The Reverse Discrimination Controversy: A Moral and Legal Analysis. Totowa, N. J.: Rowman and Littlefield, 1980.   300 p.

Examines the principles and concepts underlying the reverse discrimination controversy, with nearly a third of the book devoted to an examination of regulations, statutes, and case law related to employment discrimination. Suggests that moral equality itself does not necessarily prohibit all preferential hiring of blacks and that racial preferences need not violate basic moral principles or rights derived from them. Concludes that the Social Utility Argument, unlike the Compensatory Justice Argument and the Distributive Justice Argument, constitutes the best kind of defense of preferential hiring. Includes also notes, list of cases, and an excellent bibliography and references.

1111.   Ginsburg, R. B. "Realizing the Equality Principle. " (In item 1166; pp. 135-153.)

Discusses how affirmative action is needed to assure a more rational utilization of human resources. Affirmative action need not mean reverse discrimination nor abandonment of the merit principle. Discusses court cases relating to equality for women.

1112.   Goldman, Alan H. "Affirmative Action. " Philosophy and Public Affairs. 5 (Winter, 1976), 178-195.

Argues that the goals of affirmative action programs cannot be semantically distinguished from quotas, that in practice they encourage reverse discrimination, and that the form of reverse discrimination cannot be justified on moral grounds. Concludes with a comparison of integration in schools and housing to achieve racial balance and reverse discrimination in graduate schools and hiring, with the parallels being fewer than might first appear. (Reprinted in item 1100; pp. 192-209.)

1113.   . "Justice and Hiring by Competence." American Philosophical Quarterly. 14 (January, 1977), 17-28.

Discusses whether society has the right to impose or enforce any rule of hiring, and, if so, what principle of hiring ought to be adopted from the point of view of justice. Analyzes these questions within the context of the libertarian and egalitarian viewpoints.

1114.   . Justice and Reverse Discrimination. Princeton: Princeton University Press, 1979. 251 p.

Author's purpose is to present a sustained argument for a single coherent view on the question of preferential treatment of minority groups and women. Argues that those most competent for the position for which they apply have prima facie rights to these positions; preferential treatment is unjustified when applied indiscriminately to groups defined only by race or sex, in order merely to increase their percentage representation in various social positions; programs of affirmative action are unjust if they encourage or directly mandate group-oriented preferential policies. Nevertheless, reverse discrimination is justified in order to compensate for specific past violations of people's rights to positions based upon their competence or if they were denied equal opportunity. Preferential treatment is also justified in order to create equal opportunity in the future for the chronically deprived.

1115.   . "Limits to the Justification of Reverse Discrimination." Social Theory and Practice. 3 (Spring, 1975), 289-306.

Defines the types of groups to whom compensation can be owed according to certain formal characteristics. Women and Blacks are found not to meet such criteria. Reverse discrimination is justified as compensation only for individuals actually discriminated against in the past and can also be justified for the chronic poor to create equality of opportunity in the future. (Reprinted in item 1104; pp. 225-241.)

1116.   . "The Principle of Equal Opportunity." Southern Journal of Philosophy. 15 (Winter, 1977), 473-485.

Explains why and when equal opportunity is demanded by a moral social system. Advocates a principle which calls for eliminating advantages that result from differences in initial social positions, but not those from natural talents. Extent to which this distinction can be maintained is discussed, and ways of implementing the principle indicated.

1117.   . "Reparations to Individuals or Groups?" Analysis. 35 (April, 1975), 168-170.

Asks how high the correlation must be between group membership and past discrimination to bring about compensation. Under reverse discrimination the operation of the market for talent will give most help to those who need it least. Thus, preferential hiring must be administered on an individual basis. (Reprinted in item 1124; pp. 321-323.)

1118.   . "Reverse Discrimination and the Future: A Reply to Irving Thalberg. " The Philosophical Forum. 6 (Winter-Spring, 1974-75), 321-326.

Argues that in compensatory preferential hiring, groups which deserve such treatment must be differently and more narrowly defined than Thalberg and other supporters have defined them. Concludes that the individual himself must be deserving either because of past injustice directed toward him, or because he requires such help to have an equal opportunity in the future for himself and his children.

1119.   Goldworth, Amnon. "A Comment on John H. Bunzel's 'Rescuing Equality'. " Mimeographed. (1976) 13 ℓ.

Professor of Philosophy at San Jose State University criticizes Bunzel for his failure to clarify the word "equality. " Concludes that preferential treatment is an attempt to right unjust social practices and to create an acceptable parity among all those who would compete for desired benefits.

1120.   Golightly, Cornelius L. "Justice and 'Discrimination For' in Higher Education. " Philosophical Exchange. 1 (Summer, 1974), 5-14.

Discusses the two distinct political moralities or moral systems contained in affirmative action guidelines for higher education. Affirmative action guidelines as legal promulgations of the government introduce a policy that vests rights in the black group or black nation rather than in black individuals. This political morality is contrary to the morality of the Fourteenth Amendment which vests rights in individuals regardless of race, creed, color, or national origin. There may be a utilitarian justification for the nation to discriminate against the individual white citizen if the state has an overriding interest in providing special opportunity for the black group.

1121.   Greene, M. "Equality and Inviolability: An Approach to Compensatory Justice. " (In item 1166; pp. 176-198.)

Develops an approach to equality and justice based upon a conception of individual inviolability and critical self-consciousness. Challenges the relevancy of meritocracy compared to such characteristics as self-development, respect for persons, and self-respect. Believes that preferential treatment is harmful in academic and business employment.

1122.   Gross, Barry R.   Discrimination in Reverse: Is Turnabout Fair Play? New York: New York University Press, 1978. 168 p.

Examines various arguments made on behalf of reverse discrimination, for individuals and groups. Contends that these arguments are forms of special pleading for a substantive outcome and they should be opposed because 1) they are unsound; 2) some of their premises and certainly their conclusions violate the principles of a liberal and democratic society; 3) the substantive outcome reverse discrimination aims for is most unlikely to happen.

1123.   _____. "Is Turn About Fair Play?" Journal of Critical Analysis. 5 (January-April, 1975), 126-135.

Claims that the balance of argument weighs heavily against reverse discrimination: the procedures designed to isolate the discriminated are flawed; the consequences that flow from official sanction of race are dangerous; there is no pattern of compensation or restitution nor any mechanism for implementing reverse discrimination; and its outcome is unjust toward both those it favors and those it harms. (Reprinted in item 1124; pp. 379-388.)

1124.   _____, ed. Reverse Discrimination. New York: Prometheus, 1977. 401 p.

Compilation of the pros and cons of reverse discrimination in education and employment. Selections reprinted from various sources and includes some original articles. Contains three sections: facts and polemics, the law, and value. Section on "value" includes the following items: 1078, 1083, 1088, 1093, 1117, 1123, 1131, 1134, 1144, 1146, 1148, 1160, 1161, 1169.

1125.   Hancock, Roger. "Meritorian and Equalitarian Justice." Ethics. 80 (January, 1970), 165-169.

Contrary to recent claims that there are two opposing concepts of justice, meritorian and equalitarian, justice is a single meritorian concept, in which the distribution of a thing is proportionate to some relevant attribute which serves as the basis of distribution. Meritorian justice presupposes equality of opportunity. Other senses of equality, such as impartial enforcement of rules, are part of justice; however, they do not conflict with meritorian justice. Conflicts about justice arise over which attributes are relevant bases of distribution.

1126.   Havighurst, Robert J.   "Individual and Group Rights in a
         Democracy. " Society.   13 (January-February, 1976), 25-
         28.

         Reflects upon individual, group, and institutional rights in
         a democracy and how the 1970's is experiencing an uneasy
         equilibrium among these rights.   Suggests that the univer-
         sity's rights and obligation to work for the highest quality
         of scholarship is partially reduced by the university's ob-
         ligation to serve society by giving greater opportunities to
         women and members of certain minority groups.

1127.   Heslep, Robert D.   "Preferential Treatment and Compen-
         satory Justice. "   Educational Theory.   26 (Spring, 1976),
         147-153.

         Examines a compensatory justice argument used to defend
         college and universities.   Examines two variations to the
         compensatory justice argument.   One of them concerning
         rectificatory justice holds that minority students should be
         given preferential treatment because such treatment com-
         pensates for injuries suffered by them.   The other varia-
         tion, appealing to distributive justice, holds that prefer-
         ential treatment to minority students serves to compensate
         them for losses suffered.   Author considers factual and
         normative claims by these two variations and concludes
         that they do not justify preferential treatment.

1128.   _____.   "Preferential Treatment in Admitting Racial
         Minority Students. "   (In item 1166; pp. 33-51.)

         Discusses whether arguments based upon compensatory jus-
         tice are valid criterion for granting preferential admissions
         to minority students.   Concludes that such arguments are
         not valid.

1129.   _____.   "Response to Sokolow's 'Response to Robert
         Heslep's 'Preferential Treatment and Compensatory Jus-
         tice. '"   Educational Theory.   (Summer, 1978), 238-240.

         Answers Sokolow's criticisms by elaborating upon his orig-
         inal article.

1130.   Hill, Jim.   "What Justice Requires: Some Comments on
         Professor Schoeman's Views on Compensatory Justice. "
         Personalist.   56 (Winter, 1975), 96-103.

         Agrees with Schoeman that justice requires preferential
         treatment for those who have suffered social and economic
         discrimination but disagrees with him as to what form the
         argument should take in justifying preferential treatment.
         Criticizes Schoemen for inconsistencies in his arguments.

Concludes that compensatory justice may require preferential treatment for the disadvantaged, but preferential treatment does not require pejorative discrimination. Moreover, discrimination which can be justified for justice-respecting reasons is not pejorative discrimination.

1131.   Hoffman, Robert. "Justice, Merit, and the Good. " (In item 1124; pp. 358-72.)

Argues that justice does not require that everyone be treated equally or that everyone has equal natural talents. Any differentiation in the distribution of status, honors and the like, should be justified by individual merit or the common good.   Compensatory justice in behalf of ethnic, racial, or sexual groups or their members is immoral if it contravenes what merit and the common good require and that large-scale compensatory policies are immoral.

1132.   Jaggar, Alison. "Relaxing the Limits on Preferential Treatment. " Social Theory and Practice.   4 (Spring, 1977), 227-235.

Critical discussion of Alan H. Goldman's "Limits to the Justification of Reverse Discrimination. " Jagger refutes Goldman's four specific arguments against preferential treatment for any group defined only by race or sex.   Concludes that it is just to provide preferential treatment for blacks or women as a group, at least within our own historical situation and in the context of certain philosophical assumptions about how society should be organized.

1133.   Jones, Hardy E.   "Fairness, Meritocracy, and Reverse Discrimination. "   Social Theory and Practice.   4 (Spring, 1977), 211-226.

Defends a "counterfactual meritocracy theory" to justify reverse discrimination.   Such a theory is a natural extension of an intuitive notion of equal opportunity.   Persons are deserving within the limits specified, of jobs on the basis of what their qualifications would have been if they had been neither victims nor beneficiaries of injustice.   Responds to criticisms of reverse discrimination.

1134.   _____ .   "On the Justifiability of Reverse Discrimination. " (In item 1124; pp. 348-357.)

Lists four aims which justified reverse discrimination: to insure that discrimination ceases, to offer a symbolic denunciation of our racist and sexist past, to provide role models, and to compensate victims of discrimination. Analyzes five major objections to reverse discrimination and how they might be resolved.

1135.   Ketchum, Sara Ann. "Evidence, Statistics, and Rights: A
         Reply to Simon. " Analysis. 39 (June, 1979), 148-153.

         Responds to Simon's "Statistical Justification of Discrimina-
         tion" (Analysis, 38 (1978), 37-42). Criticizes Simon's a
         priori assumption that white males rejected for jobs under
         a policy of preferential hiring are unjustly treated.

1136.   King, Charles. "A Problem Concerning Discrimination. "
         Reason Papers. (Fall, 1975), pp. 91-96.

         Considers several possible factors justifying favored treat-
         ment of minorities in education and employment, of which
         the most important is redress for past injustice. Argues
         that as a method of redress for past injustice, favored
         treatment is both inefficient and unfair.

1137.   McGary, Howard, Jr. "Justice and Reparations. " Philo-
         sophical Forum. (Bonaron) 9 (Winter-Spring, 1977/78),
         250-263.

         Argues that Black Americans are entitled to receive pref-
         erential treatment and admissions to institutions of higher
         education as a reparation for the injustices of slavery, Jim
         Crow practices, and current discriminatory institutions.

1138.   _____ . "'Reparations' and 'Inverse Discrimination'. "
         Dialogue. (PST) 17 (October, 1974), 8-10.

         Argues that J. L. Cowan ("Inverse Discrimination") misin-
         terprets James Nickel's article ("Discrimination and Moral-
         ly Relevant Characteristics"), relating to preferential hiring
         and education policies. Suggests that preferential hiring
         and education policies are a species of reparation and that
         Black Americans are owed reparation for slavery and ille-
         gal discriminatory treatment.

1139.   Miller, S. M. "The Case for Positive Discrimination. "
         Social Policy. 4 (November-December, 1973), 65-71.

         Discusses three basic strategies--preferences, allocational
         priorities, and incentives--and four principles of positive
         discrimination--compensation and rectification, appropriate
         meritocratic criteria, the development of the discriminated
         and fairness.

1140.   Minas, Anne C. "How Reverse Discrimination Compensates
         Women. " Ethics. 88 (October, 1977), 74-79.

         Claims that discrimination takes from women self-esteem
         and esteem from others. It is this loss of esteem for
         which compensation is owed by society to all women. One
         possible form of compensation is repayment in kind, dis-

criminating now in favor of women. Such a program would
be self-defeating if people were hired only because of sex,
regardless of any qualifications they might have. Reverse
discrimination favoring women should only be used as a
criterion for selection when use of the criterion of qualification leaves a pool of the most qualified, and cannot be
of any more use in decisions of how to draw from this
pool.

1141.   Moral Problems: A Collection of Philosophical Essays.
         2nd ed. Edited by James Rachels. New York: Harper &
         Row, 1975. (See item 1172.)

1142.   Nagel, Thomas. "Equal Treatment and Compensatory Dis-
         crimination." Philosophy and Public Affairs. 2 (Summer,
         1973), 348-363.

         Suggests that compensatory discrimination need not be seri-
         ously unjust and may be warranted not by justice but by
         considerations of social utility, as for example, a discrim-
         inatory admissions or appointments policy adopted to miti-
         gate a grave social evil or to help those in an unfortunate
         social position. (Reprinted in 1100; pp. 3-18.)

1143.   _____. "The Justification of Equality." Critica. 10
         (April, 1978), 3-31.

1144.   Newton, Lisa H. "Reverse Discrimination Is Unjustified."
         Ethics. 83 (July, 1973), 308-312.

         Discusses the ideal of equality as derived from, and logi-
         cally dependent upon, the notion of political justice, which
         entails the rule of law. A program of discrimination, re-
         verse or otherwise, destroys justice in the political sense.
         Reverse discrimination undermines the foundation of the
         ideal in whose name it is advocated and destroys justice,
         law, equality, and citizenship, and replaces them with pow-
         er struggles and popularity contests. (Reprinted in item
         1124; pp. 373-378.)

1145.   Nickel, James W. "Classification by Race in Compensatory
         Programs." Ethics. 84 (January, 1974), 146-150.

         Article discusses two responses that might be made by a
         person who is criticized for inconsistency when he says that
         race is irrelevant when he condemns racial discrimination
         but says that racial classifications may be used in compen-
         satory programs, thus does not need to be held to be rele-
         vant. The other reply claims that race is relevant in this
         context, even though it is normally irrelevant. Author dis-
         cusses some difficulties in the second reply which may be
         reasons for preferring the first.

1146. _____. "Discrimination and Morally Relevant Character-
       istics. " Analysis. 32 (March, 1972), 113-114.

       Rejects the argument that special considerations need not
       be extended to blacks because this means reverse discrim-
       ination. Such an argument rests upon a false premise,
       namely, that it assumes that the characteristic which forms
       the basis for the original discrimination (race) is the same
       which forms the basis for granting special considerations.
       Concludes that compensation is possible not because of a
       person's race but because he was discriminated against.
       (Reprinted in item 1124; pp. 288-290.)

1147. _____. "Should Reparations Be to Individuals or to
       Groups?" Analysis. 34 (April, 1974), 154-160.

       Claims that it would be justifiable to design and institute
       programs of special benefits to blacks because almost all
       of them have been victimized by discrimination.   Relates
       compensatory justice to John Rawls' A Theory of Justice.
       (Reprinted in item 1124; pp. 314-320.)

1148. Nunn, William A. "Reverse Discrimination. " Analysis.
       34 (April, 1974), 151-154.

       Responds to Paul Taylor's article "Reverse Discrimination
       and Compensatory Justice. " Claims that his article con-
       tains two elementary fallacies. It is untrue that "institu-
       tionalized injustice demands institutionalized compensation, "
       because there are numerous cases in which compensation
       for past unjust discrimination is inappropriate on practical
       or logical grounds.   Moreover, Taylor's general argument
       for reverse discrimination leads to an unjust discrimination
       varying only in a periodic exchange of places between op-
       pressor and oppressed.   (Reprinted in item 1124; pp. 306-
       309.)

1149. O'Neill, Onora (Nell). "How Do We Know When Opportuni-
       ties Are Equal? " Philosophical Forum. (Boston) 5 (Fall-
       Winter, 1973), 334-346.

       Distinguishes between the formal and the substantive inter-
       pretation of equal in opportunity, explains why equal oppor-
       tunity is dependent upon balancing liberty against both equal-
       ity and efficiency, and suggests various policies to bring
       about such a balance.   Believes that affirmative action
       plans are mild compromise policies which try to achieve
       greater substantive equality of opportunity without sacrificing
       either liberty or efficiency. (Reprinted in item 1178; pp.
       334-346.) (Reprinted in item 1104; pp. 177-189.)

1150. _____. "Opportunities, Equalities and Education. " The-
       ory and Decision. 7 (October, 1976), 275-295.

Discusses recent debates on equal educational opportunities,
debates which center on divergent assumptions about human
nature. Those who see persons primarily as autonomous
choosers believe that equal educational opportunity requires
only that publicly controlled obstacles to any given level or
sort of educational attainment be made equal for all persons. Those who see persons as socially produced view
educational equality as requiring the production of equal
educational results, sometimes for all individuals, though
more often for all social groups, and so are committed to
educational policies that counterbalance the differences produced by varied abilities and choices or other factors.

1151. Oppenheim, Felix E. "Equality, Groups, and Quotas."
       American Journal of Political Science. 21 (February,
       1977), 65-70.

       Argues that the concept of egalitarianism must be separated
       into descriptive and normative terms. The only fully egali-
       tarian admissions policy would be one in which every appli-
       cant was given the same probability of admission (i. e., a
       random selection such as drawing lots). Just as it is in-
       egalitarian to discriminate on the basis of ability it is
       equally so to compensate a particular group for past depriva-
       tion.

1152. Park, Ernie Z. "Reparations and Inverse Discrimination."
       Dialogue. (PST) 17 (April, 1975), 75-76.

1153. Rawls, John. A Theory of Justice. Cambridge, Mass.:
       Harvard University Press, 1971. 607 p.

       One of the most widely discussed books on moral philosophy
       in recent times. Discusses the major theme of justice as
       fairness, elaborates upon the general principle that all so-
       cial value--liberty and opportunity, wealth and income, and
       the bases of self-respect--are to be distributed equally un-
       less an unequal distribution of any, or all, of these values
       is to the advantage of everyone. Some inequalities are
       justified which benefit the least advantaged member of so-
       ciety. The difference principle permits the allocation of
       educational resources to improve the long-term expectation
       of the least favored.

1154. Robertson, John. "Woodruff on Reverse Discrimination."
       Analysis. 39 (January, 1979), 54-57.

       Answers Paul Woodruff's arguments favoring compensatory
       discrimination. Argues that if a practice is to be compen-
       satory, it involves imposing a burden upon some group, and
       it is morally relevant whether the burden is distributed
       fairly within the group owing compensation. The burden of
       reverse discrimination falls capriciously, though the burden

of tax-based social programs need not.   The latter is thus
preferred to reverse discrimination.

1155.   Rusk, Dean.   "Preferential Treatment: Some Reflections. "
(In item 1166; pp. 154-160.)

Favors compensatory measures to overcome the results of
past discrimination, but insists upon high standards of competence for graduation.

1156.   Sasseen, Robert F.   "Affirmative Action and the Principle
of Equality. "   Studies in Philosophy and Education.   9
(Spring, 1976), 275-295.

Discusses the background of affirmative action in higher
education, Executive Orders and HEW regulations implementing these orders.   Concludes that affirmative action is
a preferential policy of proportional employment and that
such a policy assumes that no group possesses genuinely
equal opportunity unless jobs, wealth, and status are distributed in arithmetic proportion among all groups equally.
This transformation of equal opportunity into equal status
and wealth, as De Toqueville argues, leads inevitably to an
increased concentration of political power, centralization of
administration, and to a new form of Caesarism.

1157.   Schoeman, Ferdinand.   "When Is It Just to Discriminate?"
Personalist.   56 (Spring, 1975), 170-177.

Argues that pejorative discrimination can be morally justified in certain cases.   Preferential treatment is required
for the disadvantaged in order to insure fair competition.

1158.   Sher, George.   "Groups and Justice. "   Ethics.   87 (January, 1977), 174-181.

Addresses the claim that reverse discrimination can be
justified for wronged groups, as opposed to wronged individuals.   Argues that the racial and sexual groups usually
mentioned for compensatory purposes are not enough like
persons to fall under the principle of distributive justice.
Even if such groups did fall under it, that principle could
not justify preferential treatment for their current, underprivileged members and that appeals to retributive justice
must fail for analogous reasons.

1159.   _____ .   "Justifying Reverse Discrimination in Employment. "   Philosophy and Public Affairs.   4 (Winter, 1975),
159-170.

Discusses the question of whether, and if so, under what
conditions, past discrimination against a particular group
justifies the current hiring of a member of that group who

is less than the best qualified applicant for a given job. Analyzes adequate and inadequate defenses of reverse discrimination. Defends reverse discrimination to neutralize competitive disadvantages caused by past privations. (Reprinted in item 1100; pp. 49-60.)

1160.   Shiner, Roger A. "Individuals, Groups, and Inverse Discrimination." Analysis. 33 (June, 1973), 184-187.

Argues that groups can logically deserve inverse discrimination. But whether blacks, as individuals or a group, deserve such discrimination must stand not simply on their being black, but on the facts of history. (Reprinted in item 1124; pp. 310-313.)

1161.   Silvestri, Philip. "The Justification of Inverse Discrimination." Analysis. 34 (October, 1973), 31-32.

Author concedes that blackness is not directly relevant, but suggests that we would be justified in using what would otherwise be morally irrelevant if there is an almost one to one correlation between being black and having been the object of unfair discrimination. Suggests that if the reparations were voluntary, the injustices following in particular cases would not be a punishing of the innocent but only unfair reward, which would be an acceptable practice. (Reprinted in item 1124; pp. 294-295.)

1162.   Simon, Robert. "Preferential Hiring: A Reply to Judith Jarvis Thomson." Philosophy and Public Affairs. 3 (Spring, 1974), 312-320.

Objects to Thomson's defense of preferential hiring on three grounds: she has not taken adequate account of the distinction between compensating groups and individuals; she has not shown that compensation ought to be awarded according to one's marketability, but this is what preferential hiring does; she has not shown that inequity can be avoided in distributing the costs of preferential hiring policies. (Reprinted in item 1100; pp. 40-48.)

1163.   _____. "Preferential Treatment for Groups or for Individuals?" National Forum. 58 (Winter, 1978), 7-9.

Opposes claim that preferential treatment is justified to prevent the virtual exclusion of racial minorities from central areas of American life. Evaluates different proposed arguments for preferential treatment and concludes that while race sometimes may be relevant to selection of individuals for scarce benefits, such benefits should be available to equally victimized individuals, regardless of their race or group membership.

1164. _____. "Statistical Justifications of Discrimination. "
Analysis. 38 (January, 1978), 37-42.

Answers James Nickel's argument that compensatory programs favoring all members of a victimized group are
justified because most members have themselves been victimized by discrimination. Simon responds that acceptance
of Nickel's reasoning commits one to parallel but unacceptable arguments such as "We need not consider any women
for this job since most women lack the physical strength
to perform it. "

1165. Small Comforts for Hard Times: Humanists on Public Policy. Edited by Michael Mooney and Florian Stuber. New
York: Columbia University Press, 1977. (See items
1098, 1108.)

1166. Social Justice and Preferential Treatment: Women and Racial Minorities in Education and Business. Edited by William T. Blackstone and Robert D. Heslep. Athens: University of Georgia Press, 1977. 216 p.

Ten essays by philosophers, lawyers, and an historian
which address the justifiability of preferential treatment of
women and racial minorities in education and business.
(See items 1075, 1079, 1086, 1099, 1111, 1121, 1128,
1155, 1176, 1177.)

1167. Sokolow, H. Michael. "Response to Robert Heslep's
'Preferential Treatment and Compensatory Justice'. " Educational Theory. 27 (Spring, 1977), 160-165.

Reviews Heslep's argument that preferential treatment in
admissions as compensatory justice is unjustified. Sokolow
shows that what Heslep argues against as commonalities of
arguments for preferential treatment are not commonalities
at all. Heslep also begs the questions that must be addressed with reference to preferential admissions in his
attacks on preferential treatment based upon rectificatory
justice.

1168. _____. "Reverse Discrimination as Compensation for
Prior Injustice. " Philosophical Studies in Education.
(1975), pp. 102-109.

Discusses the concepts of discrimination and reverse discrimination, two principles of justice and the concept of
compensation, and a situation where reverse discrimination
serves as compensation for a prior injustice. Discusses
the key issues in the debate from aggregate and distributive
viewpoints. Justifies reverse discrimination at least in a
tie-breaking situation.

1169.   Taylor, Paul W.   "Reverse Discrimination and Compensa-
          tory Justice. " Analysis.   33 (June, 1973), 177-182.

          Argues that reverse discrimination is justified on the prin-
          ciple of compensatory justice.   Blackness and Femaleness
          have been made morally relevant characteristics because
          of the original unjust social practice of discriminating
          against blacks and women.   Institutionalized injustice de-
          mands institutionalized compensation.   (Reprinted in item
          1124; pp. 296-302.)

1170.   Thalberg, Irving.   "Justifications of Institutional Racism. "
          The Philosophical Forum.   (Boston) 3 (Winter, 1972), 243-
          263.

          Analyzes some fifteen arguments white Americans frequently
          offer against the insistence of blacks and similarly oppressed
          minorities upon redistribution of power within and between
          various institutions.   Investigates whether these arguments
          are more important considerations than ceasing major in-
          justice toward nonwhites.

1171.   _____. "Reverse Discrimination and the Future. "
          Philosophical Forum.   (Boston) 5 (Fall-Winter, 1973), 294-
          308.

          Challenges critics of reverse discrimination who believe
          such discrimination parallels traditional racism and sexism.
          Suggests that measures to bring in representative numbers
          from groups previously excluded from virtually all status-
          conferring positions is not tantamount to discrimination
          against any other group.   They also do not require a uni-
          versal quota system.   Author challenges the assumption
          that such measures must be designed to make up for past
          inequities.   They may also be future directed.   (Reprinted
          in item 1178; pp. 294-308.)

1172.   Thomson, Judith Jarvis.   "Preferential Hiring. " Philosophy
          and Public Affairs.   2 (Summer, 1973), 364-384.

          Discusses the issues of preferential hiring in universities,
          including whether an individual white male should bear the
          burden of making amends to women and blacks when he
          himself has not wronged them.   (Reprinted in item 1100;
          pp. 19-39.) (Reprinted in item 1141; pp. 144-162.)

1173.   Van Dyke, Vernon.   "The Individual, The State, and Ethnic
          Communities in Political Theory. " Journal of World Poli-
          tics.   29 (April, 1977), 343-369.

          Explains why the question of ethnic group rights needs to be
          explored and interrelationships between the rights of indi-
          viduals, of groups, and of the state need to be clarified.

Brief section on how affirmative action would be facilitated
if ethnic communities were accepted as "right-and duty-
bearing units. "

1174.   Vetterling, Mary. "Some Common Sense Notes on Prefer-
        ential Hiring. " Philosophical Forum. (Boston) 5 (Fall-
        Winter, 1973), 320-324.

        Defines both the weak and the strong sense of the term "to
        preferentially hire. " Discusses the difficulties in hiring
        the "most qualified, " "equally as qualified as, " and "less
        qualified than" another person. Advocates strong preferen-
        tial hiring as a common sense move. (Reprinted in item
        1178; pp. 320-324.)

1175.   Wade, Francis C. "Preferential Treatment of Blacks. "
        Social Theory and Practice. 4 (Spring, 1978), 445-470.

        Argues that justice is not simply equality; it is giving each
        his due. To repair injustice, compensation is not enough;
        reparations is also demanded in the name of distributive
        justice. Preferential treatment in the form of jobs and
        positions is appropriate, provided the black is qualified and
        no one's proved right is destroyed.

1176.   Wasserstrom, Richard A. "The University and the Case
        for Preferential Treatment. " American Philosophical Quar-
        terly. 13 (April, 1976), 165-170.

        Discusses the question of whether minority group member-
        ship is by itself a good reason for admitting a student or
        appointing a person to the faculty. Argues that the univer-
        sity is benefited from the presence within it of minority
        group students and teachers. Such benefit derives from the
        fact that race and sex are sufficiently central features of
        experience so that they affect in quite fundamental ways how
        it is that individuals perceive and respond to the social and
        physical world. Women and minorities add distinctive
        points of view which provides a valuable type of intellectual
        pluralism, which, in turn, fulfills one of the universities
        most important functions--the pursuit of knowledge.
        (Reprinted in item 1166.)

1177.   Wilson, Prince E. "Discrimination Against Blacks: A His-
        torical Perspective. " (In item 1166; pp. 161-175.)

        Gives a historical perspective on the issue of compensatory
        justice for blacks, with special reference to education.
        Concludes that compensatory, affirmative action programs
        are necessary to rectify past and current racism.

1178.   Women and Philosophy: Toward a Theory of Liberation.
        Edited by Carol C. Gould and Marx W. Wartofsky. New

York: G. P. Putnam's Sons, 1976. (See items 1108, 1149, 1171.)

1179.   Woodruff, Paul. "Unfair to Groups: A Reply to Klein-
        berg." Analysis. 38 (January, 1978), 62-64.

        Defends view that discrimination is wrong only when it is
        unfair, and that it is not always unfair. Discrimination is
        unfair if it helps to lower the respect in which a group is
        held below a fair level. Compensatory discrimination as
        a form of restitution is clearly unfair for discrimination
        harms groups, but the guilty are individuals. Compensatory
        discrimination, however, is not prima facie unfair if it
        serves as a counter-force to existing prejudice, a provision
        for social equilibrium.

1180.   _____. "What's Wrong with Discrimination?" Analysis.
        36 (March, 1976), 158-160.

        Argues that an act of discrimination is wrong only if part
        of a pattern that makes membership in a group burdensome
        by unfairly reducing the respect in which the group is held.
        Compensatory discrimination is not part of such a pattern.
        When discrimination is wrong, there are two wrongs to be
        righted. If people are enslaved for their race, then com-
        pensation is due to the slaves for their loss of freedom and
        to the race for its debasement. Since the latter is owed
        to a group it can only be paid by discrimination.

1181.   Wubnig, Judy. "The Merit Criterion of Employment: An
        Examination of Some Current Arguments Against Its Use."
        Humanist. 36 (September-October, 1976), 36-39.

        Examines the argument that race, ethnic groups, and sex
        are proper criteria for employment. Demonstrates the de-
        fects of the compensation argument, the percentage quota
        argument, and the biased judgment argument. Also shows
        that they are self-refuting, since each maintains that the
        merit criterion ought to be enforced by rejecting its use.

NAME INDEX

This index consists of authors, corporate entries, editors, sponsoring agencies, names of individuals or associations prominently mentioned in newspaper articles and cross references from one author to another in response to each other. The references are to item numbers, not page numbers.

Ohio University, Athens 1056
Oltman, Ruth M.   881, 1034
   see also 627, and Howard,
   785
O'Neil, Robert M.   196, 236,
   300, 317, 318, 449-451,
   748, 882
O'Neill, Onora (Nell) 1104,
   1149, 1150, 1178
Oppenheim, Felix E.   1151
Orleans, Jeffrey   345
Ornstein, Allan C.   884-886
   see also DeStefano, 645
Ortiz de Montellano, Bernard
   887   see also Weinberger,
   638

Palmieri, Patricia   548
Park, Ernie Z.   1152
Pati, Gopal C.   889
Patterson, Michelle   890
Patterson, Orlando H.   367
Payne, Charles   198
Pearson, Jessica   380
Pearson, William   381
Pelikan, Jaroslav   891   see
   also Meyers, 854
Pemberton, S. MacPherson
   31, 535, 1035, 1057
Pennsylvania University, Phila-
   delphia. Wharton School
   of Finance and Commerce
   448
Perhacs, Richard W.   452
Persson, Leonard N.   892
Petersen, John D.   453
Pettigrew, L. Eudora   893
Petty, Roy   397
Picott, J. Rupert   199
Piesco, Judith   536
Pinderhughes, Charles A.   454
Poindexter, Paula M.   276
Pollak, Frederick   434
Pollak, Louis   200, 296, 393
Pollock, Mordeca Jane   894
   see also Gross   741
Pondrom, Cyrena N.   895
Posner, Richard A.   237, 319
Potomac Institute, Washington,
   D.C.   1071/72
Pottinger, J. Stanley   201,
   518, 519, 749, 796, 896-

899, 1018   see also Hook
   772
Pottker, Janice   391, 900
Powers, Jan   456
President's Committee on Em-
   ployment of the Handicapped
   see   U. S. President's Com-
   mittee on Employment of the
   Handicapped
Pressman, Steven   458
Prestage, Jewel L.   901
Project on the Status and Edu-
   cation of Women   see   As-
   sociation of American Col-
   leges. Project on the Status
   and Education of Women
Pruitt, Anne S.   903
Public Health Service   see
   U. S. Department of Health,
   Education, and Welfare.
   Public Health Service
Pulliam, Roger I.   202
Pyles, Jackson   904

Quaglia, Paul L., Jr.   350
Quester, Aline O.   976   see
   also Johnson and Stafford,
   798

Rabinove, Samuel   203, 906
Rachels, James, ed.   1141
Rafky, David M.   907
Rand Corporation, Santa Moni-
   ca, Calif.   1069
Ratterman, David B.   459
Ravenell, Mildred W.   204-206
Rawls, John   1153   see also
   Nickel, 1147
Reagan, Barbara R.   908-909
Record, Jane Cassels   911
Record, Wilson   911
Redden, Martha Ross   520
Redish, Martin A.   320-321
Regan, Richard J.   207
Reidhaar, Donald L.   460
Remmert, James E.   461
Renfrew, Charles B.   462
Resource Center on Sex Roles
   in Education   see   U. S. De-
   partment of Health, Educa-
   tion, and Welfare. Office

TITLE INDEX